D1825579

EUROPE AND THE
MEDITERRANEAN

EUROPE AND THE MEDITERRANEAN
Published by Brassey's for Centre for European Policy Studies
33 rue Ducale, B - Brussels (Director: Peter Ludlow)

Also available from Brassey's

Books

The Annual Review of European Community Affairs 1990, edited by Peter Ludlow

The Annual Review of European Community Affairs 1991, edited by Peter Ludlow, Jørgen Mortensen, and Jacques Pelkmans

Setting European Community Priorities 1991-92, edited by Peter Ludlow

Setting European Community Priorities 1992-93, edited by Peter Ludlow (forthcoming January 1994)

German Unification in European Perspective, Wolfgang Heisenberg

The Future of Pensions in the European Community, edited by Jørgen Mortensen

European Competition Policy, Sir Leon Brittan

Papers

North-South in the EMS: Convergence and Divergence in Inflation and Real Exchange Rates, by CEPS Economic Policy Group

From Centrally-Planned to Market Economies: Issues for the Transition in Central Europe and the Soviet Union, Daniel Gros and Alfred Steinherr

Europe and North America in the 1990s, edited by Peter Ludlow

EUROPE AND THE MEDITERRANEAN

edited by
Peter Ludlow

Published by Brassey's for CEPS

BRASSEY's (UK)

LONDON * NEW YORK

Copyright © 1994 Centre for European Policy Studies

All Rights Reserved. No part of this publication may be reproduced, stored in a retrieval system or transmitted in any form or by any means: electronic, electrostatic, magnetic tape, mechanical, photocopying, recording or otherwise, without permission in writing from the publishers.

First English edition 1994

UK editorial offices: Brassey's, 165 Great Dover Street, London SE1 4YA
Orders: Marston Book Services, PO Box 87, Oxford OX2 ODT

USA orders: Macmillan Publishing Company, Front and Brown Streets, Riverside, NJ 08075

Distributed in North America to booksellers and wholesalers by the Macmillan Publishing Company, NY 10022

Library of Congress Cataloging in Publication Data
available

British Library Cataloging in Publication Data
A catalogue record for this book is
available from the British Library

Hardcover
ISBN 1-85753-059-4

Printed in Great Britain by BPCC Wheatons Ltd, Exeter

Contents

About the Authors

Maha Azzam is Associate Fellow with the Royal United Services Institute for Defence Studies in London.

Paul Clairet is Principal Administrator, DG IA, Commission of the European Communities, Brussels.

Youssef Courbage is Senior Researcher at the Institut National d'Etudes Démographiques, Paris.

Heinz Kramer is a member of the research staff at the Stiftung Wissenschaft und Politik in Ebenhausen.

Bernabé López Garcia is Professor at the Universidad Autónoma de Madrid.

Peter Ludlow is Director of the Centre for European Policy Studies in Brussels.

Edward Mortimer is Foreign Affairs Editor of the *Financial Times* in London.

Jesús A. Nuñez Villaverde is Professor at the Universidad Autónoma de Madrid.

Seyfi Tashan is Director of the Foreign Policy Institute in Ankara.

Alfred Tovias is Associate Professor in International Relations and Senior Research Fellow at the Leonard Davis Institute of International Relations at the Hebrew University of Jerusalem.

Preface

All of the papers in the present volume were submitted to a CEPS workshop on Europe and the Mediterranean in January 1993. Like virtually every other European institution, CEPS has devoted most of its time and resources over the past two to three years to work on the development on the European Union itself and its relations with the ex-Communist countries of Central and Eastern Europe. This workshop was therefore intended to serve in some measure as a corrective gesture: a reminder to ourselves and others that there were important questions concerning our neighbours and partners in the South that we would be foolish to ignore.

The design of the workshop and therefore the book that follows was deliberately wide-ranging. We wanted to examine the "big questions" and to cover the region as a whole. Hence, an opening chapter by Alfred Tovias which discusses the nature of the Mediterranean economy, another by Maha Azzam on Islam and one by Edward Mortimer on questions of Mediterranean security. All three authors highlight important themes or features characterising the riparian states in general. Tovias in particular admits to having "no particular difficulty in speaking about the Mediterranean economy".

Despite the global focus of these three essays, however, the overriding impression that emerges from all of them is the huge diversity in the region and a corresponding need for EC policy to take account of differences as well as harmonies. Many years ago, a Belgian historian Henri Pirenne wrote a celebrated book entitled *Mohammed and Charlemagne*. In it, he questioned the conventional thesis that the Roman empire had been destroyed by the invaders from the North. Although it was obviously difficult to deny the damage that the Goths and others had done in a political and physical sense, Pirenne argued -- very convincingly -- that the underlying reality of the empire, which was an integrated Mediterranean-based economy, survived these invasions and was only broken several centuries later by the emergence of Islam.

More than a thousand years later, the successors of Mohammed and Charlemagne are still in many ways divided. Alfred Tovias' tables on per capita GNP underlines that fact very well. So too do the references in the essay by Barnabé López Garcia and Jesús Nuñez to the asymmetrical relationship between the EC and its Maghreb partners. For the purposes of the present book, however, the divisions amongst Mohammed's successors are of even more practical relevance. At point after point, myths of an organised Islamic threat, or, still more widespread, of hordes of potential immigrants simply waiting for their chance to come North, driven by "demographic explosion", are called into question. Although clearly there are many common values linking Muslims from Morocco to Iran, the Islamic world is highly differentiated and the principal threat to security stems not so much from the unity of the Arab or Islamic world as from its divisions and internal tensions.

Youssef Courbage's important essay on demographic transition among the Maghreb people not only punctures the widespread illusions about population growth in North Africa, it also highlights the differences between the Arabs of the Maghreb and their co-religionists further along the Northwest African coast in Egypt. Two million Egyptians reside in the Gulf: barely 50,000 in Europe. In the case of the Maghreb, the ratio is nearly the reverse, and, as Courbage illustrates, those who do venture eastwards from the Maghreb, often return humiliated and misunderstood.

Against this background, despite the obvious appeal of a common "Mediterranean policy", the European Union is bound to approach different countries or groups of countries quite differently. That is why, in Chapters 5 to 8, the book focuses in turn on the Maghreb, the Middle East, and Turkey. As far as the Maghreb is concerned, the relationship between the EC and most if not all of the member states of the Arab Maghreb Union (AMU) is bound to be particularly close, even though, as Morocco discovered when it tried, membership of the EC is excluded by definition. In the case of Morocco itself, the last few years since the rapid rejection of its application of membership have been remarkable both in terms of the country's internal development and its relations with the EC. The EC's relations with Morocco's partners in the AMU are more complex, not least because of the obvious problems posed by the confrontation between the government and Islamic fundamentalists in Algeria. In this connection, Maha Azzam's plea, which is echoed by

Edward Mortimer, for a more tolerant and imaginative reaction to the "threat" of Islam is particularly relevant. Not only is there no evidence whatsoever that indefinite repression will work, but there is also much to suggest that, once in power, an Islamic regime would have to come to terms with the same secular problems that confronted its predecessors and would probably seek broadly-speaking the same solutions. Perhaps our top priorities should therefore be to treat the AMU as a whole as generously as possible both in terms of market access and public finance. The parameters within which policy-makers of any persuasion will have to work are, however, far from flexible.

In terms of general importance, the relationship between the European Union and Turkey has even greater significance than the relationship with the Maghreb. As Heinz Kramer's useful account of the history of EC-Turkish relations shows, the relationship has never been a particularly easy one, since the Turks always wanted more than the European Community contemplated giving. Since the Gulf War and the collapse of the Soviet Union, however, there has been a significant change in atmosphere. Turkey, having appeared initially in the immediate aftermath of the Cold War to have lost its leverage with the West in general and the European Community in particular, is now widely perceived to be vitally important in both the Middle East and Central Asia. On the Turkish side, there are many in the Westernised political and business class who still regard membership of the EC as a goal worth striving for. There does, however, seem to be a much more realistic appreciation of the unlikelihood of achieving this objective within the foreseeable future. The way is therefore open for a more fruitful partnership than there has been in the past. At the heart of it will be the customs union which gives Turkey a standing with the European Community akin to that of the EFTA countries. For the EC at any rate, however, the still more important goal is, or should be, the development of a mature political partnership in which, it goes without saying, the problems over human rights -- on both sides -- can be openly and fruitfully discussed, alongside the numerous and growing catalogue of common security interests.

Amongst the latter is of course the pacification of the Middle East, which is discussed in Paul Clairet's essay. Clairet rightly emphasises the contradiction between the EC's overwhelming economic significance for

iv

the countries in question and its much more marginal political role, both in general terms and more particularly in the context of the Middle East peace process. The reason is well expressed by the Spanish Prime Minister Philippe Gonzalez in the passage quoted by Edward Mortimer:

> The Gulf crisis was a graphic illustration of what could happen to a common foreign policy without a common defence policy. When the peace was being negotiated Europe did not exist. The US and the Soviet Union would be at the table. But Israel and other countries in the region do 70% of their trade with the EC.

Unless and until the Common Security and Foreign Policy (CSFP) develops, as provided in the Maastricht Treaty, so that it includes a common defence policy and, in time, a common defence, this contradiction is bound to endure. In these circumstances, the European Union will *de facto* have to acknowledge US leadership in the Eastern Mediterranean and Middle East. The Community does, nevertheless, as Clairet underlines, have a potentially large role to play as the region's principal trading partner and source of aid and development funds.

In conclusion, although the character of the European Union is still to a very large extent determined by the decisive shift in the balance of power towards the North and West of Europe with which the name of Charlemagne is closely associated, his successors and the successors of the Prophet can only gain by greater cooperation and integration. A principal achievement of this book is that it questions many "myths" that even well placed policy-makers in Charlemagne's Europe entertain about their neighbours to the South. In doing so, it should help to lay the bases of a maturer and more fruitful relationship.

It only remains to thank the authors for their contributions to this book, and the European Commission for the grant that made the workshop possible in the first place. As with all of CEPS' publications, the views expressed are those of the authors alone and do not reflect the opinions or policies of any institution, official or unofficial.

Peter Ludlow
Brussels

1 The Mediterranean Economy

Alfred Tovias

I. The Mediterranean as an Object of Study[1]

Is it legitimate to focus on the countries bordering the Mediterranean as if we were speaking of a single unit for research purposes? Is there a common denominator to the countries of the region apart from the obvious fact that they share the same sea and therefore enjoy access to its natural resources as well as bear responsibility for its problems (such as pollution)? Beyond this purely geographical factor, are there other commonalities that justify approaching these countries as a single unit? I believe there are at least five.

1. Commonalities of the Region

Climatic and Ecological Factors

The first commonality is the weather. The Mediterranean region experiences mild winters and hot, humid summers, particularly near the coast. These climatic conditions give rise to a typical Mediterranean landscape, vegetation and habitat. For centuries the inhabitants of the region have been growing fruit, vegetables, cotton, tobacco and rice, since its weather and land are appropriate for these crops. Inland, the weather is drier, cold in winter and torrid in summer which, combined with the (variable) distance to the sea, explains why the Mediterranean

---

[1] This paper does not deal with EC Mediterranean policy in the past, present or future, because these subjects are treated by other contributors to this volume. For additional analyses and views on Mediterranean policy, see chronologically Tovias (1978), Commission of the EC (1985), Pomfret (1986), Drevet (1986), Renier (1988), Lucron (1988), Commission of the EC (1990a), Research Group on European Affairs (1991), Aliboni (1992) and Weidenfeld (1992).

hinterlands have always been less densely populated than the coastal zones. The population in the former tends to concentrate in large towns functioning sometimes as the capital of the country (e.g. Madrid, Damascus, Jerusalem, and Ankara). Olive trees, vineyards, and grazing sheep form common features of the landscape. And of course, the Mediterranean weather combined with a proximity to a colder but richer zone confers on all coastal states tremendous possibilities for tourism development.

Another common climatic factor is the scarcity of water, a resource that is keenly sought after for a variety of competing uses: agriculture, tourism, industrialisation and urbanisation.[2] The problem is particularly severe in the Southern and Eastern rims of the Mediterranean. Countries in the south receive 15% of the region's rainfall but are home to one-half of the region's population.[3] Another common feature is the strong wind that blows from the interior lands to the coast, causing substantial soil erosion and deforestation. Clearly, there is increasing pressure on natural resources (be they water, forests or wetlands) deriving from uncontrolled population growth. Pressure is highest in the coastal areas where population and tourism concentrate.

Similar Comparative Advantage in Agriculture and Manpower Services

Proximity to Central and Northern Europe combined with the agricultural potential in perishable fruits and vegetables give rise to similar trade flows originating in the Mediterranean basin and heading north. In the same vein, the short distance to a much richer region explains the substantial labour flows from South to North.

---

[2] Of course, scarcity is a relative term. What happens is that water seems to be artificially underpriced throughout the Mediterranean region, a situation which creates tremendous aberrations. Private agents have an interest in using water-intensive methods leading many Mediterranean countries to export their water to Northern Europe in the form of water-intensive products (e.g. cotton).

[3] *The Economist*, 21 December 1991. See also Grenon and Batisse (1989); World Bank/EIB (1990).

Strategic Location between Industrialised Europe and the Energy-Rich Gulf Countries

Both European and the Gulf countries must seek acquiescence from or cooperation with Mediterranean states to efficiently transfer crude oil or its derivatives from the latter countries to the former (by ship or by pipeline). The alternative route (around Africa) is much longer and more expensive, particularly if the oil is destined for use in Southern or Central Europe.[4]

Admiration for Northern and Central European Countries

These countries are viewed in a favourable light either as political, social and economic role models or as a source of advanced technology. Additionally, they are seen as less intrusive than other political centres which possess large military arsenals, such as Moscow or Washington. The need to compensate for neutrality towards the superpowers by linking up with Europe, however, has disappeared with the end of the Cold War.

A European Sphere of Influence

For several decades now, the European Community has developed a series of policies in external relations. Being a part of Europe's hinterland and its colonial history has conferred on the Mediterranean region the privilege of receiving special treatment by the EC under single umbrella arrangements.

The foregoing presented the basic arguments in support of a common treatment of the Mediterranean region. At the same time, however, there are several factors that argue against the wisdom of a regional approach. A few are presented below.

---

[4] Note that I intentionally ignore the now obsolete role of the Mediterranean in the strategic plans of both the US and the former USSR.

2. Differences in the Region

Coexistence of Different Religions and Cultures

The fact that not all the states are secular presents some real difficulties in approaching the region as a whole. The Mediterranean is still one of the frontier areas between Islam and Christianity. In addition, many coastal states have important religious minorities (e.g. Egypt, Yugoslavia, Cyprus, and Israel).

Heterogeneous Political Regimes

The Mediterranean is a veritable laboratory for the political scientist. Working examples of parliamentary democracies, military dictatorships and quasi-feudal monarchies can all be found in the region.

Geographical Spread over Three Continents

Because the countries of the Mediterranean can be found in Europe, Africa, and Asia, the United Nations and other international institutions (such as the World Bank) treat them for the most part as members of different groupings without due consideration for the commonalities cited earlier. Virtually no institution treats the Mediterranean countries as a collective region in statistical terms.

Political and Economic Union of Europe

Progress of the European Community towards both political and economic union necessarily has the effect of dividing the coastal states between those enjoying EC member status and those that do not.

As suggested by the examples cited above, it is largely non-economic factors that lead us to discount the Mediterranean as a valid subject for regional study. Although it is difficult to generalise, the commonalities are those linked to climatic conditions, factor endowments and geography -- three factors close to the heart of the economist. Being one myself, therefore, I have no particular difficulty in speaking about "the Mediterranean economy".

II. GNP, Population and GNP per Capita in Non-EC Member Mediterranean Countries

Below is a quick assessment, using general economic indicators, of Mediterranean countries that are non-members of the European Community (MNMCs). (See Table A1 in the Annex.) The first indicator considered is the gross national product (GNP), a figure which is important for assessing both the relative economic weight as well as the relative market size of a country. Table 1 ranks Mediterranean countries (including EC members) by GNP.[5]

Several comments are worth making about the figures in Table 1. Firstly, one should note that the top six countries in the list are European, the first three of which, representing three-quarters of the Mediterranean's total GNP, are members of the European Community. Of course, one may question whether France should be considered a Mediterranean country, particularly in light of the fact that its main economic centres are located outside of the Mediterranean region. Since the time of the Roman empire, the real Mediterranean giant has been Italy, a country which is both rich and densely populated. At several points in its history, in fact, it has tried to organise economic life throughout the Mediterranean on the strength of its location.

At the lower end of the ranking are five countries (including Syria) whose economies are quite small. It is striking that the GNP of Israel is now larger than that of Egypt, Syria and Jordan combined. Israel, in fact, is now in another league altogether with Turkey, Greece and Algeria, particularly due to the influx of migrant labour into its work

---

[5] No data exist for Albania and Lebanon.

Table 1

GNP of Mediterranean Countries
(millions of US $)

Rank	Country	1990	1980
1	France	1,099,750	627,700
2	Italy	970,619	368,860
3	Spain	429,404	199,780
4	Turkey	91,742	66,080
5	Yugoslavia	72,860	58,570
6	Greece	60,245	42,190
7	Algeria	51,585	36,410
8	Israel	50,866	17,440
9	Egypt	31,381	23,140
10	Morocco	23,788	17,440
11	Libya (1989)	23,333	25,730
12	Syria	12,404	12,030
13	Tunisia	11,592	8,340
14	Cyprus	5,633	2,210
15	Jordan	3,924	3,244
16	Malta	2,342	1,190

Source: *World Bank Atlas*, 1980 and 1991, World Bank, Washington, D.C.

force (whose positive effects are not yet reflected in the 1990 figures). Cyprus' economy is larger than Jordan's. And the case of Yugoslavia is special in that one could speak until quite recently of there being one economy; the situation today is considerably complicated by the country's internal conflicts. Quite striking also is the fact that a decade ago Israel's GNP was below those of Egypt and Libya. The GNP of Syria and Libya have barely changed in this period. The economic performance of all other Mediterranean Arab countries as well as Malta have been very poor. Note as well that Italy's economy was less than two-thirds the size of France's a decade ago, but nowadays they are almost the same. Compared to the economy of the EC 12, that of MNMCs as a whole is very small. For instance in 1985, the GNP of the EC 12 was more than ten times larger than that of the MNMCs.

Population figures are a helpful indicator for assessing the size of the market for mass-consumption goods. Turkey and Egypt dominate the picture among MNMCs, but Algeria and Morocco also have large populations. All other Mediterranean non-EC member countries are quite small and two of them actually qualify as micro-states (i.e. Malta and Cyprus). Taken as a whole, however, Mediterranean non-member countries are almost as populous as the US at present. Moreover, demographers predict that in about 25 years, the Arab world will contain about 400 million people -- more than the EC 12! Annual population growth figures for 1980-88 are above the 2.5% mark for all of Northern Africa, Syria and Jordan and are fairly high for Turkey as well. This contrasts markedly with respective figures for Northern Mediterranean countries: France (0.5%), Greece (0.5%), Italy (0.2%) and Spain (0.5%).

GNP per capita is the most concise indicator for national standards of living and development levels. Table 2 ranks Mediterranean countries by this indicator for 1990 and shows the 1980 figure as well for purposes of comparison. Six out of the first seven countries listed in the table are European. The seventh (Israel) is a special case, being located in the Eastern Mediterranean. Clearly, the Mediterranean is a border zone between the industrialised and Third World. Observe that GNP per capita diminishes fairly gradually when moving eastward from France to Syria, whereas the change is abrupt when moving southward from France: Morocco's GNP per capita in 1990 was only 5% and 9% as large as that of France and Spain, respectively. We find only as shocking an economic disparity in the Eastern Mediterranean when focusing on the example of Egypt and Israel.[6] Turkey's low ranking is not surprising,

---

[6] As a point of reference, consider that the relative gap between the US and Mexico is less significant than that between the two examples cited. Mexico, however, is a newly industrialising country and enjoys a higher standard of living than either Morocco or Egypt.

given that one-half of the country, from Ankara eastward, is extremely poor and underdeveloped.

Table 2

GNP per Capita of Mediterranean Countries
(thousands of US $)

Rank	Country	1990	1980
1	France	19,480	11,730
2	Italy	16,850	6,480
3	Israel	10,970	4,500
4	Spain	10,920	5,350
5	Cyprus	8,040	3,560
6	Malta	6,630	3,470
7	Greece	6,000	4,520
8	Libya (1989)	5,310	8,640
9	Yugoslavia	3,060	2,620
10	Algeria	2,060	1,920
11	Turkey	1,630	1,460
12	Tunisia	1,420	1,310
13	Jordan	1,240	1,420
14	Syria	990	1,340
15	Morocco	950	860
16	Egypt	600	580

Source: *World Bank Atlas*, 1980 and 1991, World Bank, Washington, D.C.

How have the rankings changed in the 1980s? How have the different countries fared in the last decade? GNP per capita has practically doubled or tripled in US $ (i.e. nominal) terms for the first six countries on the list (all of which are European, except Israel). Conversely Syria, Jordan and Libya have seen their GNP per capita diminish in absolute terms, while the rest of the Mediterranean countries have seen their GNP per capita either stagnate or rise very slowly. Even Greece and

Yugoslavia are experiencing similarly poor results, a fact which is increasingly coming to the attention of international institutions. Nevertheless, their record is better than that of the North African countries, most probably because their population growth has been almost non-existent. In fact, in much of North Africa and Turkey, growth in GNP per capita has been neutralised by the population explosion occurring in those countries. Moreover, the shape of the "population pyramid" works against achieving high savings rates.

Of course, the evolution in crude-oil prices has much to do with the change in fortune of many Mediterranean countries. For instance until 1985, Libya was the second most affluent country in the region after France. More generally we observe a "scales effect" (*effet de bascule*) in the Mediterranean. When the price of oil goes up, the terms of trade of oil-poor Northern Mediterranean countries deteriorate sharply, affecting their growth record (as in the 1970s). The reverse happened in the 1980s. In turn, oil- and gas-rich Southern Mediterranean countries (e.g. Libya, Algeria and Egypt) suffered enormously from the secular decline in oil prices. In fact, GNP and GNP per capita growth rates for Egypt, Algeria, Tunisia and Yugoslavia were quite impressive in the 1970s and extremely low for Italy, Spain, France and Israel. Recent data show that the standard of living in Algeria and Yugoslavia totally stagnated or marginally decreased in the last decade. (Although the link is not proven, this may have something to do with the current turmoil in both countries.)

Note that there are many NICs (newly industrialising countries) located in the Mediterranean, although, or so it seems, fewer than there were a decade ago. It is debatable whether Spain or Israel still falls into this category. On the other hand, Algeria, Egypt and Syria, which not long ago were considered by some scholars as "incipient" NICs, are still highly dependent on mining and/or agriculture. As a matter of fact, in the mid-1970s when scholars were eager to discover clusters of NICs, the triad composed of Southeast Asia, Latin America and the Mediterranean was often cited. It was presumed that an industrialisation strategy based on oil and gas would succeed -- an expectation that has, unfortunately, proved unfounded. Not surprisingly, the Mediterranean today is rarely characterised as a viable NIC cluster.

Finally, to complete this panorama, a word about using GNP per capita figures for assessing welfare standards. According to economists at the UNDP (United Nations Development Programme), it is more appropriate to use the Human Development Index (HDI), a composite figure based on purchasing power units, life expectancy and adult literacy. The UNDP has succeeded in compiling such data for a two-year period for all the countries of the world and has ranked their populations on a scale from the "most miserable" to the "happiest". As far as the Mediterranean goes, it appears that the Northern Mediterranean countries (excluding Turkey) and Israel rank lower in terms of their HDI than in GNP per capita. Turkey holds the same position in the two rankings, whereas all other Mediterranean countries appear to be less well off than what one would think according to their GNP per capita. This is particularly the case in Libya and Algeria.[7]

Thus, the UNDP refinements only strengthen the impression of a substantial discrepancy in the development levels between Mediterranean Europe plus Israel on the one hand and the rest of the region, on the other. In fact, from the point of view of an international institution such as the World Bank, the Mediterranean is a mixed bag of countries including industrialised countries with market economies, developing countries with medium-income levels, petroleum-exporting countries and exporters of manufactured goods.

---

[7] See *The Economist*, 26 May 1990. In 1987, Algeria and Libya were ranked 91 and 103 in terms of GDP per capita, respectively (out of 130 countries) but 57 and 67, respectively, in terms of HDI.

III. The Economic Structures of MNMCs: Permanent Features, Factors of Instability and Long-Term Change[8]

1. Permanent Features

a. A large share of the *population* lives from agricultural and service activities, particularly in the most populated countries, such as Turkey, Morocco and Egypt (see Tables A2 and A7).[9] The share of the economically active population involved in agriculture is still larger than that engaged in industry in several MNMCs (Egypt, Morocco and Turkey). However, some of that share may actually be "hidden" unemployment. This applies to services as well.

b. In terms of contribution to GDP (gross domestic product), the *share of agriculture* is systematically lower than its share among the economically active population, a situation that points to low productivity in relative terms (see Table A3). The explanation lies in the typically small family farms, scarce water, lack of human capital, low mechanisation and marketing deficiencies. The "green" revolution has not yet taken root in most MNMCs. Food production per capita stagnated in the 1980s or seriously declined as in the case of Syria (see Table A7). The demographic explosion led to massive basic-food imports (cereals, meat, sugar), which have become a key element in MNMC import baskets (comprising between 20% to 30%; see Table A7).[10]

---

[8] From this point on in the paper, I shall be concerned exclusively with those countries that are the focus of the EC's Mediterranean policies. This includes some potential members (e.g. Turkey), but not Mediterranean member countries.

[9] The exceptions are Libya, Israel, Jordan, Lebanon and Malta, which, in light of their small populations, do not alter the general picture. For all other MNMCs, the share is above 20%.

[10] In Egypt, for example, more than 75% of the grain consumed is imported. An important exception to the rule is Turkey, which is self-sufficient in primary-food production.

It is important to note, nevertheless, that efficiency is very high in those agricultural sectors[11] producing for sophisticated overseas consumers in Europe (and the EC in particular).[12] The MNMCs are indisputably important actors in world trade of citrus fruit, tomatoes, avocados, raisins, dry fruit, potatoes, tobacco, cotton and olive oil (see Table A15). Many of these goods are not even thought appropriate for local consumption (see Table A14). Agricultural exports account for more than 20% and 10%, respectively, of Turkey's and Morocco's imports. Nevertheless, less than a decade ago, agricultural exports accounted for 10% or more of total exports (see Table A7) for almost every MNMC (and reached a quarter of total exports for Turkey and Cyprus). Therefore the importance of stability and predictability of future relations with the EC cannot be overestimated as key ingredients for success.

c. *Industry's share of GNP* among Mediterranean non-EC member countries is generally more than twice as high as that of agriculture (excepting Syria, where the share of industry in 1990 was less than that of agriculture). However, the share of industry in GNP composition may be somehow distorted for some MNMCs (e.g. Algeria) given that all mining activities (such as oil and phosphate extraction) are included in the category of "industry". Apart from the latter, light labour-intensive industries are the dominant feature: food processing, textiles and clothing, leather and travel goods.[13] In some MNMCs with a large capacity to absorb pollution, highly-polluting industries have been established. A certain potential exists for these industries (e.g. cement, fertilisers, plastics, and leather tanning), given the increasing environmental protection imposed by OECD countries in their own home

---

[11] Although, as noted above, this efficiency is based on unrealistically low water prices.

[12] For example, according to the Food and Agricultural Organisation (FAO) of the United Nations, about 90% of Morocco's citrus production is destined for export markets, of which 70% goes to the EC.

[13] For example, the textile industry in Tunisia employs nearly 5.5% of the active population, procures 55% of jobs in industry and accounts for 30% of the country's exports. *Telex Mediterranean*, 29 May 1992. See also Pomfret (1986).

economies and the lack of alternative uses for arid desert lands.[14]

A common feature of the MNMCs is the absence of efficient, capital-intensive heavy industry using standardised technologies, in contrast to the examples of Spain or Italy. Economies of scale may prevent their development in the smaller countries, such as Jordan, Lebanon, Cyprus, Malta or even Israel. Another explanatory factor is the lack of industrial raw materials and water for basic production of electricity in the Southern and Eastern rims of the Mediterranean. Capital-equipment industries are clearly underrepresented throughout the region, and "high-tech" industry is virtually non-existent (except in the case of Israel) due to inadequate human-capital endowments. In any case, one should not ignore the fact that more than 95% of industrial value-added in the Mediterranean originates in its northern shore (and 85% in France, Italy and Spain).

d. Most of the activity in *services* is concentrated in distribution, transport and tourism. The share of this sector in GDP (gross domestic product) is particularly high in Jordan and Egypt, 66% and 54%, respectively, in 1990 (see Table A3). Tourism alone accounts for more than 10% of GNP for Malta, Israel and Cyprus, and is close to that figure for Tunisia. For all these countries and for Morocco, tourism services account for between 10% and 20% of imports. Apart from Egypt and Israel, all other MNMCs suffer (as do Spain and Greece) from the seasonality of tourism. For instance, more than 70% of tourists arrive in Yugoslavia in the summer. In absolute numbers this country has absorbed more tourists in the past than has Greece (8.5 million in 1986), but other MNMCs had a much poorer record in the 1980s (some with as few as less than 3 million in one year). None of the MNMCs can compare yet with Italy, Spain or France in tourism. The sector has, however, been growing at very high rates over the past five years, and Turkey has now replaced Yugoslavia as the main tourist destination among MNMCs.

---

[14] Note however that with the advent of the single market, EC demand for exports of polluting intermediary or final products from MNMCs (e.g. certain kinds of fertilisers or washing powders) may diminish.

e. As a rule, MNMCs report a *negative trade balance* (except for Libya and Algeria). The export of services, migrant remittances and official transfers, however, allow for the practical balancing of the current account in many MNMCs (see Table A4). This balance was positive in 1990 for Algeria, Cyprus, Egypt, Israel, Jordan, Libya and Syria. Migrant remittances are particularly significant for Egypt (where they are larger than the amount of goods exported) as well as Yugoslavia, Jordan and Morocco (where they represent about 50% or more than exports). This is one reason why a war such as the Gulf conflict in 1991 can have drastic economic implications for many MNMCs.

f. Given the geographical proximity, historical links and contractual agreements between the EC 12 and the MNMCs, as well as their respective economic sizes, a strong *asymmetric trade interdependence* has grown up between these two groupings. This asymmetry is bound to increase further with the inevitable expansion of EC trade with Eastern Europe and the CIS (Commonwealth of Independent States, formerly the republics of the Soviet Union). Table A6 shows that the share of the EC 12 in MNMC exports ranged between 28% and 83% in 1991 (excepting Lebanon and Jordan). Export dependence is extreme (more than 67%) for all Maghreb countries (including Libya) and Malta. Southeastern Mediterranean countries are the least trade dependent on the EC.

The degree of trade dependence of MNMCs in relation to the EC 12 is comparable to other subregions which have also long-standing institutional linkages with the EC (e.g. the ACP -- African, Caribbean and Pacific -- countries). In Table A8 the average share that the EC 12 has in the total imports and exports of different subregions has been calculated for the period 1980-83. In exports the role played by the EC 12 in the MNMCs is only slightly less than the one it played in sub-Saharan Africa and much greater than in Eastern Europe or the Caribbean members of the ACP group, two subregions that have historically been very close to the EC 12. For the latter, MNMCs are a much less important trading partner than the EFTA (European Free Trade

Association), but also than the US or even Japan.[15] It is true, however, that MNMCs remain the EC's most important regional trading partners from the developing world (e.g. more than sub-Saharan Africa, Latin America, Asia or the Gulf),[16] but this is rapidly changing with the emergence of Eastern Europe and the CIS as key EC trading partners.

As shown in Table A9, the share of MNMCs in EC exports has been declining over the last decade (from 11% in 1980 to 8.2% in 1988). And although the MNMC share of EC imports has remained stable, MNMCs have now been surpassed by Southeast Asia as a supplier of the EC (4.6% and 5.6% in 1988, respectively), as per Table A10. But the EC is keen to preserve existing trade relations for the following reasons:

- The EC has accumulated a large trade-balance surplus with the MNMCs;

- MNMCs have become important clients for some EC exports subsidised under the Common Agriculture Policy (CAP); and

- MNMCs are providers of some strategic commodities (such as crude oil, natural gas, and phosphates) to the EC.

In fact, more than one-half of the EC's imports from MNMCs can be explained by one of these three reasons. Intra-MNMC trade is negligible except for Jordan, Syria and Lebanon.

g. *Accumulated external debt* is a real plague for all MNMCs, resulting from a combination of food deficits (created by the demographic explosion), armed conflict and macroeconomic mismanagement. Lack of energy cannot, in my view, explain the current high levels of external debt, given that the price of oil has been going down in real terms over the last decade. About one-quarter or more of total exports (goods and

---

[15] Japan has become a more important supplier of the European Community (accounting for 10.7% of total imports in 1988) than are MNMCs.

[16] See Aliboni (1990), p. 140.

services) were used in 1990 to cover debt service on public debt in several MNMCs (Algeria, Israel, Syria, Tunisia and Turkey). What is worse is the fact that this burden has increased systematically in the last decade (except in Morocco). Incidentally, in 1988 the external debt of Egypt and Morocco was larger than their GNP. By the end of 1989, Egypt's debt was the sixth highest among developing countries.[17]

h. *Official Development Assistance* (ODA), mostly from the US, has been an important means for Israel and Egypt to partially finance both the balance of payments and to service external debt over the past decade. Other MNMCs have had to fend for themselves. The EC has not been an important donor to the MNMCs (accounting for only 3% of ODA received), assigning to the area only 11.5% of total ODA granted between 1979 to 1987 (compared to 67% to ACP countries). Some individual EC countries (particularly France and Germany) have been more generous. Even so, the EC's bilateral and multilateral ODA was less than that of OPEC or the US. As far as private investment is concerned, however, most flows come from EC countries.[18]

2. Factors of Change and Instability

a. *Oil price instability* has a tremendous impact on the whole region and is an immensely disrupting factor. A sudden increase in relative oil prices automatically implies for one-half of the MNMCs (Algeria, Tunisia, Egypt, Libya and Syria) an improvement in the terms of trade and a shift of resources from agriculture and industry to mining. When oil prices decline, the reverse happens. Dramatic fluctuations have occurred several times in the past 25 years owing to the fact that the price of crude oil contains an important political element, heavily

---

[17] Meanwhile, Egypt has been forgiven for about one-half of its official debt as an outcome of negotiations with the International Monetary Fund (IMF) in the wake of the Gulf war in 1991.

[18] For instance in 1990, EC countries represented 70% of foreign investment in Turkey. *Telex Mediterranean*, 18 October 1991.

influenced by military tensions (such as the recent Gulf conflict) and other psychological factors.[19] From a long-term perspective, this instability is as devastating as that experienced in commodity prices for many sub-Saharan African countries.

b. Demand for *tourist* services is also highly affected by political tensions. Unfortunately, investment in tourism activities has become a high-risk proposition in a region which in the long run is ideally situated to receive large numbers of tourists seeking relief from the expensive food and accommodations available in Spain, Portugal or Greece where prices tend quite naturally to be aligned with EC averages.

c. *Migrant workers' income and remittances* represent an important means in several MNMCs for financing the trade deficit and insuring the survival of part of the population (the migrants and their families back home). This income, however, is subject to several hazards: a) legislative changes in the host country's social legislation (e.g. in the domain of work-permit renewal, visa requirements, or family reunification); b) changes in foreign-currency legislation in the migrant's home country; c) war and political turmoil in the host country (e.g. the Gulf states); and d) macroeconomic instability in the host countries (e.g. an economic slump affects migrants more drastically than nationals).

3. Long-Term Changes

a. Uncontrolled *population growth* in the Southern and Eastern rims of the Mediterranean basin if unchecked may lead to increasing poverty and ecological catastrophe. (Almost) all MNMCs are eager to attract

---

[19] Note as well that (known) oil reserves in MNMCs are much lower than in the Gulf countries: at present rates of extraction, Libya for example possesses approximately a 60-year supply compared to a 15-year supply for Egypt and Algeria. In the case of the latter, however, gas production could last for many more decades. See also Luciani (1984).

increasing numbers of tourists,[20] who tend to gravitate towards the narrow coastal strip. Additionally, the number of residents living in the coastal cities of the Southern shore will more than treble by 2025. As a result, three-quarters of the increase in demand for fresh water will come from the Southern and Eastern Mediterranean countries. Experts calculate that whereas land-based environmental degradation is now much worse in the North than in the South of the Mediterranean, this will radically change in the coming decades. Pollution and other health hazards may actually dissuade tourists to travel to MNMCs. On poverty levels, see the earlier discussion on current trends in GNP per capita.

b. The exploitation of natural comparative advantage in Mediterranean-type products has been impaired both by the EC's Common Agricultural Policy and lately by the southern enlargement of the EC.[21] Table A7 shows that *agricultural exports* from the Mediterranean region have stagnated (except in the case of Turkey). This trend should continue until 1996, when the transition period to full agricultural integration of Spain and Portugal into the EC will have ended, particularly in the areas of fruit and vegetables. Countries like Morocco should prepare themselves for a real shock since the adaptation protocols to the cooperation agreements between the Mediterranean countries and the EC, designed to account for the southern enlargement of the EC, provide zero-duty access to the EC only for "traditional exports" of fruit and vegetables, i.e. an average of what was exported in the period 1980-84.

The only possible strategy for the MNMCs (and this is viable only if Spain does not take similar steps) is to devote resources to the production of tropical or other crops (such as flowers, grapefruit or hazelnuts) that are not yet mass-produced in Spain. As far as markets are concerned, there are no real alternatives to Western Europe for Mediterranean-type

---

[20] Between 170 and 340 million tourists are expected to arrive annually on Mediterranean shores by the year 2025, up from 52 million in 1984. See Grenon and Batisse (1989).

[21] For a thorough analysis of the triangular links between the CAP, the EC's southern enlargement and the MNMCs, see Tovias (1979), Musto (1988), Yannopoulos (1988), Swinbank and Ritson (1988) and Tovias (1990).

products due to their highly perishable nature. In time (perhaps a decade), the CIS and Eastern European countries may come to partially replace the EC as a destination for Mediterranean goods.

c. Long-term trade liberalisation by OECD countries combined with preferential tariff treatment by the EC have initiated a slow but *significant shift of resources* from import-competing sectors to industries with high export potential based on an abundance of local factor endowments: labour and some raw materials (such as phosphates). This phenomenon is occurring in textiles and clothing, leather and travel goods, food processing, chemicals (and in the case of Israel in some "high-tech" industries). Table A11 shows that the average tariff rates imposed by the EC 10 in 1983 on MNMC imports were lower (1.9%) than those applied on imports from OECD countries (3.2%), former socialist countries, excluding China (2.7%) or even other developing countries, including China (2.1%).[22] The margin (in relation to former socialist or other developing countries) was particularly large for chemical, pharmaceutical and plastic products, textiles, clothing and footwear.

Not surprisingly, then, the share of manufactures in exports rose in the period 1980-1987 in Morocco (from 23.5% to 48.7%), Tunisia (from 35.8% to 60.7%) and Turkey (26.9% to 66.3%). The share was already high in 1980 for Cyprus, Malta, Yugoslavia and Israel and therefore increased more slowly (see Table A12). On the other hand, the share of mining exports dropped quite dramatically in Egypt, Tunisia and Morocco, as a result of a stabilisation or decrease in the real price of oil and phosphates.[23] MNMCs have suffered relatively less than other developing countries from non-tariff barriers (NTB) erected in the last

---

[22] 1983 was the mid-point of implementation of the Tokyo Round provisions which still prevail, but the overall pattern has not changed since then except for the important fact that former socialist countries receive much better treatment under the Europe Agreements than they had previously.

[23] Oil and gas, however, still represented 98% of Algerian exports at the end of the 1980s!

decade by the EC 12 against the import of "sensitive products" -- officially because of the MNMC position in the EC's pyramid of privilege; less officially because European companies have traditionally invested heavily in those countries and applied political pressure to safeguard their investments.

It is not at all clear that MNMCs would benefit from the abolition of the Multi-Fibre Agreement (MFA). In Table A13, information is given for each SITC division (excluding SITC 9) on the EC's NTB treatment of imports from MNMCs and other broad groups of countries (the same groupings as shown for tariffs in Table A11). The table shows a significantly lower incidence in the application of NTBs against MNMC trade than against other groups of countries and against the world in general. With respect to individual SITC divisions, there are only a few industrial products in which the share of trade from MNMCs affected by some kind of NTB is higher than that for other groups of countries (e.g. textile fibres and leather manufactures).[24] Note, however, the astronomical level of NTBs on imports of Mediterranean agricultural products, which are high even in relation to other groups of countries.

d. A radical change in industrialisation policies from import substitution to *export-led strategies* has taken place in most MNMCs -- although at different points in time. Small MNMCs, which had the most to gain, already changed gears in the 1960s or 1970s (e.g. Israel, Tunisia, Malta, Cyprus); others did it in the 1980s mostly under the guidance of the World Bank (e.g. Morocco and Turkey); and still others are trying to do it right now (e.g. Syria and Algeria). Some MNMCs have even attempted to be integrated into what I call the European system of intra-industry trade and sought export-oriented direct foreign investment (DFI).

e. The new growth perspectives in the EC announced in the Cecchini Report (Commission of the EC, 1988) and which result from the completion of the single market may motivate more than one MNMC migrant to move to an EC country to try his luck in what is perceived as

---

[24] Turkey has suffered from anti-dumping actions by the EC in several sectors.

the new El Dorado.[25]   On the other hand, most EC countries have agreed under the so-called Schengen Agreement that in order to implement the White Paper with respect to the abolition of internal border controls, they must adopt a common visa policy and strengthen control of the external Community borders. This may basically mean *common rules for the crossing of the external frontiers* of the member states.

The danger as perceived by outsiders is that the Schengen provisions and, later on, EC rules will approximate the harshest conditions presently prevailing at national level, rather than those from the more lenient regimes.[26]   MNMC citizens may reason that the later they take the plunge, the more difficult it will be to eventually secure an EC passport. The consequences of the Schengen Agreement for MNMC immigration will be substantial. Once there exists a common EC visitor's visa, an "overstayer" will have an easier time than he does now. It is much simpler to remain undetected in a population of 340 million people -- larger by far than the US (240 million) -- than in the largest EC member state, namely Germany (80 million).

In fact, the situation has been changing in the EC since the mid-1980s following a decade of relative stability in immigration (due, in large part, to the strict measures taken by European governments in the aftermath of the first oil crisis of 1973). Between 1979 and 1987, the number of legal immigrants in the EC, which are not citizens of one of its members, has doubled from 4 to 8 million (see Figures A1 and A2 for more data on net Community immigration). Of that figure, more than 4.5 million originated in MNMCs, representing about 2% of the EC's population. More than 50% of these individuals are economically active. It is

---

[25] See *The Economist*, 16 March 1991.

[26] The requirement that North African nationals obtain a visa to visit any EC country appears particularly discriminatory at a time when these same countries have abolished one after another visa-entry requirements for East European nationals. For more information on this sensitive subject, see Callovi (1990), Commission of the EC (1990b), ILO (1989), and Martin and Honekopp (1990).

estimated that in 1989, an additional 3 million were illegally residing in the southern part of the EC mostly originating from the Maghreb, Yugoslavia and Turkey. Egyptians and Palestinians tend to migrate to other Arab countries (for the present). The destination of Tunisian migrants is mixed (both to the EC and to Arab countries).

f. The prospect of a real single market of 340 million consumers has attracted and will continue to attract to the EC not only immigrants but also *investment capital* at a significantly higher level than existed before the Community's 1992 programme was launched in 1985. A new investor who intends to market his product in the EC will know that if he locates his investment on EC territory, he will not have to contend with NTBs, which he would immediately confront if trying to penetrate the EC market from outside, e.g. from a MNMC.

In that respect, the completion of the single market is bound to influence decisions of those investors who focus on a product (a good or service) that 1) can be produced competitively either in the EC or a MNMC, and 2) faced significant NTBs in intra-EC trade before 1993, but that now can move freely from market to market within the EC. There are many products in the MNMC-export basket that meet both conditions (e.g. all foodstuffs), while the first condition also applies to clothing and fertilisers. The fact that in most cases the overlap in comparative advantage is between MNMCs on the one hand, and Spain and Portugal on the other, leads some experts to attribute investment diversion in favour of the latter (e.g. in agro-industry projects) to their entry into the EC.

This analysis is only partially true. Without the prospect of the single market, agro-business investments in Spain and Portugal would have been perceived as much less attractive. A counter-argument frequently made in MNMCs predicts a rapid rise in labour costs in the Iberian Peninsula as a result of the completion of a single labour market for EC nationals, thereby increasing the labour-cost differential in favour of MNMCs. But this overlooks the fact that the level of non-qualified labour unemployment in Spain is the highest of all the OECD countries. Nevertheless, Spain may be prepared in the future to import workers from across the Straight of Gibraltar, at least on a temporary or seasonal basis, in order to decelerate rising wage rates. The experience of the 1960s and 1970s has shown as well that the freedom of movement by workers under the Treaty of Rome did not lead to massive migrations from Italy to the other five EC members.

But the argument is right in one respect, namely that Spanish and Portuguese firms will have to comply with higher standards than presently apply in the realm of social legislation. Thus it would make sense for MNMCs to liberalise (further) their foreign investment laws. Secondly, in some cases the amount of investment in the EC that a MNMC firm (whether locally- or foreign-owned) will be required to make in order to overcome the problem of market access may be relatively small -- ranging from establishing a simple representation in the EC to forming a joint venture with an EC firm. Even enterprises from capital-poor countries, like MNMCs, can try these routes, although they would require a further relaxation of exchange controls.

g. The economic periphery of Western Europe has been enlarged substantially with the end of the Cold War. In practical terms, this means that footloose European investors now have more alternatives than before for *locating labour-intensive activities* closer to home. Eastern European countries will compete with MNMCs in subcontracting, which has been a real boon in the past for Malta, Tunisia and Morocco. Although less important for MNMCs (excepting Israel and maybe Turkey), the creation of the European Economic Area (EEA) as of January 1994, further erodes their relative attractiveness to potential investors.

IV. Concluding Remarks

The economic fate of the MNMCs is a function both of their socio-economic policies and what will eventually transpire in Europe. To begin with the latter, the sensitivity of almost all of the MNMCs to any institutional change in the Community follows from their economic interdependence with the EC 12. Therefore, MNMCs cannot accept easily the view that the completion of the single market or the creation of a European Economic Area is a purely domestic European affair. On the other hand, it is also inappropriate to blame those developments for past or future erosion of MNMC privileges and status in the EC market resulting from other commitments which the Community may have undertaken in the course of time (such as its enlargement to include Spain and Portugal or the new association agreements with Eastern European countries).

By and large, these events portend bad news for the MNMCs and there is no point in avoiding that fact. On the contrary, the sooner the MNMCs take notice of the new reality, the earlier they can begin adapting to it. Domestically this means proceeding with economic reform and adjustment (including privatisation, deregulation, etc.). But the demographic explosion in the Maghreb, the Mashreq and in Turkey critically undermines the benefits that could normally be expected to accrue from the introduction of adjustment and economic reform policies in most of these countries. This conclusion also should not be hidden. MNMCs should have the courage to recognise that Europe is neither going to engage in a massive transfer of resources to MNMCs nor accept massive migration from the region, just because the latter countries are unable to contain uncontrolled population growth.

Nevertheless, this is not to say that there is nothing the EC can do to help the MNMCs and is therefore justified in giving priority to Eastern Europe and the republics of the former Soviet Union. On the contrary; rising fundamentalism, fuelled by the frustrations prevalent in some MNMCs, is at least as important a challenge to liberal democracies in the European Community as is economic mismanagement.[27] The latter has afflicted Eastern Europe and the CIS; the former, sometimes together with the latter, afflicts Europe's southern periphery. Moreover, as we have seen, many of the unwanted, long-term changes which will affect future MNMC economic structures will originate in Europe. In conclusion, the Community has the means to change the course of events provided it can summon up the necessary political will.

---

[27] For more on this subject, see Tovias (1992a).

Statistical Annex

Table A1
General Economic Indicators
of the Mediterranean States, 1990

Country	GNP (mil. of US $)	GNP Real Growth Rate 1980-90 (%)	GNP/Capita (US $)	GNP/Capita Growth Rate 1988-90 (%)	Population (thousands)	Population Growth Rate 1980-90 (%)
Algeria	51,585	2.7	2,060	-2.0	25,056	3.0
Cyprus	5,633	6.0	8,040	5.4	701	1.1
Egypt	31,381	4.7	600	-1.2	52,061	2.5
Israel	50,866	3.2	10,970	0.6	4,636	1.7
Jordan	3,924	-0.4	1,240	-13.7	3,154	3.6
Lebanon	n.a.	n.a.	n.a.	n.a.	n.a.	n.a.
Libya[a]	23,333	-5.4	5,310	-9.2	4,395	4.1
Malta	2,342	3.1	6,630	6.4	353	-0.5
Morocco	23,788	4.3	950	0.1	25,091	2.7
Syria	12,404	1.4	990	-0.9	12,533	3.6
Tunisia	11,592	3.4	1,420	3.8	8,175	2.5
Turkey	91,742	5.5	1,630	3.4	56,277	2.4
Yugoslavia	72,860	-0.2	3,060	-3.3	23,800	0.7

[a] Data for 1989.

Table A2
Shares of the Economically Active Population (%)

Country	Year	Agriculture[a]	Industry[b]	Services	Not Adequately Defined
Algeria	1981	25	25	50	-
	1987	17	31	46	6
Cyprus	1980	19	34	47	-
	1989	14	28	52	6
Egypt	1981	50	30	20	-
	1986	38	22	38	2
Israel	1981	7	36	57	-
	1990	4	28	67	1
Jordan	1979	11	26	63	-
Lebanon	1981	11	27	62	-
Libya	1981	19	28	53	-
Malta	1980	6	39	55	-
	1989	0.4	5.6	94	-
Morocco	1981	52	21	27	-
Syria	1981	33	31	36	-
	1989	23	29	48	-
Tunisia	1981	35	32	33	-
	1989	26	34	38	2
Turkey	1981	54	13	33	-
	1989	49	21	30	-
Yugoslavia	1981	29	35	36	-

[a] Agriculture includes hunting, forestry and fishing.
[b] Industry includes mining and quarrying, manufacturing, electricity, gas and water and construction.

Sources: ILO, *Yearbook of Labour Statistics*, Geneva, 1985, 1987 and 1991.

Table A3

Structure of Production: Distribution of GDP (%)

Country	Agriculture			Industry			Services		
	1965	1990		1965	1990		1965	1990	
Algeria	15	13		34	47		51	40	
Cyprus	-	7		-	-		-	-	
Egypt	29	17		27	29		44	54	
Israel[a]	-	5		-	-		-	-	
Jordan	-	8		-	26		-	66	
Lebanon[a]	12	9		21	-		67	-	
Libya[a]	5	4		63	-		32	-	
Malta	-	4		-	-		-	-	
Morocco	23	16		28	33		49	51	
Syria	29	28		22	22		49	50	
Tunisia	22	16		24	32		54	52	
Turkey	34	18		25	33		41	49	
Yugoslavia	23	12		42	48		35	40	

[a] Data for 1990 is a World Bank estimate.

Sources: World Bank, *World Development Report*, 1992 and *World Bank Atlas*, Washington, D.C., 1991.

Table A4
Current Account Summaries (millions of US $)

Country	Year	Merchandise Trade		Export of Services			Private Unrequited Transfers		Official Unrequited Transfers	Current Account
		Export of Goods	Trade Balance	Total	Shipment	Travel	Total	From Migrants and Workers		
Algeria	1983	12,742	3,226	679	278	152	237	235[b]	1	-85
	1990	12,964	4,187	498	126	64	332	321[b]	1	1,420
Cyprus	1983	438.1	-655.5	684.7	16.1	331.9	23.4	20.5[c]	50.9	-184.6
	1990	846.5	-1,458.3	2,082.6	16.2	1,251.8	21.9	19.6[c]	18.7	45.7
Egypt	1983	3,693	-4,558	3,133	-	285	3,688	3,666[b]	817	-330
	1990	4,650	-8,643	8,109	33	1,419	5,527	5,527[b]	1,444	237
Israel	1983	5,655	-3,149	2,732	551	1,017	809	103[c]	1,899	-1,941
	1990	12,260	-2,890	4,379	834	1,382	1,982	545[c]	3,807	702
Jordan	1982	751.6	-2,127	1,112.1	47.7	521.3	932.9	905.3[b]	1,033.5	-322.7
	1989	1,109.4	-773	1,239.2	20	545.8	565.5	536[b]	613.2	384.9
Lebanon	1983	-	-	-	-	-	-	-	-	-
	1990	-	-	-	-	-	-	-	-	-
Libya	1984	-	3,458[a]	170	-	4	-2,110[a]	-2,085[a]	-80	-1,456
	1990	-	-	117	-	6	-	-	-35	2,203
Malta	1982	421	-288.2	330.5	6.8	189.5	37.1	15.1	37.6	16.3
	1989	866.3	-461.4	669.2	23	412.6	54.8	31.9	49.6	-3.2
Morocco	1983	2,058	-1,243	861	98	457	888	879	98	-891
	1990	4,210	-2,071	2,024	154	1,280	2,012	1,990	320	-200
Syria	1983	1,918	-2,106	560	17	198	387	387[b]	1,302	-844
	1990	4,221	2,159	839	43	305	375	375[b]	80	1,827
Tunisia	1983	1,850	-1,073	1,015	59	611	346	343	41	-578
	1990	3,515	-1,678	1,680	110	1,018	593	584	215	-500
Turkey	1983	5,905	-2,990	1,939	564	420	1,549	1,513[b]	211	-1,923
	1990	13,026	-9,554	7,141	833	3,225	3,349	3,246[b]	1,162	-2,616
Yugoslavia	1983	9,917	-1,231	3,128	463	947	3,653	3,429[b]	-2	275
	1990	14,308	-2,676	6,374	669	2,774	9,830	9,360[b]	-2	-2,364

[a] Data for 1983.   [b] Workers only.   [c] Migrants only.

Source: IMF, *Balance of Payments Statistics Yearbook*, Washington, D.C., 1988 and 1991.

Table A5
External Public Debt (millions of US $)

Country	Public and Publicly Guaranteed Debt		Service Payments on Public and Publicly Guaranteed Debt		Service Payments on Public and Publicly Guaranteed Debt as a % of Exports of Goods and Services	
	1980	1990	1980	1990	1980	1990
Algeria	17,052	24,316	3,917	8,070	26.3	58.1
Cyprus	398	1,542	60	218	5.4	6.9
Egypt	16,273	34,242	749	2,769	8.1	20.9
Israel[a]	n.a.	22,495	n.a.	3,499	n.a.	25.3
Jordan	1,491	6,486	182	620	7.3	21.5
Lebanon	196.7	545	12.5	88	-	-
Libya	-	-	-	-	-	-
Malta	86.2	80.1[b]	3.1	9.3[b]	0.3	0.5[b]
Morocco	8,325	22,097	1,172	1,616	27.1	19.4
Syria	2,918	14,959	302	1,375	9.0	25.2
Tunisia	3,211	6,506	428	1,308	11.6	22.2
Turkey	15,040	38,595	1,053	6,188	18.3	24.6
Yugoslavia	4,580	13,492	616	2,042	3.4	6.6

[a] The data for Israel is from the World Bank, *World Development Report 1989*, and it is for total long-term debt for the year 1987.
[b] Data for 1989.

Source: World Bank, *World Debt Tables*, Washington, D.C., 1991-92.

Table A6
Destination of MNMC Exports to the World and the EC, 1981 and 1991

Country	Exports to the World (millions of US $)		Exports to the EC as a % of Total Exports	
	1981	1991	1981	1991
Algeria	13,296	12,314	51.0	67.7
Cyprus	562.4	975.2	30.2	44.1
Egypt	3,232.6	3,838.2	44.2	28.3
Israel	5,673.3	11,598.3	35.8	34.4
Jordan	540.8	879.2	1.6	3.1
Lebanon	1,001.7	490.2	4.5	22.7
Libya	15,575	10,775	52.7	83.8
Malta	449.6	1,140.7	70.4	71.8
Morocco	2,286.5	5,148.8	57.9	67.8
Syria	2,101.9	3,699.8	65.5	45.7
Tunisia	2,463.7	3,826.7	61.4	73.8
Turkey	4,695.6	13,334.9	33.4	50.8
Yugoslavia	10,929	16,235	23.3	56.0

Source: IMF, *Direction of Trade Statistics Yearbook*, Washington, D.C., 1988 and 1992.

Table A7
The Role of Agriculture in the Economy of the Mediterranean, 1987 - 1989

Country	Agric. Pop. as % of Total Pop. (1988)	Agric. Exports as % of Total Exports (1988)	Agric. Imports as % of Total Imports (1988)	Share of Total Imports Financed by Agric. Exports (1988)	Public Commitment to Agric. in US $ per Capita (1987)	Index of Food Production per Capita (1979-81=100) (1989)	Index of Total Agric. Production per Capita (1979-81=100) (1989)	Index of Value of Agric. Exports (1979-81=100) (1985-87)
Algeria	25	-	31	-	3.1	94	95	100
Cyprus	22	28	11	11	0.1	100	100	107
Egypt	42	12	22	3	8.1	108	101	138
Israel	5	10	8	8	-	101	92	86
Jordan	7	9	21	4	9.2	103	103	105
Lebanon	10	24	33	7	-	132	130	83
Libya	14	-	23	-	-	110	110	-
Malta	4	4	12	2	-	109	109	74
Morocco	38	16	15	12	17.7	125	126	129
Syria	25	13	20	8	1.5	62	65	101
Tunisia	26	8	18	5	64.8	94	94	81
Turkey	46	26	7	21	5.2	93	93	331
Yugoslavia	21	9	10	9	-	95	95	76

Sources: FAO, *The State of Food and Agriculture 1989, World Review*, Rome, 1990 and *The State of Food and Agriculture 1990, World Review*, Rome, 1991.

31

Table A8[a]
Trade with the EC 12 as a Percentage of Trade with the World

	1980-1983 Average	
	Imports from the EC 12	Exports to the EC 12
EC 12 (intra-EC share)	49.9	54.5
Sub-Saharan Africa	53.5	44.4
EFTA	55.4	53.2
Mediterranean Countries	43.5	42.6
Eastern Europe excl. USSR	16.1	17.1
USSR (EC 12 as a Reporter)	21.4	36.0
Caribbean under ACP	10.0	20.6
South-Central America plus Mexico	17.8	23.7
South East Asia	12.4	13.6

[a] This table also appears in a publication by the author entitled "The European Community's Single Market: The Challenge of 1992 for Sub-Saharan Africa", World Bank Discussion Papers, No. 100, 1990.

Note: Country groupings are defined as follows:

Sub-Saharan Africa: Burundi, Ethiopia, Kenya, Madagascar, Malawi, Mauritius, Rwanda, Seychelles, Somalia, Sudan, Tanzania, Uganda, Zaire, Niger, Nigeria, Senegal, Sierra Leone, Togo, Zambia, Zimbabwe, Benin, Burkina Faso, Cameroon, Central African Republic, Congo, Ivory Coast, Gabon, Gambia, Ghana, Liberia, Mali, Mauritania, Angola, Comoros, Djibouti, Mozambique, Cape Verde, Chad, Equatorial Guinea, Guinea, Guinea Bisseau and Sao Tome and Principe.

EFTA: Norway, Iceland, Finland, Sweden, Switzerland and Austria.

Mediterranean Countries: Yugoslavia, Syria, Lebanon, Turkey, Malta, Cyprus, Israel, Jordan, Egypt, Morocco, Algeria and Tunisia.

Eastern Europe excluding the USSR: Albania, Bulgaria, Czechoslovakia, East Germany, Hungary, Poland and Romania.

Caribbean under ACP: Antigua and Barbuda, Bahamas, Barbados, Belize, Dominica, Grenada, Guyana, Jamaica, St. Christopher and Nevis, St. Lucia, St. Vincent and the Grenadines, Trinidad and Tobago and Suriname.

Central-South America plus Mexico: Bolivia, Chile, Colombia, Costa Rica, Ecuador, El Salvador, Guatemala, Nicaragua, Paraguay, Peru, Argentina, Brazil, Mexico, Uruguay, Venezuela, Honduras and Panama.

South East Asia: Thailand, Kampuchea, Laos, Socialist Rep. of Vietnam, Indonesia, Macau, Malaysia, Philippines, Singapore, Brunei and Hong Kong.

Source: Comtrade data base, Geneva.

Table A9[a]

EC 12 Exports by Geographical Destination and Shares of Different Partners in Extra-EC Exports
(thousands of US $)

EC 12 Exports to:	1980	1981	1982	1983	1984	1985	1986	1987	1988
Sub-Saharan Africa	22,435,188	21,177,202	18,306,242	14,291,354	13,048,033	13,877,555	14,693,376	15,021,522	2,153,758
EFTA	75,598,716	61,340,233	58,807,030	58,222,581	59,409,286	64,309,711	85,080,001	103,700,369	9,079,294
Mediterranean Countries	33,552,015	32,413,424	30,479,794	30,260,401	29,943,324	30,480,738	32,813,504	36,132,872	4,030,674
Eastern Europe excl. USSR	13,061,472	10,950,622	8,376,642	7,606,859	7,563,797	8,414,907	10,173,857	11,564,254	1,176,753
USSR	10,836,183	9,173,051	9,041,605	11,051,561	9,839,763	9,509,898	9,693,321	10,617,005	684,580
Caribbean under ACP	1,144,109	1,347,560	1,139,482	974,391	1,072,670	790,851	1,053,762	974,478	205,748
Central-South America + Mexico	18,048,696	17,993,210	14,222,049	10,711,369	10,990,368	10,843,306	13,306,968	15,220,613	2,096,087
South East Asia	10,857,351	11,291,447	11,622,682	11,393,600	11,109,625	10,955,730	12,514,453	15,828,794	1,953,274
World	687,846,563	630,146,020	607,679,210	594,616,468	607,599,665	643,902,843	788,354,610	950,831,645	162,399,213
Intra-EC 12 based on Exports	383,824,944	334,185,439	329,840,533	325,511,041	329,799,229	352,260,607	450,034,321	559,158,974	113,223,508
Extra-EC Trade (World-Intra-EC)	304,021,619	295,960,581	277,838,655	269,105,427	277,800,436	291,642,236	338,320,289	391,672,671	49,175,705
Shares as a Percentage of Extra-EC 12									
Sub-Saharan Africa	7.4	7.2	6.6	5.3	4.7	4.8	4.3	3.8	4.4
EFTA	24.9	20.7	21.2	21.6	21.4	22.1	25.1	26.5	18.5
Mediterranean Countries	11.0	11.0	11.0	11.2	10.8	10.3	9.7	9.2	8.2
Eastern Europe excl. USSR	4.3	3.7	3.0	2.8	2.7	2.9	3.0	3.0	2.4
USSR	3.6	3.1	3.3	4.1	3.5	3.3	2.9	2.7	1.4
Caribbean under ACP	0.4	0.5	0.4	0.4	0.4	0.3	0.3	0.2	0.4
Central-South America + Mexico	5.9	6.1	5.1	4.0	4.0	3.7	3.9	3.9	4.3
South East Asia	3.6	3.8	4.2	4.2	4.0	3.8	3.7	4.0	4.0

[a] This table also appears in a publication by the author entitled "The European Community's Single Market: The Challenge of 1992 for Sub-Saharan Africa", World Bank Discussion Papers, No. 100, 1990.

See Note in Table A8 for an explanation of the country groupings.

Source: Comtrade data base, Geneva.

Table A10[a]

EC 12 Imports by Geographical Origin and Shares of Different Partners in Extra-EC Imports

(thousands of US $)

EC 12 Imports from:	1980	1981	1982	1983	1984	1985	1986	1987	1988
Sub-Saharan Africa	25,795,901	18,508,666	17,371,947	17,534,381	20,279,651	21,593,035	17,281,335	16,821,319	3,651,732
EFTA	66,275,911	57,129,076	54,624,016	56,735,947	58,654,734	61,129,593	75,861,953	93,889,083	10,410,008
Mediterranean Countries	22,986,415	22,634,911	23,378,962	22,183,898	23,282,492	25,514,399	23,887,840	28,589,463	3,131,730
Eastern Europe excl. USSR	12,537,133	10,123,504	9,524,376	9,134,832	10,057,671	10,100,873	11,466,582	13,123,185	1,483,778
USSR	15,996,381	15,401,126	17,140,587	16,822,942	18,333,752	15,810,164	13,688,734	14,947,512	2,294,653
Caribbean under ACP	2,321,831	1,557,202	1,500,268	1,062,560	975,180	1,082,425	1,046,115	1,093,953	220,686
Central-South America + Mexico	22,498,440	22,345,466	21,058,315	21,643,152	22,198,889	22,833,865	19,573,322	21,879,053	5,618,908
South East Asia	14,690,468	12,849,286	11,876,193	11,898,623	13,006,706	12,442,402	15,274,263	20,049,665	3,814,128
World	768,523,977	679,567,593	649,663,667	622,317,843	633,412,390	659,853,291	776,818,196	949,692,002	175,735,150
Intra-EC 12 based on Imports	379,681,632	330,877,244	326,334,330	321,658,412	325,456,525	348,848,056	444,805,080	552,537,582	108,187,233
Extra-EC Trade (World-Intra-EC)	388,842,345	348,690,349	323,329,337	300,659,431	307,953,865	311,005,235	332,013,116	397,154,420	67,547,917
Shares as a Percentage of Extra-EC 12									
Sub-Saharan Africa	6.6	5.3	5.4	5.8	6.6	6.9	5.2	4.2	5.4
EFTA	17.0	16.4	16.9	18.9	19.0	19.7	22.8	23.6	15.4
Mediterranean Countries	5.9	6.5	7.2	7.4	7.6	8.2	7.2	7.2	4.6
Eastern Europe excl. USSR	3.2	2.9	2.9	3.0	3.3	3.2	3.5	3.3	2.2
USSR	4.1	4.4	5.3	5.6	6.0	5.1	4.1	3.8	3.4
Caribbean under ACP	0.6	0.4	0.5	0.4	0.3	0.3	0.3	0.3	0.3
Central-South America + Mexico	5.8	6.4	6.5	7.2	7.2	7.3	5.9	5.5	8.3
South East Asia	3.8	3.7	3.7	4.0	4.2	4.0	4.6	5.0	5.6

[a] This table also appears in a publication by the author entitled "The European Community's Single Market: The Challenge of 1992 for Sub-Saharan Africa", World Bank Discussion Papers, No. 100, 1990.

See Note in Table A8 for an explanation of the country groupings.

Source: Comtrade data base, Geneva.

Table A11

EC Tariffs Applied in 1983 against Groups of Exporters (%)

SITC	Description	World	OECD	Soc.	LDCs	Med.	EFTA	Hungary
all	Total Trade	2.6	3.2	2.7	2.1	1.9	0.3	6.8
00	Live Animals	2.2	0.6	4.6	5.6	5.4	1.8	4.8
01	Meat and Preparations	13.2	13.2	9.5	14.3	14.2	9.1	9.6
02	Dairy Products and Eggs	10.8	11.1	3.3	1.9	12.0	11.4	12.0
03	Fish and Preparations	8.2	6.8	12.7	11.5	10.2	3.4	3.3
04	Cereals and Preparations	0.0	0.0	0.0	0.0	0.0	0.0	0.0
05	Fruit and Vegetables	8.3	7.1	13.0	9.7	5.7	16.6	14.2
06	Sugar, Preparations and Honey	25.9	27.0	26.6	25.9	15.2	26.3	27.0
07	Coffee, Tea, Cocoa, Spices	2.5	1.9	2.8	2.5	3.5	8.0	11.6
08	Animal Feeding Stuff	1.7	0.1	0.3	2.3	0.6	1.6	0.2
09	Misc. Food Preparations	12.6	10.7	7.3	14.2	1.5	7.1	4.6
11	Beverages	12.4	7.1	21.3	22.4	16.7	9.0	20.1
12	Tobacco and Manufactures thereof	61.8	66.1	48.7	45.5	70.0	88.2	-
21	Hides, Skins, incl. Fur, Undressed	0.0	0.0	0.0	0.0	0.0	0.0	0.0
22	Oil Seeds, Nuts, Kernels	0.0	0.0	0.0	0.0	0.0	0.0	0.0
23	Rubber Crude, Synthetic	0.0	0.0	0.1	0.0	0.1	0.0	1.2
24	Wood, Lumber and Cork	0.1	0.1	0.0	0.1	0.0	0.0	0.1
25	Pulp and Waste Paper	0.0	0.0	0.0	0.0	0.0	0.0	0.0
26	Textile Fibres (not Yarn, Thread)	0.6	0.6	1.6	0.6	0.1	0.0	2.6
27	Crude Fertilisers and Minerals	0.0	0.0	0.2	0.0	0.0	0.0	0.0
28	Metalliferous Ores, Metal Scrap	0.0	0.0	0.0	0.0	0.0	0.0	0.0
29	Crude Animal Veg. Materials	3.6	3.8	0.8	2.7	7.9	1.7	0.7
32	Coal, Coke, Briquettes	2.9	3.0	2.8	2.7	1.8	0.0	0.9
33	Petroleum and Petroleum Products	0.2	0.4	0.6	0.2	0.4	0.0	3.5
34	Gas Natural and Manufactured	0.1	0.6	0.1	0.1	0.1	0.0	1.0
35	Electric Energy	0.0	0.0	0.0	0.0	0.0	0.0	-
41	Animal Oils and Fats	0.5	0.6	2.4	0.2	0.7	0.5	2.2
42	Fixed Vegetable Oils and Fats	6.7	9.9	7.4	6.5	8.4	8.8	8.9
43	Processed Animal, Veg. Oil and Fats	9.2	9.3	0.7	9.5	0.1	13.8	0.5
51	Chemical Elements and Compounds	3.3	3.2	4.1	4.0	3.6	0.2	3.0
52	Mineral Tar and Crude Chemicals	0.3	0.1	0.8	0.3	0.1	0.0	1.1

53	Dyeing, Tanning and Colouring Materials	2.7	2.5	8.8	3.9	3.4	0.0	10.0
54	Medicinal and Pharm. Products	2.7	2.5	5.7	5.0	3.6	0.1	6.8
55	Essential Oils and Perfume Materials	2.3	2.5	0.7	1.6	1.1	0.0	3.2
56	Fertilisers Manufactured	2.5	2.4	3.6	4.1	3.0	0.0	7.5
57	Explosives, Pyrotech Products	3.9	3.1	5.7	5.4	2.3	0.0	8.9
58	Plastic Materials, etc.	5.7	5.6	12.5	8.7	3.6	0.0	13.4
59	Chemicals	3.4	3.3	5.2	4.0	0.9	0.0	6.8
61	Leather/Furs incl. Manufactures	2.1	1.2	3.7	2.8	3.2	0.0	5.1
62	Rubber Manufactures	2.9	2.3	6.6	4.3	2.9	0.0	6.8
63	Wood and Cork Manufactures	4.1	2.8	8.3	5.9	4.2	0.0	6.4
64	Paper/Board and Manufactures	2.7	2.6	8.9	6.7	6.3	1.4	10.5
65	Textile Yarn, Fabrics and Articles	5.3	3.2	10.1	7.6	3.0	0.1	12.0
66	Non-Metallic Mineral Manufactures	2.0	2.0	4.2	1.1	0.7	0.0	8.6
67	Iron and Steel	2.3	1.7	5.8	3.3	3.8	0.0	6.0
68	Non-Ferrous Metals	0.6	0.8	0.5	0.5	3.1	0.0	4.1
69	Metal Manufactures	3.0	2.5	5.3	4.9	2.5	0.0	6.1
71	Machines Non-Electric	3.3	3.3	5.5	3.9	2.4	0.0	5.3
72	Machinery Electric	6.0	5.7	6.2	7.0	3.5	0.0	6.3
73	Transport Equipment	4.7	4.8	8.9	3.4	6.0	0.0	16.9
81	Sanitary, Plumbing, Heating, Lighting Equip.	2.2	0.9	6.8	4.7	4.3	0.0	8.5
82	Furniture	3.2	0.9	6.6	5.4	4.2	0.0	6.7
83	Travel Goods, Handbags	4.9	3.3	5.1	4.3	4.2	0.0	6.1
84	Clothing	7.3	2.1	10.5	9.3	5.4	0.0	13.2
85	Footwear	6.5	0.7	9.6	9.1	5.9	0.0	11.7
86	Professional Scientific Instruments	6.1	6.2	6.9	4.4	1.5	0.0	6.9
89	Misc. Manufactures	5.1	4.9	6.0	5.0	2.4	0.2	5.5

Notes: A missing value implies no imports in that category.

Soc. refers to "Socialist" countries of Asia and Eastern Europe plus the USSR and Cuba, excluding China and Hungary.

Med. refers to Mediterranean countries, not elsewhere included.

LDCs refer to developing countries, not elsewhere included, including China.

OECD refers to OECD countries, including Spain and Portugal, excluding Turkey.

EFTA refers to Austria, Finland, Norway, Sweden, Switzerland and Iceland.

Source: Calculations by the author using GATT data. To the extent possible, account has been taken of preferential rates and their usage.

Table A12
Export Shares by Major Category, 1980 and 1987

Country	Agriculture Shares[a]		Mining Shares[b]		Manufactures Shares[c]	
	1980	1987	1980	1987	1980	1987
Algeria	0.8	0.4	98.9	97.9	0.3	1.7
Cyprus	33.5	32.1	11.0	8.4	55.4	59.5
Egypt	6.4	11.3	82.6	54.3	10.9	34.4
Israel	11.5	9.4	6.4	5.2	82.1	85.4
Jordan	24.9	14.8	41.3	37.2	33.8	48.0
Lebanon	27.5	n.a.	12.0	n.a.	60.5	n.a.
Libya	n.a.	n.a.	1.1	1.9	n.a.	n.a.
Malta	5.3	4.6	1.1	1.9	93.6	93.5
Morocco	28.4	27.6	48.0	23.7	23.5	48.7
Syria	4.2	n.a.	89.2	n.a.	6.6	n.a.
Tunisia	7.2	12.7	57.0	26.6	35.8	60.7
Turkey	50.8	25.2	22.3	8.5	26.9	66.3
Yugoslavia	11.6	8.8	15.2	12.7	73.2	78.5

[a] SITC 0 + 1 + 4.
[b] SITC 2 + 3 + 68.
[c] SITC 5 + 6 + 7 + 8 + 9 - 68.

Source: Comtrade data base, Geneva.

37

Table A13
EC Imports from Partner Groups Affected by NTBs in 1988 (%)

SITC	Description	World	OECD	Soc.	LDCs	Med.	EFTA	Hungary
all	Total Trade	13.8	16.0	21.4	20.7	7.5	6.7	35.2
00	Live Animals	59.9	11.3	80.3	55.7	9.8	87.4	88.3
01	Meat and Preparations	83.1	89.0	85.3	74.6	47.6	95.7	39.7
02	Dairy Products and Eggs	83.0	85.0	75.7	60.8	38.4	69.7	89.8
03	Fish and Preparations	3.0	34.8	40.9	60.3	48.7	63.6	7.9
04	Cereals and Preparations	100.0	100.0	100.0	100.0	100.0	100.0	100.0
05	Fruit and Vegetables	53.3	68.4	56.7	38.0	61.7	46.4	61.5
06	Sugar, Preparations and Honey	98.1	78.1	87.7	99.3	94.8	74.2	58.1
07	Coffee, Tea, Cocoa, Spices	27.2	37.2	37.5	22.1	9.7	59.9	65.5
08	Animal Feeding Stuff	29.2	43.7	24.2	23.0	63.7	4.6	39.8
09	Misc. Food Preparations	49.9	50.1	61.1	14.0	62.4	81.3	85.4
11	Beverages	2.1	3.5	0.8	0.2	0.2	0.5	0.3
12	Tobacco and Manufactures thereof	0.0	0.0	0.0	0.0	0.0	0.0	0.0
21	Hides, Skins, incl. Fur, Undressed	0.0	0.0	0.0	0.0	0.0	0.0	0.0
22	Oil Seeds, Nuts, Kernels	1.2	2.7	0.8	0.1	0.0	2.7	9.6
23	Rubber Crude, Synthetic	0.4	0.0	7.4	0.1	0.0	0.0	6.8
24	Wood, Lumber and Cork	0.0	0.0	0.0	0.0	0.0	0.0	0.1
25	Pulp and Waste Paper	0.0	0.0	0.0	0.0	0.0	0.0	0.0
26	Textile Fibres (not Yarn, Thread)	12.8	8.7	18.3	12.8	45.5	7.0	18.9
27	Crude Fertilisers and Minerals	18.3	3.1	17.1	16.4	3.5	17.7	40.0
28	Metalliferous Ores, Metal Scrap	7.4	12.2	1.9	3.7	0.9	2.5	5.2
29	Crude Animal Veg. Materials	18.0	14.0	30.2	19.4	14.7	16.1	21.9
32	Coal, Coke, Briquettes	0.0	0.0	0.0	0.0	0.0	0.0	0.0
33	Petroleum and Petroleum Products	12.3	17.2	28.1	10.5	14.0	4.3	32.6
34	Gas Natural and Manufactured	1.2	0.0	11.1	0.0	0.0	0.0	0.5
35	Electric Energy	1.5	0.0	11.1	0.0	-	0.0	-
41	Animal Oils and Fats	6.6	10.3	2.2	0.2	0.0	1.2	34.4
42	Fixed Vegetable Oils and Fats	6.4	2.2	0.2	0.1	98.7	0.2	0.0
43	Processed Animal, Veg. Oil and Fats	0.0	0.0	0.1	0.0	0.0	0.0	4.2
51	Chemical Elements and Compounds	1.8	2.6	4.0	0.9	0.0	2.6	1.2
52	Mineral Tar and Crude Chemicals	0.8	0.1	3.0	1.0	0.0	0.0	2.9

53	Dyeing, Tanning and Colouring Materials	0.9	0.7	15.1	5.1	0.0	0.0	7.3
54	Medicinal and Pharm. Products	5.3	5.4	4.9	2.7	4.4	6.8	7.1
55	Essential Oils and Perfume Materials	0.8	0.5	0.1	2.0	0.0	0.0	0.0
56	Fertilisers Manufactured	1.7	6.6	11.6	0.0	0.0	0.0	11.5
57	Explosives, Pyrotech Products	0.4	0.0	21.7	5.6	0.0	0.0	24.8
58	Plastic Materials, etc.	1.5	1.1	20.2	1.9	0.0	0.0	9.1
59	Chemicals	8.2	14.3	6.6	19.4	8.7	1.7	5.5
61	Leather/Furs incl. Manufactures	16.4	11.2	32.1	12.1	92.7	3.5	43.1
62	Rubber Manufactures	6.2	0.9	26.4	14.9	0.0	0.0	16.6
63	Wood and Cork Manufactures	33.5	23.8	52.1	46.3	4.6	23.2	16.7
64	Paper/Board and Manufactures	35.4	42.2	27.0	12.7	0.0	12.7	78.6
65	Textile Yarn, Fabrics and Articles	29.6	1.4	77.6	69.7	0.1	0.6	96.9
66	Non-Metallic Mineral Manufactures	7.3	5.0	36.4	4.6	11.0	0.1	32.7
67	Iron and Steel	32.7	19.2	57.9	28.7	8.9	44.5	61.4
68	Non-Ferrous Metals	2.0	4.4	0.4	0.5	0.1	1.5	5.8
69	Metal Manufactures	2.5	1.5	7.6	3.5	5.7	2.1	4.3
71	Machines Non-Electric	4.2	6.6	7.5	0.8	0.1	0.5	11.2
72	Machinery Electric	6.8	9.9	18.9	7.1	5.4	3.7	7.0
73	Transport Equipment	11.0	34.3	11.0	3.3	3.4	3.1	7.4
81	Sanitary, Plumbing, Heating, Lighting Equip.	3.1	1.1	1.6	5.3	0.2	0.3	62.5
82	Furniture	13.1	8.0	21.6	11.5	10.6	9.8	19.6
83	Travel Goods, Handbags	0.2	0.0	2.7	0.0	0.0	0.0	4.2
84	Clothing	52.9	0.2	93.7	77.3	0.3	0.3	90.2
85	Footwear	40.5	22.7	69.0	45.4	21.3	25.9	66.7
86	Professional Scientific Instruments	5.4	7.5	24.1	1.5	0.9	1.6	3.9
89	Misc. Manufactures	3.4	5.5	8.5	3.1	0.1	0.5	3.2

Notes: A missing value implies no imports in that category.

Soc. refers to "Socialist" countries of Asia and Eastern Europe plus the USSR and Cuba, excluding China and Hungary.

Med. refers to Mediterranean countries, not elsewhere included.

LDCs refer to developing countries, not elsewhere included, including China.

OECD refers to OECD countries, including Spain and Portugal, excluding Turkey.

EFTA refers to Austria, Finland, Norway, Sweden, Switzerland and Iceland.

Source: UNCTAD computerised files on NTBs (non-tariff barriers).

Table A14
Exports of Some Major Agricultural Products, 1988
(millions of US $)

	Potatoes	Olive Oil	Tomatoes	Onions	Citrus	Apples	Raisins	Wine	Cotton	Tobacco
World	1,048,140	941,808	1,587,980	59,619	3,402,517	1,597,070	653,239	6,779,370	7,858,883	4,174,840
Mediterranean	395,590	911,975	422,896	6,122	1,613,713	594,684	264,530	5,510,896	837,394	791,898
Mediterranean[a]	141,200	117,319	109,702	367	266,926	41,838	142,069	98,248	628,575	329,285
(% World = 100)										
Mediterranean	37.7%	96.8%	26.6%	10.3%	47.4%	37.2%	40.5%	81.3%	10.7%	19.0%
Mediterranean[a]	13.5%	12.5%	6.9%	0.6%	7.8%	2.6%	21.7%	1.4%	8.0%	7.9%
Morocco	3.0%	-	11.3%	0.2%	-	-	-	0.1%	1.9%	-
Algeria	0.1%	-	-	-	-	-	-	0.4%	-	-
Tunisia	0.3%	9.1%	0.1%	0.8%	-	-	-	0.1%	-	0.1%
Malta	0.3%	-	-	-	-	-	-	-	-	0.2%
Libya	-	-	-	-	-	-	-	-	-	-
Egypt	15.0%	-	1.3%	-	-	-	-	-	38.2%	-
Israel	2.2%	0.2%	2.3%	-	11.0%	-	-	0.1%	9.9%	-
Jordan	0.3%	-	3.6%	-	-	-	-	-	-	-
Lebanon	3.5%	-	0.7%	-	-	3.5%	-	-	-	0.9%
Syria	0.9%	-	0.7%	-	-	0.4%	-	-	5.8%	-
Turkey	1.3%	3.6%	5.8%	5.0%	5.6%	2.7%	52.7%	-	18.9%	33.6%
Cyprus	8.8%	-	0.1%	-	-	0.0%	0.9%	0.2%	-	-
Yugoslavia	0.1%	8.8%	0.1%	-	-	0.3%	-	0.9%	0.3%	6.7%
Greece	0.9%	52.6%	-	-	-	0.4%	44.6%	0.8%	15.0%	38.7%
Spain	7.6%	2.9%	64.0%	-	76.1%	1.5%	0.5%	9.4%	4.7%	1.4%
Portugal	0.2%	-	0.2%	-	-	0.3%	0.5%	6.2%	0.4%	0.5%
Italy	25.4%	21.5%	4.2%	7.1%	5.3%	28.2%	-	18.9%	1.9%	13.0%
France	30.2%	1.3%	5.7%	86.9%	2.0%	62.5%	0.7%	63.0%	2.9%	4.8%

[a] Mediterranean refers to the Mediterranean region minus the contributions of France, Greece, Italy, Spain and Portugal.

Source: FAO trade data base.

Table A15
Share in Output of Major Agricultural Exports, 1988
(% by volume)

	Potatoes	Olive Oil	Tomatoes	Onions	Citrus	Apples	Raisins	Wine	Cotton[a]	Tobacco
World	2.4%	33.7%	3.6%	5.7%	11.4%	8.7%	50.1%	16.0%	27.5%	20.3%
Mediterranean	6.5%	33.2%	3.5%	2.5%	29.6%	13.3%	49.3%	21.4%	31.7%	50.1%
Mediterranean[b]	4.7%	23.7%	2.8%	1.0%	23.3%	4.1%	39.6%	20.1%	27.1%	31.2%
Morocco	8.3%	0.6%	22.4%	0.4%	45.5%	-	0.1%	11.0%	55.5%	-
Algeria	0.1%	-	-	-	2.1%	-	-	40.0%	c	-
Tunisia	2.9%	85.5%	0.2%	0.1%	20.3%	-	-	34.8%	-	21.5%
Malta	22.1%	-	-	-	-	-	-	3.8%	-	-
Libya	-	-	-	-	-	-	-	-	-	-
Egypt	9.8%	-	0.3%	-	5.8%	-	-	0.5%	27.0%	-
Israel	12.6%	-	2.1%	-	40.0%	-	-	17.9%	63.0%	-
Jordan	12.7%	15.8%	53.2%	-	50.7%	3.3%	0.5%	-	-	0.7%
Lebanon	20.2%	-	6.4%	-	13.1%	50.0%	-	-	-	c
Syria	3.1%	-	1.1%	-	-	2.7%	2.2%	-	23.6%	0.1%
Turkey	1.1%	20.2%	2.8%	1.9%	21.6%	3.3%	41.9%	14.6%	23.2%	36.7%
Cyprus	83.2%	6.9%	0.7%	-	61.9%	0.3%	46.3%	28.3%	-	4.3%
Yugoslavia	-	0.1%	0.1%	-	4.5%	2.8%	-	17.5%	c	26.7%
Greece	1.1%	12.9%	-	-	29.5%	1.7%	68.8%	10.1%	44.7%	80.5%
Spain	2.5%	67.7%	15.5%	-	56.8%	2.2%	22.5%	20.0%	24.3%	15.1%
Portugal	0.4%	78.4%	0.2%	-	0.6%	5.6%	-	41.4%	c	50.7%
Italy	11.8%	20.6%	0.5%	c	8.7%	14.6%	c	20.7%	c	68.1%
France	12.4%	c	3.5%	22.3%	c	28.6%	-	22.5%	c	42.1%

a Cotton includes cotton waste.
b Mediterranean refers to the Mediterranean region minus the contributions of France, Greece, Italy, Spain and Portugal.
c Exports exceed production figures.

Source: FAO trade and production data bases.

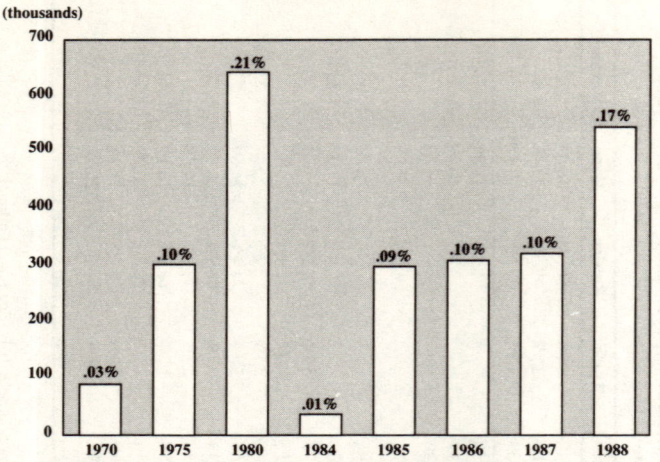

Figure A1
Net Community Immigration
1970-1988

Source: Commission of the European Communities, *Employment in Europe 1990*, Brussels, 1990.

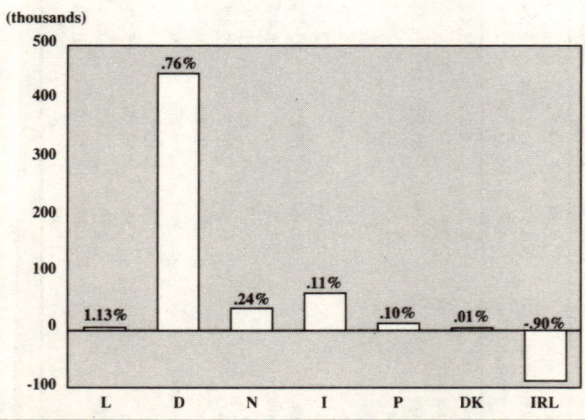

Figure A2
Net Immigration in the Member States
1988

Source: Commission of the European Communities, *Employment in Europe 1990*, Brussels, 1990.

Bibliography

Aliboni, R. (1990), "The Mediterranean Scenario: Economy and Security in the Regions South of the EC", *The International Spectator*, Vol. 25, No. 2, 1990, pp. 138-54.

Aliboni, R. (1992), "The Mediterranean Dimension" in Wallace, W. (ed.), *The Dynamics of European Integration* (London: Pinter, for the Royal Institute of International Affairs, 1992).

Bohning, W.R. and Werquin, J. (1990), "Some Economic, Social and Human Rights Considerations concerning the Future Status of Third-Country Nationals in the Single European Market", International Labour Organisation, World Employment Programme, Working Paper MIG WP 46.E, April 1990.

Callovi, G. (1990), "Regulating Immigration in the European Community", Paper presented at the 7th Biennial Conference of Europeanists, Washington, D.C., 23-25 March 1990.

Commission of the European Communities (1985), *The European Community and the Mediterranean* (Luxembourg: Office of Official Publications of the European Communities, 1985).

Commission of the European Communities (1988), "The Economics of 1992", *European Economy*, No. 35, March 1988.

Commission of the European Communities (1989), *Employment in Europe* (Brussels: Directorate General for Employment, Industrial Relations and Social Affairs, 1989).

Commission of the European Communities (1990a), *Redirecting the Community's Mediterranean Policy. Proposals for the Period 1992-96*, Communication from the Commission to the Council, SEC(90)812 final, 1 June 1990.

Commission of the European Communities (1990b), *Employment in Europe* (Brussels: Directorate General for Employment, Industrial Relations and Social Affairs).

Drevet, J. (1986), *La Méditerranée, nouvelle frontière pour l'Europe des Douze* (Karthala).

Grenon, M. and Batisse, M. (1989), *Futures for the Mediterranean Basin: The Blue Plan* (Oxford: Oxford University Press).

ILO (1989), "Informal Consultation Meeting on Migrants from Non-EEC Countries in The Single European Market after 1992", Informal Summary Record, Geneva, 27-28 April.

Koekkoek, A., *et al.* (1990), "Europe 1992 and the Developing Countries: An Overview", *Journal of Common Market Studies*, Vol. 29, No. 2, December, pp. 111-32.

Luciani, G. (1984), *The Mediterranean Region* (Beckenham: Croom Helm).

Lucron, C. (1988), "Méditerranée, Lomé: Des politiques globales?", *Revue du Marché Commun*, No. 318, pp. 321-7.

Martin, P. and Honekopp, E. (1990), "Europe 1992: Effects on Labor Migration", *International Migration Review*, Vol. 24, Fall, pp. 591-603.

Musto, S. (1988), "The Common Agricultural Policy and the Mediterranean", *The Jerusalem Journal of International Relations*, Vol. 10., No. 3, pp. 55-83.

Nonneman, Gerd (ed.), (1992), *The Middle East and Europe: An Integrated Communities Approach* (London: Federal Trust for Education and Research).

Pomfret, R. (1986), *Mediterranean Policy of the European Community* (London: Macmillan).

Renier, Y. (1988), "L'Europe et le Sud de la Méditerranée", *Le Courrier*, No. 108, pp. 53-55.

Research Group on European Affairs (1991), *Challenges in the Mediterranean: The European Response* (Gutersloh: Bertelsmann Foundation).

Rousset, M. (1992), *La Méditerranée occidentale, espace de coopération,* Grenoble, Cahiers du CEDSI, No. 12.

Swinbank, A. and Ritson, Ch. (1988), "The Common Agricultural Policy, Customs Unions and the Mediterranean Basin", *Journal of Common Market Studies*, Vol. 27, No. 2, pp. 97-112.

Tovias, A. (1978), *Tariff Preferences in Mediterranean Diplomacy* (New York: St. Martin's Press).

Tovias A. (1979), *EEC Enlargement: The Southern Neighbours*, Brighton, Sussex European Papers, No. 5.

Tovias, A. (1988), "Les effets extérieurs des politiques domestiques communautaires sur les pays non membres: le cas des pays méditerranéens", *Journal of European Integration*, Vol. 12, No. 1, pp. 51-70.

Tovias, A. (1990), *Foreign Economic Relations of the European Community: The Impact of Spain and Portugal* (Boulder, CO: Lynne Rienner Publishers).

Tovias, A. (1992a), "The EC's Contribution to Peace and Prosperity in the Mediterranean and the Middle East: Some Proposals", *Jerusalem Journal of International Relations*, Vol. 14, No. 2, pp. 123-32.

Tovias, A. (1992b), "The Single Market and Labour Mobility", *Journal of Development Planning*, No. 22, pp. 103-14.

Weidenfeld, W. (ed.), (1992), *Herausforderung Mittelmeer: Aufgaben,*

Ziele und Strategien europäischer Politik (Gutersloh: Verlag Bertelsmann Stiftung).

World Bank/EIB (1990), *The Environmental Program for the Mediterranean*, (Washington, D.C.: World Bank).

Yannopoulos, G. (1988), *Customs Unions and Trade Conflicts. The Enlargement of the European Community* (London: Routledge).

2 Demographic Transition among the Maghreb Peoples of North Africa and in the Emigrant Community Abroad

Youssef Courbage

Introduction

Without undue concern for distinctions, the Southern Mediterranean is frequently portrayed in the mass media and occasionally in scientific publications[1] as an indiscriminate melting pot of high-fertility rates and baby booms, not to mention the source of a nearly inexhaustible supply of migrants. Unfortunately, the full significance does not seem to have been drawn from the pointers given by recent data, which actually indicate a deceleration in population growth from the banks of the Bosphorus to the Strait of Gibraltar -- a development that tends to invalidate certain predictions. In its movement towards economic and political union, the Maghreb[2] in particular, is increasingly emerging as an intermediate demographic area between the Mashreq and Europe.[3] The realities of demography and migration in the Maghreb region give

---

[1] Standing at the crossroads of the mass media and science is a recent report by the Agnelli Foundation entitled *The 21st Century: Living on the Mediterranean*, Number 4, February 1992, the product of a research programme on the Mediterranean and the Arab world. According to the report, the programme "originated in the conviction that different demographic trends, international migration, and different ethnic groups and cultures living together have created a series of problems which will continue to grow in the last part of the century, to the point of becoming one of the main causes of political and social conflict (if not actual war)".

[2] For these purposes, the Maghreb is to be understood as the group of countries comprising Morocco, Algeria and Tunisia. The greater Maghreb also includes Mauritania and Libya.

[3] Morocco, a member of the Union of the Arab Maghreb founded in 1989, has even applied for membership in the European Community.

lie to a large body of received wisdom -- represented by those very preconceptions that all too readily ease scientific debate into the political arena. Emerging trends suggest a less gloomy demographic outlook than that commonly predicted.

This paper first describes the demographic transition currently under way in the Maghreb countries, with particular emphasis on fertility rates. It then goes on to discuss the endogenous and exogenous factors which determine the pace of that transition. In the process, the contribution of the Maghreb communities to immigration into Europe is reevaluated in light of recent data, which also serves to highlight the effect of emigration on the accelerating pace of fertility transition in the Maghreb. It concludes with a few words on the outlook for the future.

I. Demographic Transition in the Maghreb: Nascent Convergences

Population growth is determined by three parameters: birthrates, deathrates and international migration. Arithmetically-speaking, the impact of the deathrate in the Maghreb is now of an order of magnitude four times lower than the birthrate, following the dramatic decline in sickness and death which began at the turn of the century and accelerated from about the mid-century onwards. Even in the mass-migration periods of the 1960s, for example, the effect of international emigration on population growth was one-twentieth that of the birthrate. In the recent past, and for the next generation -- or for about the first quarter of the next century -- the birthrate has been and will remain far and away the prime determinant of population growth in the Maghreb. Hence, the central place it occupies in this paper.

In the immediate aftermath of independence, fertility[4] remained very high with slight variations between the three Maghreb countries, where

---

[4] Since crude birthrates can be affected by the age structure of the population, natality will be analysed throughout this paper on the basis of a more accurate indicator -- the fertility rate.

the post-war resumption of births produced an exceptional fertility of 8.36 children per woman in Algeria. While more attenuated, fertility in Morocco and Tunisia nonetheless exceeded 7 children per woman. The demographic landscape in all three countries has now been transformed without exception; Maghreb women now bear only one-half the number of children they once did. In Tunisia in 1991, the fertility rate had fallen to 3.29 children, and for the same period, in Morocco it was in all probability 3.86 children.[5] Even in the most prolific of the three countries -- Algeria -- fertility fell by one-half over a period of 30 years to 4.71 children in 1990. See Figure 1.

Without exception, the governments of all three countries introduced population policies, although at markedly different points in time, which would explain the variations in fertility trends between Algeria, Morocco and Tunisia. The latter two countries sanctioned and approved birth control policies in the mid-1960s -- a step taken by Algeria only 20 years later in 1983 when it came to fear the consequences of rapid population growth at a time of depleting oil and gas reserves. Social demand, however, had anticipated the official family-planning programme: one out of every three women were using contraception to limit births and/or to regulate the interval between births. Just as in Morocco with its longer experience in demographic interventionism, Algerian civil society had taken the lead, and declining fertility gathered pace within three years following the programme's introduction.

The decrease in fertility in the Maghreb countries is now acknowledged, notably by the United Nations and World Bank, whose projections in the

---

[5] The existence in Algeria and Tunisia of near-exhaustive records of birth, marriage and death enables the trend of birth and fertility indicators to be tracked year after year. The decline in birthrates in Morocco is extracted from regularly repeated censuses and surveys. Pending its full processing, the most recent such survey (Government of Morocco, Department of Statistics, *Niveaux de vie des ménages 1990-91*, Rabat, 1992) enables a fertility rate of 3.86 children per woman to be deduced from the proportion of children under 15 years of age (37.7%). In 1986, the proportion was 41.4%, and fertility was determined to be 4.46 children per woman.

Figure 1
Fertility Rates of Maghreb Women in Their
Country of Origin and in France, 1962-1990

Algerian Women

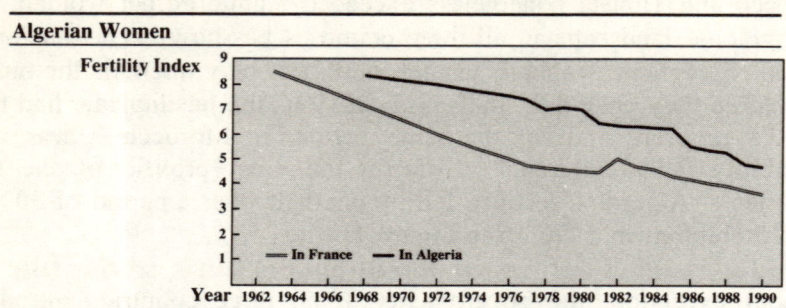

Moroccan Women

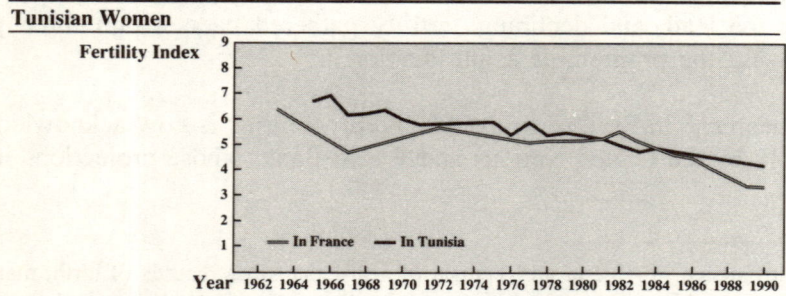

Tunisian Women

Sources: Data for countries of origin extracted from official population surveys and national censuses. Data for France taken from Guy Desplanques, "Nuptialité et fécondité des étrangères", *Economiques et statistiques*, No. 179, 1985, and for the period after 1982, Michèle Tribalat, "Chronique de l'immigration", *Population*, No. 1, 1988. Provisional estimate for 1990, M. Tribalat.

matter are authoritative. But the international organisations have not yet taken the full measure of the magnitude of the decline. Using its own projections (1985-1990), the United Nations[6] overestimates fertility in Algeria (5.43 rather than 5.08), Morocco (4.82 instead of 4.46) and Tunisia (4.10 rather than 3.82) alike. Although these may at first sight appear to be minor overestimations, their cumulative medium-term effects will be very tangible indeed, particularly by the end of the first quarter of the 21st century.

II. Endogenous Factors in Declining Fertility among the Populations of the Maghreb

National populations are heterogeneous. Different social groups rarely display uniform reproductive behaviour. Some segments of the population -- often out of self-interest, sometimes from ignorance -- are more fertile than others: they marry earlier, and contraception -- or any other birth-prevention method -- is little used. A multiplicity of factors -- an urban or rural place of residence, level of affluence, husband's occupation, wife's occupation, ethnic background, religion -- may all result in different patterns of reproduction.

Major upheavals in the Maghreb societies have shifted entire swathes of the population from a pronatalist philosophy towards a more Malthusian ethos -- from the large family to the small family. These changes were perhaps even more of a driving force behind the decrease in national fertility than were the birth-control programmes which, far from creating, were merely responding to the growing demand for smaller families. With the increased child-survival rate brought about by improved hygiene and nutrition (not to mention medical progress),[7] parents became

---

[6] United Nations, *World Population Prospects 1990*, New York, 1992.

[7] Algeria's infant-mortality rate fell from 179 per 1,000 in 1960 to 58 in 1990; Morocco's from 130 in 1957 to 74 in 1987; and Tunisia's from 137 in 1957 to 50 in 1985.

increasingly inclined towards fewer births as the survival of children to adulthood became a near-certainty.[8]

Three revolutions -- urban, educational and social -- accelerated these trends in the space of a single generation. At the time of independence and the dawn of the 1960s, the great majority of people in the Maghreb were still living in a rural society. Occasional slight variations aside -- Tunisia was slightly more urbanised and Morocco more rural -- overall, some 70% of the population was rural. Illiteracy -- particularly among women -- was the general rule: 96% in Tunisia and Morocco, 85% in Algeria.[9] Educated women were insignificant in number, and their education rarely went beyond primary school. Less than 10% of the female population were engaged in paid work outside the home.

A generation later, these populations were, without exception, more urbanised and better educated, and women -- except in Algeria -- were far more present in the labour market. Over one-half of the population -- particularly women of reproductive age -- had fled the countryside for the towns.[10] Female illiteracy has not yet been eradicated, but in 1992, over one-half of all Algerian (53%) and Tunisian (58%) and over one-third of all Moroccan (38%) women of reproductive age have emerged from cultural obscurantism.[11] With a lower education-participation rate than their sisters in the other countries, Moroccan women could have found themselves sidelined in society. But their rush into the labour market mitigated the adverse effects of their educational lag. They are

---

[8] At present mortality rates, more than 9 out of 10 children are still living when their parents reach the age of 65.

[9] Illiterate female population aged 10 and over recorded in the Tunisian 1956 census, the Moroccan 1960 census and the Algerian 1966 census.

[10] In Morocco, in 1990, the rural/urban split in the total population was 53% to 47%, while the balance for women of reproductive age was tilted 51% to 49% in favour of town-dwellers.

[11] Figures updated for 1992 from recent censuses and surveys.

developing a higher profile in areas of public life, hitherto an exclusively male preserve.

Changes in fertility therefore depend on the extent to which women are present in towns, classrooms, factories and offices. In Morocco, for example, but also throughout Algeria and Tunisia, recent data show town-dwelling to be irreconcilable with large families.[12] In 1987, the average rural woman had a family of nearly 6 children (5.97), while her urban counterpart -- all conurbations together -- was much less fertile, with fewer than 3 children (2.85). Today, five years later, she has reduced this to the minimum-population replacement level of just 2.1 children per mother. See Table 1.

The demand for education changes as women's status improves, making up for many decades of ground lost to men. Educated women marry later and are more inclined to use contraception. This cultural revolution, which increased literacy among women and closed the gap with men, became the main -- but far from the only -- key to controlling reproduction. The difference in fertility between a Maghreb woman with just a few years of primary education and a wholly illiterate one is marked: 3.15 compared with 5.20 in Morocco, for example; the gap widens still further with those entering secondary education: just 2.34 children.[13] As yet, however, secondary education remains the preserve of a very small percentage of the population -- just 15% of the population of Moroccan (but not Algerian or Tunisian) women of child-bearing age. Nevertheless, the ineluctable advance of women's education will soon increase that. For example, in Morocco, which is the least well

---

[12] This is a recent correlation; rural Moroccans have traditionally had smaller families than their urban counterpart: 6.91 children against 7.7. See Centre d'Etudes et de Recherches Démographiques, *Analyses et tendances démographiques au Maroc*, Rabat, 1986.

[13] The figures for differential fertility in Morocco derive from the two most recent surveys: Ministry of Public Health, *Enquête nationale sur la planification familiale, la fécondité et la santé de la population -- 1987*, Rabat, 1989, and Department of Statistics, *Enquête démographique nationale 1986-1988 -- Rapport préliminaire*, Rabat, 1989.

Table 1
Differential Fertility in the Maghreb
by Selected Socioeconomic Determinants

Algeria (1983)	Live Births per Woman
Education	
No Education	7.34
Primary School	4.95
Secondary School or Higher	3.39
Residence	
Rural	7.11
Secondary Towns	5.64
Major Towns and Cities	3.44
Standard of Living	
Low	8.95
Below Average	7.53
Above Average	4.90
High	5.38

Morocco (1982-87)	Live Births per Woman
Education	
No Education	5.20
Primary School	3.15
Secondary School or Higher	2.34
Residence	
Urban	5.97
Rural	2.85
Labour Force Participation (1982)	
Urban Non-Working	5.01
Urban Working	2.40
Agriculture Non-Working	6.06
Agriculture Working	6.05

Tunisia (1988)	Live Births per Woman
Education	
No Education	5.10
Primary School	3.90
Secondary School or Higher	2.40
Residence	
Urban	5.70
Rural	3.40

Sources: Data for Algeria extracted from CENEAP, *Enquête nationale algérienne sur la fécon-dité 1986*, Algiers, 1989.

Data for Morocco taken from Department of Statistics, *Enquête démographique natio-nale 1986-1988* (Preliminary Report), Rabat, 1989; Centre d'Etudes et de Recherches

Démographiques, *Ménages - Variables socio-démographiques*, Rabat, 1990; and Ministry of Public Health, *Enquête nationale sur la planification familiale, la fécondité et la santé de la population au Maroc*, Rabat 1989.
Data for Tunisia appears in Ministry of Public Health, *Enquête démographique et de santé en Tunisie 1988*, Tunis, 1989.

endowed of the three Maghreb countries, the number of girls in secondary education is increasing geometrically: only 11.7% of women born between 1952 and 1956 entered secondary education compared to 15.3% of the 1957-1961 birth cohort and 25.1% of the 1962-1966 cohort.

There can be no doubting the effect of place of residence and educational attainment on fertility. By contrast, the effects of women's labour-force participation are ambivalent. In Maghreb rural society -- more specifically, in the farming community -- a woman may be both a permanent family worker and bring up a large family; reproductive behaviour is barely affected by women's participation in agricultural activities, where the farm is at once the place of residence and place of work.[14] But as soon as pregnancy and childcare begin to compete with paid work and pose a threat to household resources (opportunity cost), fertility declines dramatically. Now-outdated Moroccan data from 1982 show that fertility among working women (educated or otherwise) in towns was already nearing the replacement level with 2.40 children, just one-half the level of non-working mothers (5.01). Ten years on, what is the position? To judge by the particularly rapid pace of demographic transition in Morocco, fertility among urban working women has now fallen below the replacement level. Heretofore very much in the minority, this segment of the population now includes over 15% of women of child-bearing age in Morocco.[15] To summarise, fertility tends to decrease as women's lot improves, in towns and cities, where the gender gap in education and jobs is being closed.

---

[14] The total fertility rate in 1982 was 6.86 children for a non-working rural woman compared to 6.22 for a woman farm-worker. See "Activité féminine, état matrimonial et fécondité" in Centre d'Etudes et de Recherches Démographiques, *Ménages - Variables socio-démographiques*, Rabat, 1990.

[15] Urban women account for 51% of all Moroccan women in the peak-fertility age group, 30% of urban women between the ages of 20 and 44 were economically active in 1990; this low-fertility category therefore accounts for 15.3% of all Moroccan women of child-bearing age. Government of Morocco, *op. cit.* A record among the Arab countries.

III. Fertility among Maghreb Women in the Arab World and Europe

The processes of rapid urbanisation, education and women's labour-force participation are not peculiar to the Maghreb. Many other countries in the Arab region are experiencing similar advances to a greater or lesser degree. And while those advances could have steered fertility to levels approximating those of their Western neighbours, such has not been the case. Unlike the demographic situation of the 1960s when reproductive behaviour throughout the region was relatively uniform from east (7.22) to west (7.25), the late 20th century Arab world is increasingly sharply divided with Libya falling roughly in the middle. In the Mashreq (120 million inhabitants), from Egypt to Iraq, fertility has levelled-off at a high rate of more than 6 children per woman (6.19), including world peaks (Yemen, 8.62). In the Maghreb, by contrast (population, 60 million), it has fallen below 4 children and presently (1992) stands at 3.66. The speed of the transition in the Maghreb contrasts with the hesitancy of the process in the Mashreq.

Where are we to look for the causes of such a fundamental discrepancy between the members of an Arab world thought to be united by language, religion, family structures and, until recently, demography? An elementary statistical analysis could help identify the "why" of the demographic differential between the Maghreb and the Mashreq. But the Arab world as defined by the Arab League includes not only the Maghreb and the Mashreq proper, but also a number of countries and population groups which prudence dictates should be excluded from any such statistical analysis. While Mauritania, Sudan, Somalia and Djibouti may be politically part of the Arab world, geographically and culturally, they are no less a part of sub-Saharan Africa. Lebanon[16] and Sudan[17]

---

[16] Fertility of the order of 2.1 children per woman among the Christians, who account for 43% of the total population, see Youssef Courbage and Philippe Fargues, *Chrétiens et Juifs dans l'Islam arabe et turc* (Paris: Fayard, 1992). The findings of the last national survey conducted in 1987, however, show that declining fertility now affects all denominational groups in the country. National fertility was on the order of approximately 2.9 around 1985, in Robert Kasparian and André Beaudouin,

have sizeable non-Muslim Christian and animist minorities. Among the Palestinians of the Occupied Territories (Left Bank and Gaza Strip) and among Israeli Arabs,[18] fertility is determined as much by the political context as by economic and social norms. Libya, finally, straddles the two worlds of the east and the Maghreb (and its statistics are very incomplete).[19]

The countries analysed in Table 2 are classified by level of fertility and various determinants of fertility: urbanisation, literacy, women's participation in the non-farm labour market, and infant mortality. Gross Domestic Product (GDP -- expressed in US dollars) and purchasing power parity (PPP) is also included. But the inherent defects of this indicator prevent it from being an effective tool.

Despite the respective values of the proximate determinants (identical infant mortality of 65 deaths per 1000 of population, urbanisation rates of 49.6% and 51.8%, female literacy 43.8% and 41.4%), fertility in the Maghreb contrasts markedly with that of Arabic countries in the east. Maghreb women differ from those of the east by their higher participation in the non-domestic labour force -- 17% compared to 11% -- although this remains very low compared to the levels attained by the highly industrialised nations (approximately 45%). Both parts of the Arab world are still far from having channelled all their human resources into productive activities.

La population déplacée au Liban: 1975-1982 (Beirut: Université Saint-Joseph, 1992).

[17] 52% Arabic-speakers (see Rafic Boustani and Philippe Fargues, *Atlas du monde arabe - Géopolitique et société*, Paris: Bordas, 1990) and 28% animists and Christians.

[18] Record levels of fertility were recorded in Palestinian women in Gaza (9.6 children per woman in 1990) and on the Left Bank (7.23 children in 1985-1989), despite the very high degree of urbanisation and education among women; fertility among Israeli Arabs has recently increased (4.70 in 1990). See Youssef Courbage and Philippe Fargues, *Chrétiens et Juifs dans l'Islam arabe et turc, op. cit.*

[19] The inclusion of these countries in the regression analysis in no way affects the results of the analysis, however.

Table 2

Fertility Rates and Selected Determinants of Fertility in Arab Countries

Country	Population (millions)	Fertility Rate (1960 - 65)	Fertility Rate (1985 - 90)	Fertility Rate (1992)	Infant Mortality (per 1,000)	GDP (US $ PPP)	Urban (%)	Literacy among Women (%)	Women in Non-Farming Occupations (%)
Egypt	54.6	7.07	5.75	5.78	63	2,099	43.9	33.8	13.8
Iraq	17.1	7.17	6.15	6.15	62	3,730	71.0	49.3	10.8
Saudi Arabia	15.5	7.26	7.01	6.85	65	8,705	71.0	48.1	7.5
Syria	12.8	7.46	6.44	5.49	52	3,508	50.6	50.8	11.2
Yemen	10.1	7.61	8.62	8.62	121	1,745	18.5	29.1	4.7
Jordan	3.4	7.99	6.49	5.87	42	3,062	66.2	70.3	11.9
UAR	2.4	6.87	6.72	5.99	28	21,665	86.6	56.3	6.1
Oman	1.6	7.17	6.73	6.42	66	15,546	10.0	38.6	0.7
Kuwait	1.4	7.31	6.21	5.96	14	10,865	94.0	56.3	19.8
Bahrain	0.5	7.17	5.79	5.32	33	10,384	82.0	69.3	22.5
Qatar	0.5	7.17	5.41	5.54	24	18,475	88.0	72.5	11.4
Subtotal	119.9	7.22	6.34	6.19	65	4,110	51.8	41.4	11.2
Morocco	26.0	7.15	4.46	3.40	74	1,730	46.2	38.0	21.1
Algeria	26.0	7.38	5.18	4.12	60	2,964	50.0	45.5	12.0
Tunisia	8.4	7.17	4.30	3.04	50	2,736	58.8	56.3	20.3
Subtotal	60.4	7.25	4.75	3.66	65	2,401	49.6	43.8	17.1

Sources: Data for Mashreq countries (except Syria) extracted from United Nations Economic and Social Commission for Western Asia, Demographic and Socio-Data Sheets, as assessed in 1988, Amman, 1989.
Data for Syria appeared in Youssef Courbage et Philippe Fargues, *L'avenir démographique de la rive sud de la Méditerranée: Algérie, Egypte, Maroc, Syrie, Turquie, Tunisie - Projections de la population et réflexions sur la migration*, Plan Bleu, 1992.
Data for the Maghreb countries taken from national statistics.

While these socioeconomic variables fully account for the fertility spread within a country, they do not really explain the country-to-country differences -- barely 56%.[20] More than 44% of these inter-Arab variations remain unexplained if infant mortality, urbanisation, literacy and women's labour force participation are taken as the sole factors.

By contrast, introducing what is fundamentally the very simple regional criterion -- Maghreb or Mashreq -- into the equation significantly increases the explanatory potential of this statistical model to 77% of variations in fertility -- 21% more than with the determinants previously mentioned. Whatever the performances of the socioeconomic indicators -- of proven effect on fertility -- the regional variable adds a further dimension to the explanation. Within the Arab world, the contours of the Maghreb or the Western Mediterranean delimit an area of lower fertility.

A brief historical detour may not be without interest. The decrease in fertility in the Mediterranean region occurred in successive waves, spread by contagion as it were. Beginning in France, the decline in the birthrate, which fell below the barrier of 30 births per 1000 of population in 1831-1835, took close to a century to cross the Alps and Pyrenees (less than 30 births per 1000 of population in Italy and Spain in 1921-1930). A decade later, the same level was found in Portugal, Greece and the Balkans. Fifty years on, the wave has now crossed the narrow strip of sea which separates the Latin crescent from North Africa: in the space of a decade, the birthrate in all the Maghreb countries has fallen below 30 births per 1000 of population.

From the Strait of Gibraltar (12 kilometres wide) to the Strait of Messina between Sicily and the mainland (150 kilometres), Morocco, Algeria and Tunisia are the only Arab countries so closely adjacent -- attached almost -- to the low-fertility countries of Europe and elsewhere. This geographical proximity has led to many pages of common history being

---

[20] Square of the multiple regression coefficient using the total fertility rate as a dependent variable, and the infant mortality rate, per capita GDP (as purchasing power parity), urbanisation, female literacy and women's labour force participation as independent variables.

written, often but not solely in blood.[21] After the colonial interlude, a series of networks for interchange -- economic,[22] cultural,[23] and linguistic[24] -- grew up between the Maghreb and Europe, and more particularly with France. A demographic exchange, too, with the post-independence flow-back, where the 2 million Europeans in the Maghreb were succeeded by 2 million Maghrebins in Europe. The accelerated pace of demographic transition in the Maghreb may be the -- unexpected -- result of the Maghrebin presence in Europe.

IV. Characteristics of Maghrebin Migration to Europe

International migration has entailed a flow of people that is, numerically-speaking, marginal compared to the populations of the countries of emigration and receiving (or host) countries. Emigrants of Maghreb origin -- Algerian (1.1 million), Moroccan (1.0 million), Tunisian (0.3 million) -- account at the most for no more than 4% of all Maghrebins on both sides of the Mediterranean Sea. Conversely France, the preferred

---

[21] For the history of relations between the two shores of the Mediterranean, and especially the Maghreb, see Chapter II: "La déchristianisation de l'Afrique du Nord" and Chapter IV: "L'Islam dominé du Maghreb colonial" in Youssef Courbage and Philippe Fargues, *Chrétiens et Juifs dans l'Islam arabe et turc, op. cit.*

[22] In 1990, 81% of Morocco's foreign trade (imports and exports) was conducted with the European Economic Community and just 18% with the Arab world, including the Union of the Arab Maghreb. See Government of Morocco, Department of Statistics, *Annuaire statistique du Maroc 1991*, Rabat, 1991.

[23] French and other European newspapers and magazines are widely circulated; dish aerials bring European television programmes from satellite channels.

[24] At the dawn of independence, the three Maghreb countries had 2.3 million French-speakers; today, there are 23 million. This many-fold increase is less the consequence of population growth than the spread of education, where French is the language of choice. See Youssef Courbage and Philippe Fargues, *Chrétiens et Juifs dans l'Islam arabe et turc, op. cit.* Spanish and Italian are also widely spoken in northern Morocco and Tunisia.

elective home of Maghrebins and host country to nearly 80%[25] of the emigrants from the Maghreb, had only 2 to 2.2 million in 1990,[26] or no more than 3.5-3.8% of the population of France. Algerian emigrants (98%) go no further than France; nor do most Tunisians (78%). Only Moroccan expatriates spread more widely throughout Europe (59% in France). See Table 3 below.

Table 3
**Ethnic Minority Population of Maghreb Nationality
in European Community Member States, 1990**

Country	Algerians	Moroccans	Tunisians	Total
France	619,923	584,708	207,496	1,412,127
Belgium	10,644	138,417	6,247	155,308
Netherlands	569	147,975	2,441	150,985
Italy	4,041	77,971	41,234	123,246
Germany	5,924	61,848	24,292	92,064
Spain	702	16,665	n.a.	17,367
Denmark	315	2,703	281	3,299
Greece	201	250	317	768
Luxembourg	92	130	138	360
Portugal	33	71	17	121
UK	n.a.	n.a.	n.a.	n.a.
Ireland	n.a.	n.a.	n.a.	n.a.
Total	642,444	1,030,738	282,463	1,955,645

Source: Eurostat, *Demographic Statistics 1992*, Luxembourg, 1992.

[25] Eurostat data reports only non-naturalised Maghrebins -- i.e., 1,412,000 Maghrebins in France for 1,956,000 in the EC as a whole, or 72%. If French nationals of Maghrebin origin are included, the total rises to nearly 1,990,000 Maghrebins in France out of 2,533,000 in the EC, or 79%.

[26] 1,072,000 Algerians of Algerian nationality, French by birth but of Algerian origin, or having acquired French nationality; 653,000 Moroccans, of whom 68,000 had acquired French nationality; 265,000 Tunisians of whom 57,000 had acquired French nationality. The inclusion of unregistered Maghrebins would not significantly affect these orders of magnitude: unregistered immigrants can be estimated in 1990 at 89,000 Algerians, 45,000 Moroccans and 22,000 Tunisians. See Youssef Courbage and Philippe Fargues, *L'avenir démographique de la rive sud de la Méditerranée: Algérie, Egypte, Maroc, Syrie, Turquie, Tunisie - Projections de la population et réflexions sur la migration*, Plan Bleu, 1992.

Europe is, almost without exception, the favoured destination of Maghrebin migrants. So modest are the flows from the Maghreb to other parts of the Arab world by contrast -- 50 to 100,000 migrants a year at the outside -- that they barely feature in the official statistics. Shunning the oil-rich lands, emigrants show a marked preference for the north over the east. The geographical distance and high travel costs, loneliness (migrant families are rarely given permission to reunite), difficulty in learning the languages of the Mashreq and so on have all weighed more in the choices of migrants than the admittedly high wages paid in the Gulf, or even the satisfaction of sharing a common religion. "I would add certain comments on the lot of other Arab and Muslim emigrants -- those working in Arab countries . . . Trenchant and bitter tales abound of humiliations, or at least misunderstandings", is the disillusioned observation of a Tunisian intellectual on the situation of his fellow-countrymen who have emigrated to Arab countries.[27]

The other main-destination country in the Arab world -- Egypt, with a resident and expatriate population broadly identical to that of the three Maghreb countries -- reveals the opposite: barely 50,000 Egyptians reside in Europe compared to some 2 million in the Gulf. The demographic import of this geographically-differentiated pattern of emigration will be examined later.

As the primary destination of Maghrebin emigrants, France is naturally a greater source than any other country of demographic data on communities of North African origin. Table 4 shows the Maghreb population in France (thousands) and as a percentage of selected ethnic minority populations.

The relative slowdown is manifest, even if naturalised migrants are included. From 1982 to 1990, the Maghreb population increased by 203,000 -- a very marked reduction in the Algerian community as a result of automatic acquisitions of French nationality, but also appreciable

---

[27] Azzedine Guellouz, Chapter 8: "Migration des hommes, mouvements des peuples" in Dominique Chevallier, *et al.*, *Les Arabes, l'Islam et l'Europe* (Paris: Flammarion, 1991).

Table 4
Maghreb and Other Foreign National Populations in France,
Native-Born and Naturalised, 1982 and 1990

	1982 (thousands)	1990 (thousands)	Change	Percentage Growth 1982-90
Algerians	639.8	634.0	-5.8	-1.1
Native-Born	565.0	522.0	-43.0	-9.9
Naturalised	74.8	112.0	37.2	50.5
Moroccans	472.8	653.0	180.2	40.4
Native-Born	441.3	584.7	143.4	35.2
Naturalised	31.5	68.3	36.8	96.7
Tunisians	236.3	264.8	28.5	14.2
Native-Born	190.8	207.5	16.7	10.5
Naturalised	45.5	57.3	11.8	28.8
Total Maghreb	1,348.9	1,551.8	202.9	17.5
Native-Born	1,197.1	1,314.2	117.1	11.7
Naturalised	151.8	237.6	85.8	56.0
Other Nationalities [a]	958.8	1,290.5	331.7	37.1
Native-Born	614.4	807.3	192.9	34.1
Naturalised	344.4	483.2	138.8	42.3
Total	2,307.7	2,842.3	534.6	26.0
Native-Born	1,811.5	2,121.5	310.0	19.7
Naturalised	496.2	720.8	224.6	46.7
% Maghreb	58.5	54.6	38.0	
Native-Born	66.1	61.9	37.8	
Naturalised	30.6	33.0	38.2	

[a] Turkey, Eastern Europe, Africa (excluding the Maghreb), Latin America and Asia (excluding Japan).

Sources: Adjusted data from the 1982 and 1990 French censuses.
1982: INSEE, *Recensement général de la population de 1982, Les étrangers*, La documentation française, Paris, 1988.
1990: INSEE, *Recensement de la population de 1990-Nationalités*, Paris, 1992.

among Tunisians. Only Morocco has a positive migratory balance. The percentage of Maghreb immigrants (born outside France), whether or not naturalised French, fell as a percentage of all job-seekers and refugees originating in other Third World (Turkey, sub-Saharan Africa, Asia, Latin America) and Eastern European countries: from 56.7% of the total in 1982, they accounted for no more than 51.6% in 1990. See Table 5.

Table 5
Immigrants, Foreign Nationals and Naturalised French Citizens
of Maghrebin and Other Nationalities, 1982 and 1990

	1982 (thousands)	1990 (thousands)	Change
Algerians	584	542	-42
Native-Born	524	473	-51
Naturalised	60	69	9
Moroccans	358	447	89
Native-Born	328	396	68
Naturalised	30	51	21
Tunisians	177	182	5
Native-Born	134	135	1
Naturalised	43	47	4
Total Maghreb	1,119	1,171	52
Native-Born	986	1,004	18
Naturalised	133	167	34
Other Nationalities [a]	853	1,100	247
Native-Born	570	723	153
Naturalised	283	377	94
Total	1,972	2,271	299
Native-Born	1,556	1,727	171
Naturalised	416	544	128
% Maghreb	56.7	51.6	17.4
Native-Born	63.4	58.1	10.5
Naturalised	32.0	30.7	26.6

[a] Turks, Eastern Europeans, Africans (excluding Maghrebins), Americans and Asians.

Source: Calculations taken from Jean-Claude Labat, *La population étrangère en 1990 par nationalité*, INSEE Première, No. 217, July 1992.

Natural increases aside, labour immigration has now become a minimal source of growth; that honour goes to family immigration alone: 92,607 individuals between 1986 and 1990. Over the same period, the three countries of the Maghreb exported only 5,543 workers to France (far fewer than Lebanon: 7,515 workers originating from a country with just one-twentieth of the population!).[28]

---

[28] Michèle Tribalat, "Chronique de l'immigration", *Population*, No. 1, 1992.

Tightly sealed frontiers and visa requirements are disincentives to legal emigration, but are naturally without effect on illegal emigration. Information circulating rapidly between the two shores of the same sea, however, assures a degree of transparency in the labour market. Europe-bound prospective illegal immigrants know nothing of the niceties of Europe's unemployment figures. They are certainly unaware that 23% of Algerians, 22% of Moroccans and 23% of Tunisians in France are unemployed -- appreciably more than in their own countries: 22% in Algeria, 17% in Morocco and 15% in Tunisia.[29] But advised by his emigrant friends and relatives, who are informed by the foreign and local media of the precarious economic plight of the destination country, an aspiring illegal migrant often decides to forgo such a costly and highly risky undertaking[30] at the end of which he has little chance of finding work while at the same time forfeiting the safety net of family support. Table 6 illustrates the rates of unemployment and increased female participation in the Maghrebin working population in France.

Family reunion -- mainly spouses and children, occasionally relatives -- opens up wider migratory prospects than labour migration, whether legal or illegal. But the absorptive capacities of "bridgeheads" established since the 1960s are also dwindling. The sex ratio (number of males to that of females) gives an admittedly approximate gauge for the expected migration potential of family reunion. A high ratio points to a surplus of males, a local marriage squeeze and a consequent need to import one's spouse from elsewhere, usually the country of origin. A narrow-based population pyramid likewise indicates that the children of immigrants left behind in the country of birth may be in the process of reuniting with their expatriate parents.

---

[29] Figures for males only (urban males only in Morocco) taken from the 1987 Algerian census, Tunisia's 1989 employment survey, and the 1990-91 standards of living survey in Morocco.

[30] Many of the boat-people who endeavour to cross the Strait of Gibraltar are not in fact Maghrebins at all, but from countries in sub-Saharan Africa.

Table 6
Unemployment and Increased Female Participation Rates in the
Maghrebin Working Population in France, 1982 - 1990

	Unemployment Rate (%)					
	Both Sexes		Men		Women	
	1982	1990	1982	1990	1982	1990
Foreign Nationals						
Algerians	21.9	27.6	18.6	23.1	44.8	42.4
Moroccans	15.2	26.5	12.7	21.8	35.5	43.3
Tunisians	18.2	26.4	16.3	22.5	35.5	42.7
Naturalised						
Algerians	n.a.	29.1	n.a.	25.1	n.a.	34.9
Moroccans	n.a.	20.9	n.a.	16.7	n.a.	27.7
Tunisians	n.a.	17.1	n.a.	12.6	n.a.	24.8

Female Participation Rate in the Work Force (%)		
Foreign Nationals	**1982**	**1990**
Algerians	9	18.4
Moroccans	8.3	16.6
Tunisians	8	14.8
Naturalised		
Algerians	n.a.	37.3
Moroccans	n.a.	35.3
Tunisians	n.a.	33.6

Sources: French census data, 1982 and 1990.
   1982: INSEE, *Recensement général de la population de 1982, Les étrangers*,
   La documentation française, Paris, 1988.
   1990: INSEE, *Recensement de la population de 1990-Nationalités*, Paris, 1992.

French data, however, clearly show that the cumulative effects of migrations linked to these various forms of family reunion have already contributed to "standardise" what were highly irregular age-sex structures: a 1982 survey found 1.85 Algerian men, 1.52 Moroccan men and 1.47 Tunisian men for each Maghrebin woman. By 1990, the gap had narrowed to 1.38, 1.25 and 1.29, respectively. See Figure 2.

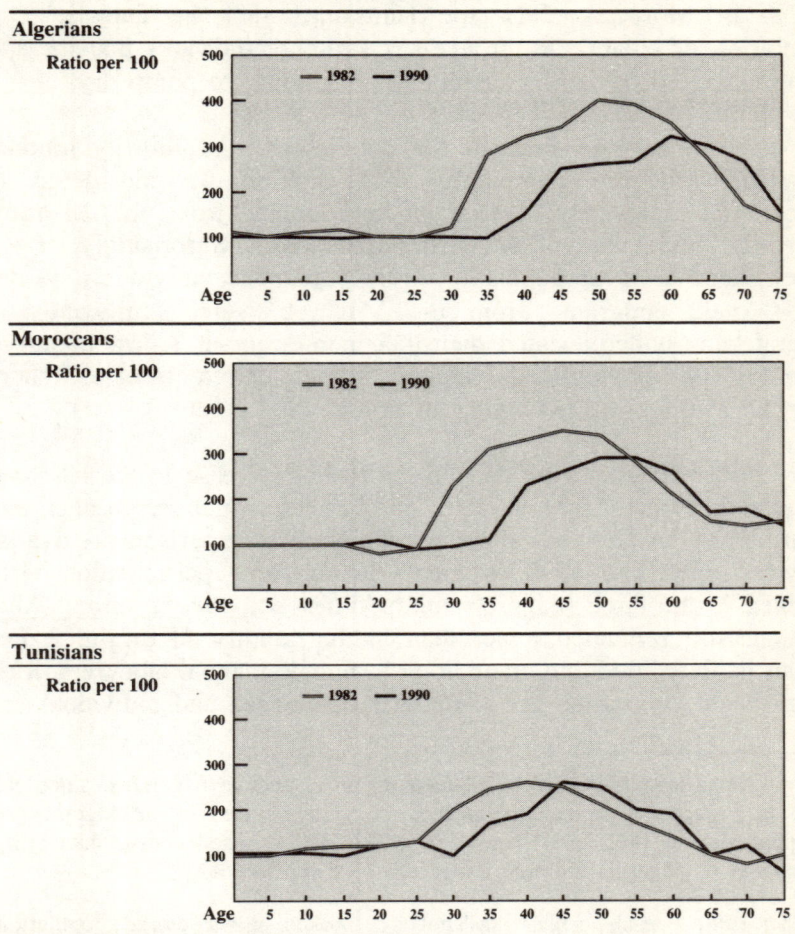

Figure 2
Sex Ratios in the Maghrebin Population[a]
in France, 1982 and 1990

[a] Includes native-born and naturalised Maghrebins in France.

Furthermore, one age group previously omitted from the population pyramid -- children of immigrant communities -- is now almost as greatly represented in France as in the Maghreb: 34% for Moroccans in France, 37.7% in Morocco; 28% for Tunisians, 35% in Tunisia.[31] This restoration of balance in the age-sex structure indicates that the suction pump activated by family reunions is beginning to pump dry.

Let us now turn to some of the determinants of fertility among the dispersed Maghreb community, the first to be considered being educational attainment. That of immigrants from the Maghreb is evidently below that of the host populations. Surprisingly, it is also lower than that of the population in the country of emigration. A decade ago,[32] male emigrants from the Maghreb were significantly more illiterate and undereducated than their non-emigrant fellow countrymen. Illiteracy also predominated among women emigrants at a higher rate than the average in the country of origin. See Figure 3.

More information is available on the recent increase in the labour-force participation rate of Maghrebin immigrants, which represents another determinant of fertility, where two points of comparison are available. Between 1982 and 1990, women's labour-force participation virtually doubled in the three Maghreb communities but, except among Algerian women, still remained lower than in the country of origin.[33] Female labour is diversified and, in addition to female manual labourers, includes a significant proportion of non-manual employees and individual service

---

[31] The comparison is devoid of all meaning in respect to Algerians, since children born in France to parents themselves born in France (or in Algeria prior to independence in 1962) are French by birth. The corrected census data brings the proportion of Algerian children under age 15 down to 8%.

[32] The 1990 French census has not yet broken down ethnic populations by educational level.

[33] The percentage of women in the economically active population was 18.4% among Algerian women living in France compared to 12.0% in Algeria (1987), 16.6% among Moroccan women in France compared to 21.1% in Morocco (1990-91), and 14.8% among Tunisian women in France compared to 20.3% in Tunisia (1989). These figures relate solely to non-agricultural labour.

Figure 3
Comparative Educational Levels of Algerian, Moroccan and Tunisian
Men and Women[a] in Their Native Countries and in France, 1982

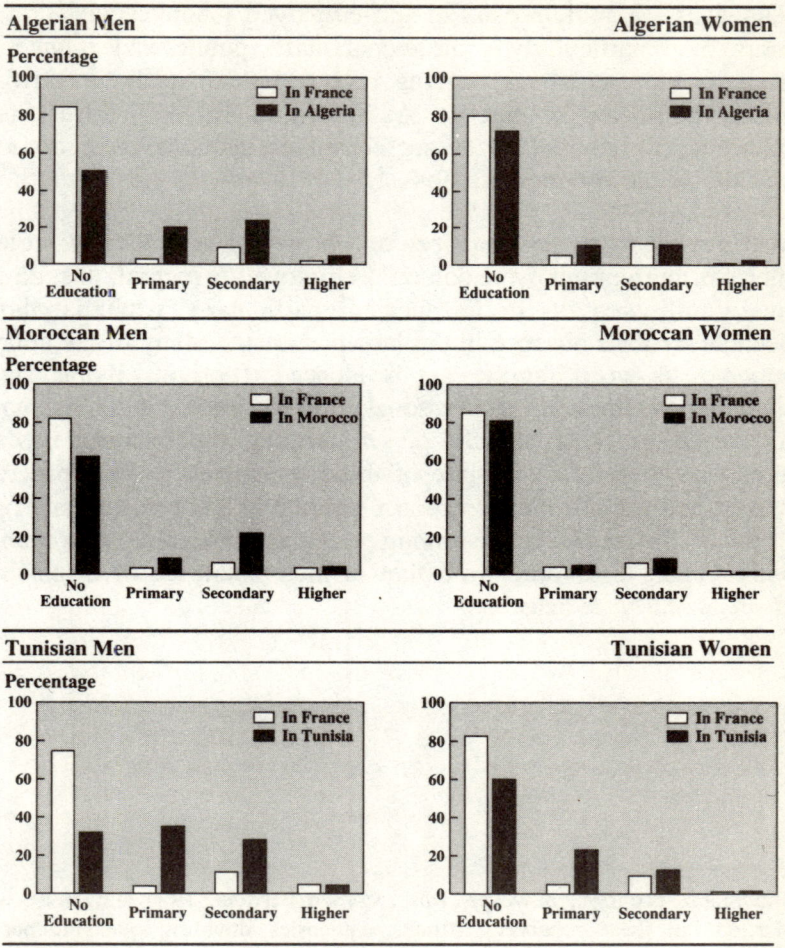

a Aged 15 to 49 years.

Sources: Calculations based on censuses: Algeria, 1987; Morocco, 1982; and Tunisia, 1984.
French data appears in Joëlle Affichard et Françoise Guillot, *Recensement général de la population de 1982 - Formation,* INSEE, Paris, 1985.

providers, unlike male labour where extreme specialisation remains the rule. Male Maghrebin workers are manual labourers, predominantly unskilled or agricultural: 78% of Algerians, 83% of Moroccans and 74% of Tunisians. A middle class of self-employed (shopkeepers, craftsmen, farmers) and particularly professional staff (public and private sector managers, representatives, agents and technical staff) is slowly and painfully beginning to emerge: As shown in Table 7, fewer than one Maghrebin in eight fell in the social and occupational categories at the top of the social pyramid in 1990.[34]

Drawn mostly from the small peasant-farmer class and rural proletariat, Maghrebin immigrants were naturally employed in menial, unskilled jobs. Virtually all were ill- or uneducated, particularly women, who were noticeable by their absence in the labour market. Many of the conditions conducive to large families -- residence of origin, living standard, husband's occupation, educational level and wife's labour-force participation -- were already present among the expatriate Maghreb community, therefore. In spite of these incentives to high procreation, however, and despite the European Community's subsidisation of part of the cost of children, fertility among emigrant Maghrebin women fairly quickly began to diverge from that in their countries of origin[35] in the form of an early decrease.

---

[34] Undeniable progress, however, was recorded between 1982 and 1990, with the proportions of these relatively affluent categories doubling over the period for Algerians, Moroccans and Tunisians alike. Hence, the category which includes management staff, agents, representatives, technical staff and members of the professions increased from 2.4% to 7.1% among Algerians, 2.4% to 6.3% among Moroccans and 5.3% to 9.1% among Tunisians.

[35] Except among Tunisians since 1985, the decrease in fertility is now more pronounced in Tunisia than among Tunisian women in France.

Table 7
Breakdown (%) by Nationality and Sex of the Maghreb Labour Force
in France, 1982 and 1990

Algerians, Men and Women	1982	1990
Farmers	0.0	0.0
Craftsmen	1.1	1.9
Wholesale/Retail Traders	2.9	4.0
Businessmen, Professionals	2.7	8.2
Supervisors	0.7	0.9
Non-Manual Workers	11.5	11.2
Services	3.6	6.6
Manual Workers	77.4	67.2
Total	**100.0**	**100.0**

Algerians, Men	1982	1990
Farmers	0.0	0.0
Craftsmen	1.2	2.2
Wholesale/Retail Traders	3.0	4.4
Businessmen, Professionals	2.4	7.1
Supervisors	0.8	1.1
Non-Manual Workers	8.1	4.3
Services	2.5	3.1
Manual Workers	82.1	77.7
Total	**100.0**	**100.0**

Algerians, Women	1982	1990
Farmers	0.0	0.1
Craftsmen	0.3	0.9
Wholesale/Retail Traders	2.9	2.3
Businessmen, Professionals	5.5	12.4
Supervisors	0.2	0.2
Non-Manual Workers	40.3	36.8
Services	13.3	19.5
Manual Workers	37.6	27.8
Total	**100.0**	**100.0**

Table 7, cont.

Moroccans, Men and Women	1982	1990
Farmers	0.1	0.4
Craftsmen	0.6	1.2
Wholesale/Retail Traders	1.4	2.3
Businessmen, Professionals	2.5	7.0
Supervisors	0.4	0.6
Non-Manual Workers	7.3	8.8
Services	3.8	6.6
Manual Workers	83.9	73.2
Total	**100.0**	**100.0**
Moroccans, Men	**1982**	**1990**
Farmers	0.1	0.5
Craftsmen	0.6	1.4
Wholesale/Retail Traders	1.4	2.4
Businessmen, Professionals	2.4	6.3
Supervisors	0.4	0.7
Non-Manual Workers	5.7	3.5
Services	1.6	2.5
Manual Workers	87.7	82.7
Total	**100.0**	**100.0**
Moroccans, Women	**1982**	**1990**
Farmers	0.0	0.2
Craftsmen	0.5	0.3
Wholesale/Retail Traders	1.0	1.8
Businessmen, Professionals	3.6	9.8
Supervisors	0.0	0.2
Non-Manual Workers	22.4	30.6
Services	24.4	23.7
Manual Workers	48.1	33.5
Total	**100.0**	**100.0**

Table 7, cont.

Tunisians, Men and Women	1982	1990
Farmers	0.2	0.1
Craftsmen	1.3	3.1
Wholesale/Retail Traders	3.0	3.6
Businessmen, Professionals	5.4	9.2
Supervisors	1.0	1.3
Non-Manual Workers	10.8	9.4
Services	5.0	7.0
Manual Workers	73.3	66.3
Total	**100.0**	**100.0**

Tunisians, Men	1982	1990
Farmers	0.2	0.1
Craftsmen	1.3	3.4
Wholesale/Retail Traders	3.0	3.9
Businessmen, Professionals	5.3	9.1
Supervisors	1.1	1.5
Non-Manual Workers	9.3	5.0
Services	3.2	3.7
Manual Workers	76.6	73.5
Total	**100.0**	**100.0**

Tunisians, Women	1982	1990
Farmers	0.3	0.1
Craftsmen	0.6	1.8
Wholesale/Retail Traders	2.7	2.4
Businessmen, Professionals	6.7	9.5
Supervisors	0.0	0.4
Non-Manual Workers	26.8	31.3
Services	23.2	23.6
Manual Workers	39.6	30.7
Total	**100.0**	**100.0**

Sources: French census data, 1982 and 1990.
> 1982: INSEE, *Recensement général de la population de 1982, Les étrangers,* La documentation française, Paris, 1988.
> 1990: INSEE, *Recensement de la population de 1990-Nationalités,* Paris, 1992.

V. International Migration as a Cause of Accelerating Fertility Transition?

Figure 1 showed fertility rates among Algerian, Moroccan and Tunisian women in their country of origin and in France for the period 1962 to 1991. The decline in fertility affects immigrant and national communities alike, with the onset of demographic transition occurring slightly earlier in the immigrant communities. Between the 1960s and very early 1980s (around 1985 in Algeria), the pace of transition was faster among the immigrant communities than in France. Lately, however, the rate of transition in the countries of emigration has overtaken that of immigrants.

Can a link be discerned between these demographic transitions on the two shores of the Mediterranean? More specifically, have Maghrebin immigrants contributed to the acceleration of demographic transition in their country of origin? The lone migrants of the 1960s, unmarried workers or married workers travelling without their families, and who were unclear about their ultimate plans -- whether to return to the country of birth or settle in the host country -- were assuredly imbued with a single, inherited family model -- the pronatalist model -- the very model which predominated in the Maghreb. They would certainly have aspired to have as many children as if they had never left their villages. But the effect of disruptions due to emigration on ultimate family size left the reality somewhat short of the intention.[36]

A generation later, a society has been born of immigration whose values are no longer strictly congruent with those of its founding fathers. While not yet fully integrated into the host society, its representatives have a realistic, perhaps even disabused, assessment of the radical development which sets them apart from their fellow countrymen in the Maghreb:

> The populations which are the product of immigration -- and thinking of the Moroccans (or all Maghrebins) in particular -

---

[36] Michèle Tribalat, *Cent ans d'immigration, étrangers d'hier Français d'aujourd'hui*, Travaux et Documents, Cahier No. 131, INED, Paris, 1991.

- the Moroccans who live in France are not the same as those who live in Morocco (or the Maghreb) . . . We do not have the same characteristics as the populations living in our parents' or our own countries of origin".[37]

But being different does not entail absolute alienation. Relative proximity and comparatively cheap travel and communication costs have favoured the proliferation of networks of interchange in the Mediterranean, perhaps more than between any other expatriate community and the region of origin. Maghrebin emigrants generate substantial flows of funds which are both essential to the survival of their families and the national balance-of-payments. In Morocco, for example, migrants' visible transfers[38] approached a tidy $2 billion in 1990; over 10% of aggregate annual private-consumption expenditure in Morocco is funded by migrants' remittances! Infinitely more if just those families who have sent one family member abroad are taken into account. Migrant remittances may sometimes be a source of new stratifications which place question marks over long-established social pyramids: the emergence of the Soussi group as a sub-element of the Moroccan bourgeoisie is a case in point.[39]

---

[37] Statement by Bouamana, "Espace culturel et citoyenneté en Europe", in *La communauté marocaine en France, quelles évolutions? Quelles perspectives?* ATMF national conference, January 1989. Jean-Claude Barreau, *De l'immigration en général et de la nation française en particulier*, Le pré au clercs, Paris, 1992, confirms: "These young Maghrebins, Muslims, like the Portuguese, Italians and Poles before them, think of themselves as French".

[38] That is, discounting remittances by non-bank channels, cash and consumer goods brought back on holidays. Visible transfers probably account for no more than 50% to 66% of all transfers.

[39] The Soussi migratory model (Souss is a region of southern Morocco) has contributed to an undeniable although hard to quantify extent to the social mobility of individuals originating from the region within the Moroccan sphere itself, notably through the formation of the Soussi middle class, which now runs not only a number of commercial but also industrial sectors of Morocco. See Hassan Haj Nasser, "Les mutations de la société française: emploi/formation", *La communauté marocaine en France, op. cit.*

Through redistributed earnings and consumer durables whose acquisition they facilitate or which they regularly introduce, emigrants wreak profound changes to patterns of consumption. Knowingly or unknowingly, they encourage aspirations for improved conditions and a reevaluation of the net value (costs and benefits) of children. In village communities and even urban lower-income families, where horizons were confined to family life and the rearing of large families, this radical change in patterns of consumption represents an initial break with traditional patterns of thinking and leads to a change in family choices and less pronatalist attitudes. Increased income raises aspirations for social mobility, resulting in a heightened desire to acquire consumer goods which compete with the additional child for family resources.[40]

Still more lasting than the effects of the consumer goods which cram emigrants' cars on the mass summer trek homewards are the effects of the ideas and values which they bring with them across the Mediterranean. On their return home -- annually for holidays, and occasionally but increasingly rarely permanently -- first-, and especially second-generation immigrants tend to propagate a more modern, more relaxed attitude towards family life, relations between the sexes, and, indeed, reproduction. These essentially are values to which they have become habituated in Europe. Basking in the prestige attaching to his superior material situation, the returned migrant gradually establishes a dependency relationship with his immediate circle and sooner or later develops into a key player in the local scene, an opinion former, most frequently of non-traditional opinions. He becomes the arbiter on fundamental issues relating to health, marriage, family size (parity), contraception and especially that keystone of future demographic trends, formal education for girls.

---

[40] Julian Simon, "Income, Wealth and their Distribution as Policy Tools in Fertility Control", in Ronald Ridker (ed.), *Population and Development* (Baltimore, MD: The Johns Hopkins University Press, 1976). See also Robert Repetto, *Economic Equality and Fertility in Developing Countries* (Cambridge, MA: Harvard University Press, 1979).

In the still largely unlettered Europe of yore, "cultural advances were not the result of central-government decisions but of local demands rooted in village life rather than an overall social structure. Even schools seem to be a village rather than a state invention".[41]   As regards the dissemination of education, the Maghreb today resembles the Europe of yesteryear in all points. This is confirmed by the Moroccan figures, which clearly point to under-education being more the result of a lack of public demand than a failing by the state.

Questioned as to why they did not send their daughters to school, Moroccan rural parents -- the last bulwark of female under-education and its corollary of high fertility[42] -- most frequently cited lack of ability to pay the costs of education (30%) and secondly, their antipathy to the values conveyed by school, or to mixed education (23%).[43] Reasons attaching to the failings of the state system were less important: the school being too far away (8.9%) or the absence of a school in the vicinity (14.3%). Emigrant remittances attenuate the material difficulties, since family solidarity remains resistant to the separation brought by emigration. The migrant him (or her)self will be better placed than anyone to overcome the moral misgivings about education for girls. On returning to the village, he (she) will be able to persuade his (her) family and friends that if young Maghrebin emigrants all attend school -- and mixed schools, to boot[44] -- "over there", there is no reason why the same situation should not obtain "back here".[45] The process of village-

---

[41] Emmanuel Todd, *L'enfance du monde-Structures familiales et développement* (Paris: Seuil, 1984).

[42] Only 30% of rural girls aged 7-13 years attend school.

[43] Government of Morocco, *op. cit.*

[44] Where girls perform better than boys, incidentally. As yet unpublished French Ministry of Education statistics show a higher proportion of girls entering first-year secondary, followed by an equally higher rate of continuity through the various levels of secondary education to the final year of higher secondary education.

[45] "Over there" and "back here" are the demotic terms used by Maghrebins to refer to the receiving or host country, and country of origin, respectively.

to-village contagion by which mass literacy slowly spread through rural Europe is now gathering pace in the Maghreb through that other form of contagion born of the emergence of a powerful centre for the dissemination of culture -- emigrant Maghrebin communities residing abroad.[46]

But through the urbanisation of their immediate kith and kin, immigrants also indirectly affect education for girls and women's fertility. One side-effect of international migration has often been an increased rate of internal migration. Originally, the families of lone migrants moved to the towns, the quicker to draw the benefits of the savings remitted from abroad. Through contact, the cultural -- then fertility -- behaviour of these internal migrants is increasingly tending to align with those of town-dwellers. Unlike rural areas, compulsory education is the rule for all -- or nearly all -- urban children, regardless of sex.[47] Parents can only educate all their children of both sexes by having fewer.

Through the feedback effect of mentalities acquired abroad, emigration may accelerate or restrain demographic transition. The endogenous data alone cannot explain why demographic transition in the Maghreb should be more pronounced than elsewhere in the Arab world. A brief glance at that other major focal point of emigration -- Egypt -- offers a reverse illustration of the potential role of international emigration, where it appears rather to be deferring the demographic transition. As the first Arab country to make a restrictionist (birth control) policy part of its development objectives, the 1960s heralded a decline in fertility of 1.7 children in Egypt: from 7 children per woman in 1961 to 5.3 in 1972. Since then, however, and particularly throughout the 1980s, the trend is once more upwards, levelling off at 5.5 in recent years.

---

[46] Immigrants have been markedly more in favour of formal education for girls -- 65% compared to 50% of non-migrants -- since 1975, i.e., before the emergence of second-generation immigrants; see A. Berrada, B. Hamdouch et. al., *Migration de développement, Migration de sous-développement?*, INSEA, Rabat, 1979.

[47] In 1990, primary school attendance rates (ages 7-13) were 88% for boys and 85% for girls in Moroccan towns, compared with 58% and 30%, respectively, in rural areas. Department of Statistics, *Niveaux de vie des ménages 1990-91, op. cit.*

The very slight inroads made by women in the labour market -- for purely domestic reasons -- have assuredly acted as a brake on transition. But no less evident in this demographic regression is the effect of the huge dispersion of Egyptian emigrants, returning imbued with the traditional values of Gulf societies, the most pronatalist in the Arab world. "The massive emigration of village men to the Gulf states has influenced ways of thinking ... The women over there, they say, are all demure and veiled, unlike our strident and voluble talkers who are happy to flaunt themselves. Consequently, this new generation wished the women confined at home, believing, unlike their fathers, that a woman's presence in the marketplace was a shameful and indecent exhibition". [48] The savings remitted by Egyptian emigrants in the Gulf, by boosting consumer spending on the banks of the Nile, could doubtlessly have instigated an eventual decrease in Egyptian fertility similar to that currently under way in the Maghreb. The decline in Egyptian fertility not having been confirmed, it must be assumed that the acquired values imported from the host societies -- seclusion of women/large families -- prevailed by obliterating the normal processes derived from the demographic impact of economics (increased income/decreased fertility). [49]

Through its antithetical effects -- delaying demographic transition in the Mashreq and accelerating it in the Maghreb -- international migration is already affecting demographic developments of the next century, more by its indirect effects on fertility in the countries of emigration than by any direct effect.

---

[48] Mona Abazza, "La femme dans la campagne égyptienne", *Peuples Méditérranéens*, No. 41-42, cited by Hinde Taariji, *Les voilées de l'Islam* (Paris: Balland, 1991).

[49] According to Carla Makhlouf Obermeyer, "Where substantial declines in fertility have taken place, they have invariably been associated with broader political changes; and where setbacks to women's status are observed, they too have accompanied a re-traditionalisation of political structures and the abandonment of an egalitarian definition of society". See "Islam, Women and Politics: The Demography of Arab Countries", *Population and Development Review*, March 1992.

VI. Prospects

Access to urban facilities, paid employment and especially schools, the opening-up to Europe brought about by geography and the work of their expatriate populations, will encourage a faster rate of fertility decline and slower population growth in the Maghreb. To take only one element of the complex of proximate determinants of reproductive behaviour, it must be concluded that the educational system will each year steadily add more literate young girls educated to the level of secondary school or higher to the group of women of reproductive age.

At the foreseeable rate of increase in the educated female population, illiteracy will affect no more than a marginal segment of women in the reproductive age groups by the not-too-distant year 2025 -- the span of a single generation: 8% in Algeria and Tunisia, 29% in Morocco. See Figure 4. By contrast, 8 out of every 10 Algerian and Tunisian women, and more than one-half of all Moroccan women, will by then have been educated to secondary or a higher standard in national schools. Given the high correlation between a woman's educational attainment and the number of children she will bear, the fertility of Maghrebin women will decrease more sharply than forecast by international organisations.

There can be no doubt that fertility in the three Maghreb countries will decline. That assumption is built into United Nations projections.[50] But taking into account the restructuring of the population by educational attainment and the certainty that declining fertility today encompasses all women -- including illiterates -- means reconsidering the rates of decline. The interaction of these two changes suggests a more optimistic trend than that depicted by the UN projections.[51] Fertility will decrease more

---

[50] United Nations, *World Population Prospects 1990*, New York, 1991.

[51] Further details of the methodology and results of population projections for the Maghreb countries can be found in Youssef Courbage and Philippe Fargues, *L'avenir démographique de la rive sud de la Méditerranée, op. cit.*

Figure 4
Projected Educational Levels of Women[a] in
Algeria, Morocco and Tunisia, 1990-2025

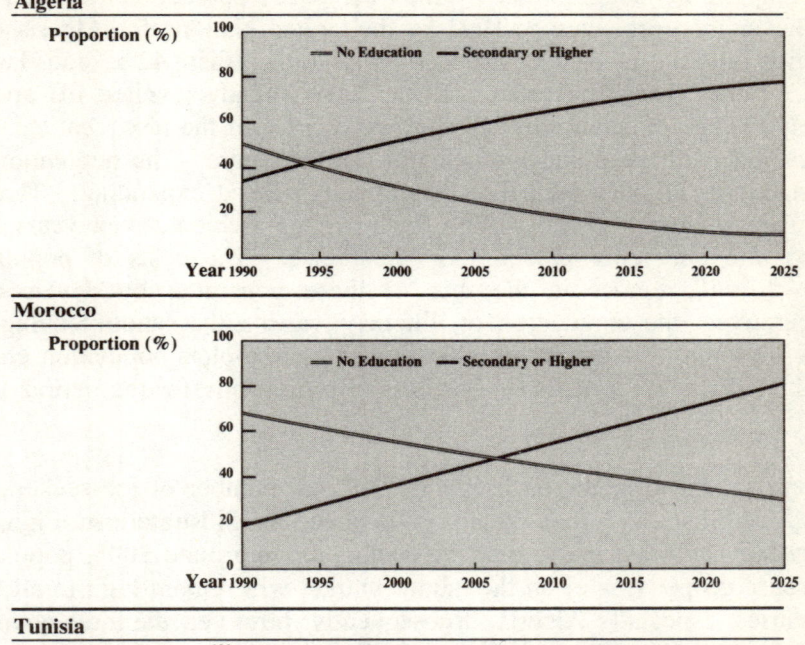

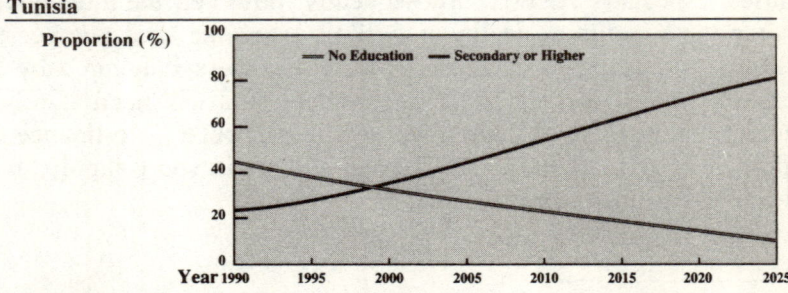

a   Aged 15 to 49 years.

Source: Calculations taken from Youssef Courbage and Philippe Farques, *L'avenir démographi-que de la rive sud de la Méditerranée: Algérie, Egypte, Maroc, Syrie, Turquie, Tunisie - Projections de la population et réfléxions sur la migration,* Plan Bleu, 1992.

rapidly and the replacement level (arbitrarily fixed at 2.07 children per woman[52]) will be more quickly crossed. See Figure 5.

Fertility trends suggest that by the year 2025, population numbers will be lower than projected in 1992 by the United Nations for Algeria (44.8 million instead of 51.8), Morocco (40.0 rather than 42.5) and Tunisia (12.7 rather than 13.4) alike. Births have already levelled off and are likely to remain stable through the first quarter of the next century. It is a reversal with profound implications for the future. The population-led demand for primary education has already ceased expanding. That for secondary education will follow in a similar fashion seven years from now, and university places 15 years hence. The costs of population growth will regress in the face of those generated by development imperatives: the eradication of illiteracy, raising the school-leaving age and improving the quality of education. Figure 6 plots population change in the Maghreb according to two sets of projections for the period 1995-2025.

Twenty years after the birth events, the total number of job-seekers will itself stabilise and then begin to decline, as illustrated in Figure 7. Between 1990 and the turn of the century up to around 2005, population pressure proper (male) on the labour market will remain high in all three countries, especially Algeria. Subsequently, however, the three countries will reap the benefits of declining fertility, when the total number of job applicants will begin to decrease. Just as Europe's bulging baby-boom generation leaves working life for retirement, and will need to rely on a sufficient labour force -- foreign workers in particular -- to finance it, the Maghreb labour markets, where labour will be in short supply, will be hard-pressed to meet export demands.

---

[52] Setting the number of children below which fertility will cease to decline at 2.07 is a purely arbitrary threshold. A continuation of existing trends even below the reproductive threshold is not beyond the bounds of imagination. Who, after all, would have thought 30 years ago to see a staunchly Catholic Southern Europe declining to the present fertility levels of 1.3 to 1.5 children? As we have seen, the total fertility rate in Morocco has recently fallen below 2 children among the urban working population.

Figure 5
Trends in Fertility in the Maghreb according to
Two Sets of Projections, 1995-2025

Algeria

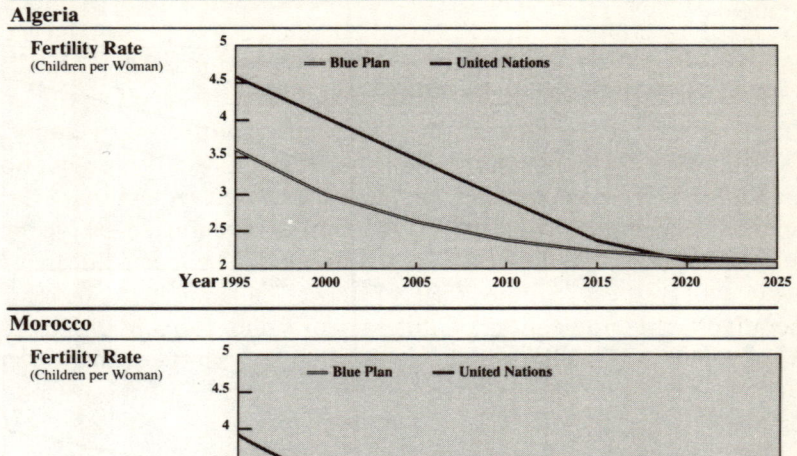

Morocco

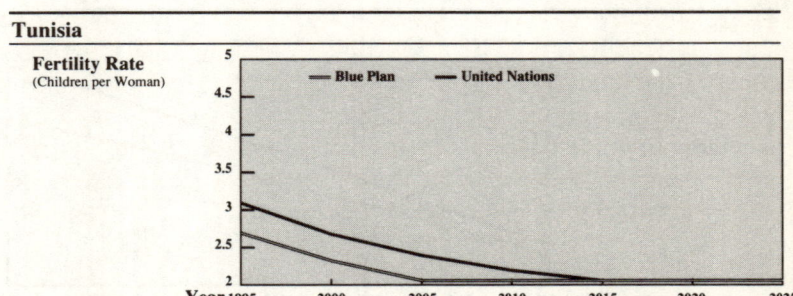

Tunisia

Sources: Blue Plan Projections: Youssef Courbage and Philippe Fargues, *L'avenir démographique de la rive sud de la Méditerranée: Algérie, Egypte, Maroc, Syrie, Turquie, Tunisie - Projections de la population et réfléxions sur la migration*, Plan Bleu, 1992.
United Nations Projections: United Nations, *World Population Prospects 1990*, New York, 1991.

Figure 6
Total Population Projections
in Algeria, Morocco and Tunisia, 1995-2025

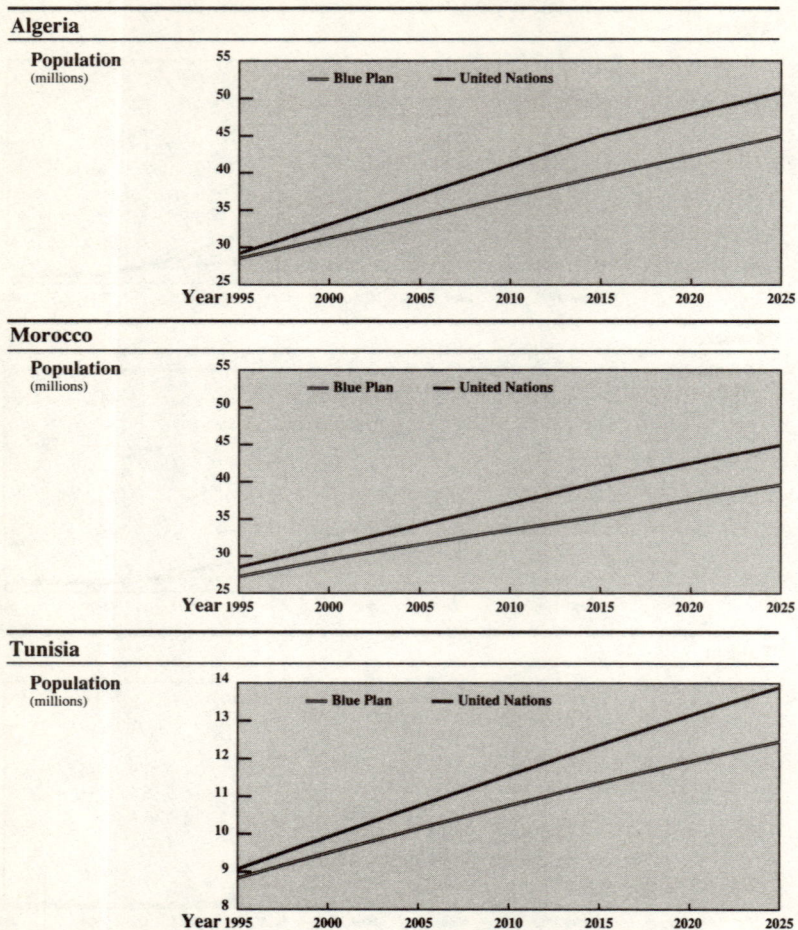

Sources: Blue Plan Projections: Youssef Courbage and Philippe Fargues, *L'avenir démographi-*
que de la rive sud de la Méditerranée: Algérie, Egypte, Maroc, Syrie, Turquie, Tunisie -
Projections de la population et réfléxions sur la migration, Plan Bleu, 1992.
United Nations Projections: United Nations, *World Population Prospects 1990,* New
York, 1991.

Figure 7
Annual Male Entrants to the Labour Market
1990-2025

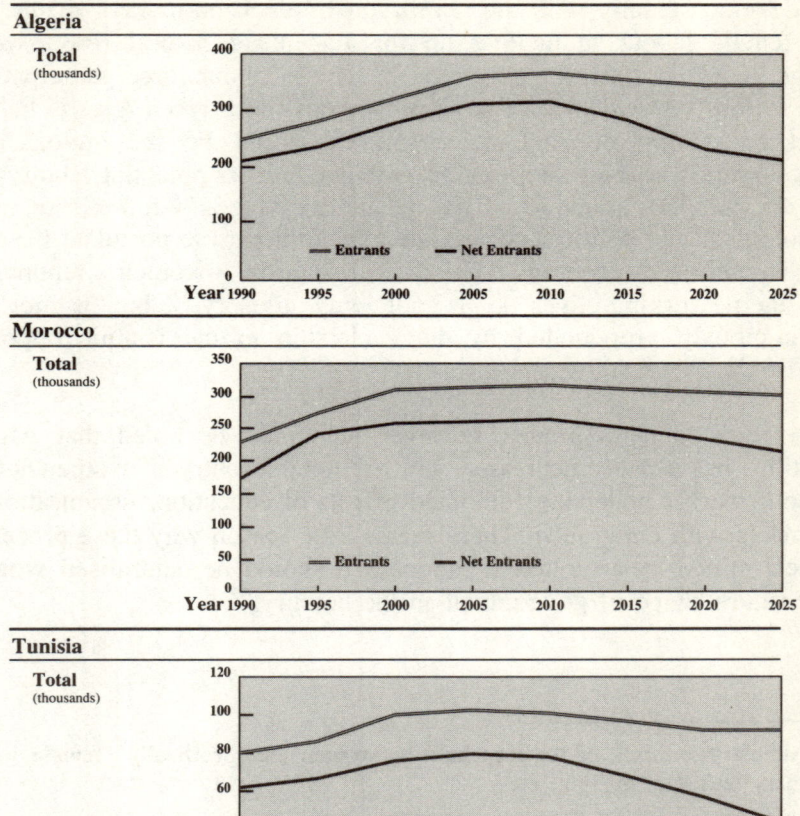

Sources: Annual entrants estimated at 1/5 of the population in the 20-24 age bracket; Annual
          departures estimated at 1/5 of the 65-69 age bracket.
          Calculations taken from Youssef Courbage and Philippe Fargues, *L'avenir démographi-*
          que de la rive sud de la Méditerranée: Algérie, Egypte, Maroc, Syrie, Turquie, Tunisie -
          Projections de la population et réfléxions sur la migration, Plan Bleu, 1992.

To what extent will women participate in the labour force? In Morocco and Tunisia, increased urbanisation and education will be accompanied by an increased penetration of the labour market by women; this is likely to develop steadily with the realisation by decision-makers of the value of female labour in making up for inadequate natural resources. In Algeria, by contrast, the very modest female labour force participation is the serious consequence of more prosperous times when Algeria believed that its natural oil and gas resources would be the motor for its development without the need to mobilise half its potential labour force. In the complex situation of the debate on Algeria's future, the myriad ideological and political uncertainties make it hard to postulate the future for women in its economy. The radical solution -- women's renunciation of their working lives -- is not only illusory,[53] but is not even unanimously propounded by the leadership of the Islamic opposition parties.[54]

To return to demography, however, it should be noted that Algerian fertility has already decreased with no notable entry of women into the labour market under the combined effects of education, urbanisation and contacts with emigrants. There seems little reason why these processes -- determined by an inherent rationale -- should be neutralised whatever the future shape of government in the country.[55]

---

[53] Almost two-thirds of the jobs held by women are specifically "female jobs" in primary teaching, nursing, etc.

[54] Abassi Madani, a leader of the Algerian FIS, said: "Women's employment is a woman's right ... provided it is done in the right conditions (segregated)", while at virtually the same time his second-in-command, Ali Belhadj, was affirming that: "If we are to live in a truly Islamic society, it is not woman's lot to work and the Head of State must allocate them remuneration from the coffers of the state. She will then remain at home to devote herself to the sublime task of educating men", cited by Hinde Taariji, *Les voilées de l'Islam, op. cit.*

[55] Note the policy in two Islamic states: in Saudi Arabia, contraception is tolerated, while in Iran, all methods of family planning, including tubal ligation and vasectomy, are officially permitted.

VI. General Survey

The received wisdom is that a Maghrebin population explosion is in progress both south and north of the Mediterranean. By some form of osmosis, the overflow from the natural increase in North Africa will be drained off by migrations to Europe. Uncontrolled fertility and a declining deathrate suggest that the upward curve will continue until the middle of the next century.

A reappraisal of the facts is essential for the indigenous and expatriate populations alike. This shows that following a historical phase of pronounced growth, demographic transition is now firmly under way. There is every likelihood that the accelerating decline in fertility will continue for the time being under the impulsion of social and geographical restructuring. An intermediate demographic area between Europe and the other Arab countries is increasingly taking shape, delimited by the three principal Maghreb countries.

The Maghreb owes this situation to geography, history and its dispersed emigrant community in Europe. For thirty glorious years, Europe's exceptional economic boom, which created a demand for foreign labour swiftly followed by the emigration of spouses and children, helped reduce the immense population pressure on the resources of the Maghreb countries. At the close of the century, with emigration tending to level off, their aggregate demographic balance shows that national populations have lost some 2.4 million inhabitants, or 4% of their total populations.

But the presence of expatriate communities in Europe has a significant, albeit not precisely quantifiable, import. Without emigration leading to the remittance of savings, sending of consumer goods, and above all the transfer of values and outlooks, the transition to lower fertility rates would have been much less rapid. In fact, the concrete evidence is lacking to explain why fertility in the Maghreb, heretofore in line with that of the Arab world, should have begun to diverge from it two decades ago. Similar developments leading to changed reproductive behaviour were under way in both the east and west of the Arab world. Infant mortality has regressed generally, urban growth has continued and girls have competed with boys, firstly in the schools, then in the labour market. Family-planning services and over-the-counter sales of contraceptives are now commonplace. Were it to have emulated that of the Middle East, the average birthrate in the Maghreb over the past 20 years should have been around 43 births per 1000 population. In fact, it has been markedly lower at 39 births per 1000 population. See Figure 8.

Figure 8
Comparative Birthrates in the Maghreb and the Mashreq
1960-1995

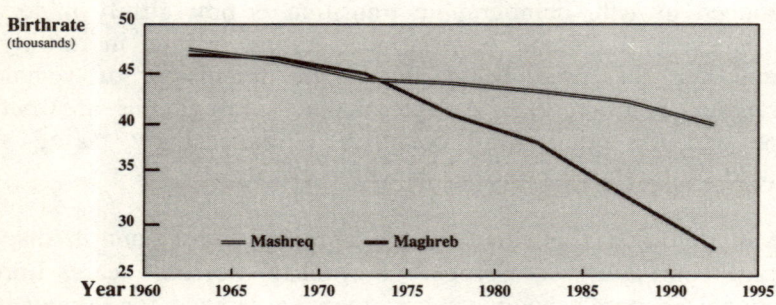

A four-point difference in the birthrate represents nearly 3.7 million averted births.[56] If we take as the lowest assumption that only one-half of these averted births are attributable to the multiple effects of international migration, that still accounts for 1.85 million fewer births in the Maghreb -- almost as great as the direct reduction due to emigration. Perhaps not the least of the paradoxes may be that the very international migration which was hitherto considered a vicissitude of the population explosion has in fact become a powerful vector of demographic transition in the Maghreb.

---

[56] Average population of the Maghreb between 1970-90: 45.9 million from the difference between the birth rates of 43 per 1000 population and 39 per 1000 population, i.e., 4 births per 1000 population over the 20 years between 1970 and 1990.

3 Islam: Political Implications for Europe and the Middle East

Maha Azzam

The widespread manifestation of Islam as a political force in the Muslim world will increasingly shape the nature of relations between Europe and the Mediterranean countries. Islam as a form of political protest has developed throughout much of this century in the context of political, economic and social dynamics particular to an individual country while also sharing many features that pertain to more than one country. Islamic protest constitutes the main opposition to regimes in the Middle East (the region of concern in this paper), and its influence is likely to increase in the 21st century.

This paper will examine the nature and role of Islam as a political force in terms of its implications for both Europe and the Middle East. First, the different trends of political Islam will be discussed as well as its relationship to democracy. Secondly, aspects of the compatibility or tension between Islam and capitalism will be examined. Finally, the implications of a number of central issues relating to the region and the EC will be discussed.

I. Islamic Protest

In academic circles, the notion of Islam as a monolithic force has by and large been replaced by the recognition that there exists a "variety of Islams".[1] This approach has the advantage of acknowledging the various traditions and interpretations of Islam specific to each Muslim society and helps to distinguish between different Islamic strains, such as, the traditionalist and modernist or the quietist and the activist. While succeeding in steering us away from one conceptual extreme, which

---

[1] P. Bannerman, *Islam in Perspective* (London: Routledge, 1988).

views Islam as monolithic, this latter approach, however, is also flawed in that it substitutes another extreme, which admits of a wide variety of trends and interpretations of Islam. Although it is extremely important to take into account the different political interpretations of Islam, the stress on differences tends to undermine the importance of the shared perception of identity and challenges that is essential to understanding contemporary Islamic protest.

The vast majority of Muslims view their religious beliefs as an integrated body of injunctions and teachings that form a unified faith. It is with the nature and interpretation of the political role to be given to Islam that the consensus breaks down and there emerges a growing struggle, primarily between those in power and those in opposition and between secularists and Islamists.

The relationship between Islam and politics has several dimensions. On one level, the two can be considered inextricably linked because of the association between Islam and the state from the time of the Prophet in 7th century Arabia and through the many centuries of Islamic history. On another, Islam can be seen as having become increasingly removed from political power, particularly in the course of the present century, with its major influence remaining primarily in the social sphere especially in relation to family law. In Muslim countries there is increasing demand for the implementation of Islamic law (*Shari'a*) to replace secular legal systems which although incorporating aspects of the *Shari'a* are based either on French or English law.

The implementation of Islamic law at the national level does not necessarily result in a militant Islamic system of government that is anti-Western. While Iran and the Sudan offer examples of *Shari'a*-based systems of government that are considered extremist by the West, Saudi Arabia, the Gulf states and Pakistan represent examples of states in which Islam is an integral part of the body politic but the government is clearly a Western ally.[2] The division between secularism and Islam is

---

[2] J. Piscatori (ed.), *Islam in the Political Process* (Cambridge: Cambridge University Press, 1983).

not easily definable in Muslim societies where the boundary where one begins and the other ends is often blurred. A process of Islamisation has been on the increase in most Muslim countries at a popular and even some governmental levels over the past two to three decades; at the same time, however, secularisation and Westernisation have also made great inroads into the very fabric of Muslim society in the course of this century.

Both Western and several Middle Eastern governments share a perceived threat not so much from Islam per se but from its use as the basis for formulating a radical political and economic philosophy that challenges (and potentially can overthrow) governments in power. As a consequence, the West is not particularly interested in the relative merits of secularism versus Islam, but rather how best to maintain a political regime that will safeguard Western interests regardless of its ideological orientation.

The belief that security and stability are offered by existing regimes, in contrast to the instability that would ensue if Islamically-oriented regimes came to power in the Middle East, raises a number of issues. First, it is becoming increasingly apparent that security and stability in the Middle East are linked to the governments' response to public demands for accountability, greater representation and respect for the rule of law and human rights. While these are essential components of the West's understanding of democracy, the emphasis among Islamists and other political opposition groups tends to be on liberties (*hurriyat*) in the political rather than the social sphere. A fundamental difference that helps define the Islamists' position on democracy is that sovereignty for them lies with God alone and the *Shari'a* is paramount; the *Shari'a* -- comprising the *Qur'an* and *Sunna*, and not the sovereignty of the electorate -- is the source of legislation and policy. Government is seen as a trust which an elected assembly carries out in accordance with the *Shari'a*.[3] Islamists will argue that there can be a whole spectrum of political opinion represented within the constitutional framework of Islam. If the search is for long-term stability in these societies, then the

---

[3] *A Model of an Islamic Constitution*, Islamic Council, London, 1983.

increasing demand for a different political order, whether or not it represents Western-style democracy, will need to be addressed.

Secondly, the argument that an Islamic system of government is to be resisted because it is unlikely to be democratic appears weak in light of the fact that the vast majority of Middle Eastern regimes are themselves undemocratic. Thirdly, Western fears of increased immigration to Europe as a result of growing economic and political hardship should be seen in the context of the existing economic situation in which corruption is rife and poverty widespread. One can construct a scenario where a popular Islamic regime that is committed to weeding out corruption and instigating development, and if unhindered by outside forces, could win the "hearts and minds" of its people and realise results that existing unpopular regimes have failed to accomplish. This in turn would not increase the internal pressures to migrate to the West. It is also possible that many of the Muslim immigrants in the West who face increasing racism might feel the urge to return to participate in establishing a state towards which they may feel less alienated.

The call for political liberalisation has been fuelled by secular and Islamist forces, but it is clearly the latter that will benefit if a process of democratisation gets under way. However, it is highly unlikely that Middle Eastern regimes will allow any degree of real democratic reform that permits the participation of Islamists, given that the popular strength of these forces, once unleashed, would lead to a change in government. It is not so much that the political opposition in the Middle East is often of an Islamist orientation that makes it unpalatable to regimes in power but, rather, that this opposition has the capacity to overthrow existing regimes.

Dictatorships, continued poverty and extended war have left the people of the region disillusioned with regimes and ideologies that have failed to realise their promises in terms of economic development, political participation, regional unity and the defeat of Israel. The unhappy legacy of colonialism and the demoralisation of continued political and economic decline need to be set against the Muslim self-image of having been a powerful and advanced civilisation in the past. The Islamists place the blame on Muslims themselves -- for having turned away from their religion -- on their rulers and on the West.

Islamists draw little distinction between one regime in the Middle East and another, although they have received some financial support in the past from Saudi Arabia and more recently from Iran, both of which governments lay claim to Islam as the basis of their political legitimacy. This financial assistance in part reflects the need of the two regimes to forestall opposition and to compete for the support of Islamist elements (most recently in Central Asia).

The funding of certain Islamist groups has always been problematic because it helps them to survive and spread. Then at a later date and depending on the political climate, they may turn against their donors despite a continued need for funding, as happened during the Gulf war. The level of Iran's financial backing of Islamist groups has been exaggerated, except for its support for Hizbollah and possibly other *shi'a* groups in the Gulf states. Involvement by the Iranian government with sunni Islamist groups seems to have been limited primarily to providing moral support and modest financial assistance. Clearly, Islamist groups are indigenous and have developed independently of Iranian backing. These groups are themselves often sceptical of Iran's claim to being Islamic on the ground that it is *shi'a* and because of its support in the past for the Syrian regime, despite its massacre of thousands of Muslim Brotherhood members in Hama in 1982.

The Islamist groups represent independent, non-governmental opposition. A policy designed to financially starve them, particularly the moderate elements such as the Muslim Brotherhood, will only have the effect of inhibiting the beneficial educational and social welfare services they perform and leave room for smaller, more extreme groups to carry out acts of terrorism.[4]

There is something of a pattern to the development and activities of

---

[4] For a study of militant Islamist groups in Egypt, see R. Rubin, *Islamic Fundamentalism in Egyptian Politics* (London: Macmillan, 1990).

Islamist groups in many Middle Eastern countries. Their growth was encouraged by regimes in the 1970s and 1980s as a counterweight to the leftists and to both the leftists and Nasserists in the case of Egypt. And in the Occupied Territories, the Israeli government saw them as a possible counterweight to the PLO. In most cases, Islamist groups -- whether university-based or organised in small underground cells -- have survived or new groups have emerged, despite attempts by governments to suppress their more extreme elements and by some governments to accommodate the moderates. Even in Saudi Arabia, owing to a combination of factors -- the need for participation, resentment at the lack of accountability of the ruling family, the Gulf war and Saudi Arabia's involvement in it and the traditionalists' fear of Westernisation -- there has developed an Islamist presence of some strength. The government experienced a dramatic expression of Islamist opposition in 1979 with the siege of the Great Mosque. And following the Gulf war, there has been a growing Islamist fervour that has employed many tactics similar to those being used by other Islamist groups in the Middle East.

Among Islamists there is a shared ideology aiming at the implementation of the *Shari'a* and the establishment of an Islamic state, as well as shared tactics for communicating their message. These tactics are far-ranging. They include the sponsorship of welfare programmes, the use of the Friday sermon to spread their message, recruitment on university campuses, assassination of political figures and more recently in Egypt, attacks on tourists.

Dissention and violence instigated by Islamists in urban areas (although in Egypt it is also taking place in the countryside) are already on the rise and represent attempts to strike out at the state by any means possible. Islamist groups justify their own actions as a legitimate response to the long-standing violence that the state has committed against them, while the state views them as a security threat that needs to be contained by whatever measures are required, even draconian ones. Several Arab states, including Egypt, Algeria, Tunisia and Saudi Arabia, have recently begun to coordinate political policy and security measures with a view towards crushing Islamist groups.[5]   The experience to date, however, of the Algerian and Egyptian governments is that a policy of confrontation does not stem, but, on the contrary, actually incites more violence.

The main strength of the Islamists is that they are not functioning in a vacuum nor are they or their message marginal. They are active within societies where religious fervour and Islamisation are intensifying. Whether in the Maghreb, Egypt, Jordan, or the Occupied Territories, Islam is capturing the imagination of people, particularly among the young who constitute very high percentages of the populations.   In attempts to control religion and to encourage the spread of a moderate, non-activist brand of Islam, governments have inadvertently helped in the general Islamisation of society.   In the case of Egypt, for example, religious topics predominate in the government-controlled media, with the effect that there is a greater awareness within society of religion in general.   The magnitude of economic and social problems facing the Middle East today makes it easy for a Muslim to cross the line between being an non-activist and an activist.

The appeal of political Islam has been aided by the apparent bankruptcy of secular alternatives.   There is a search for the realisation of the unfulfilled promises by regimes in the areas of economic development and political participation.

To date, radical Islamists have only been in a position of protest against the government in power, except in the cases of Iran and Sudan. However, if the Islamists come to power, they will face the same set of economic and social problems that have afflicted their societies for the greater part of this century.   The reality of the situation would most likely moderate their views, although increased political and economic pressures from Western governments could possibly provoke anti-Western feelings that would also be reflected in government policy.

---

[5] See "Arabs Urge Unity against Muslim Zealots", *The Independent*, 6 January 1993.

II. Compatibility between Islam and Modernity

One of the main questions that arises in the context of Islam and modernity is whether Islam is compatible with the capitalist development model. One often hears the question: does there exist anywhere in the world a single modern industrialised Islamic state? The answer to this question, however, is more likely to be found in the conditions of underdevelopment prevalent in the Third World than in the suitability of Islam as a basis for industrial development.

Historically, Islamic law has been an integral part of the body politic of Muslim society and has provided the basis of political legitimacy and authority of the leaders over an advanced civilisation. Therefore, when Islamists say that "Islam is the solution", it is partly because there is a belief that it was central to their "golden age". The political system that contemporary Islamists are attempting to establish is different in terms of its *raison d'être* and its level of advancement compared to past Muslim societies. Despite their emphasis on the past, Islamists are very much a product of contemporary political and socioeconomic conditions.

Another major concern is the influence of the economic situation on the appeal and growth of Islamist groups. It is often argued that economic progress in the region and increased economic aid would help remove one of the main reasons for the success of the Islamists. Although it is true that the Islamists have established various welfare programmes and other facilities where governments have failed to do so, and in turn have enlarged their support, it is an oversimplification to argue that the upsurge in the Islamic following is due to economic factors. Support for the Islamists has become widespread, and it is unlikely that it would be significantly diminished if there were a reversal in the economic fortunes of these states. In addition to economic considerations, it is clear that Islam responds to the search for political participation and government accountability coupled with the desire to preserve tradition and values. Economic development and financial assistance should not be seen just as a way of combating Islamic radicalism, but as a necessity for long-term domestic and regional security.

For Islamists, the problem in the economic sphere is not one of choosing between modernisation and tradition (although that may be the essential choice in the social sphere). On the contrary, the problem has been that too little modernisation and technological development has left these states weak and poor. The call by the developing countries in the early 1970s for a "New International Economic Order", in fact, encompasses some of the most fundamental economic concerns still held by both Islamists and non-Islamists in the developing world.

Islamist attitudes towards free-market economics have a number of facets. On the one hand, Islamists acknowledge that the socialist experiments undertaken in many Muslim states have largely failed, but on the other, they hold the policies of economic liberalisation responsible for the corruption and excessive consumerism evident in these societies and for widening the gap between the rich and the poor. In addition, the philosophical tenets of social welfare have permeated the political discourse of the Islamists via the nationalist and socialist experiments of the post-colonial era and have been combined, at the same time, with the Islamic commitment to social justice. Thus, a government is judged to have fundamentally failed if it does not provide a basic level of welfare for the poorer members of its population. In this climate, the Islamists' promotion of welfare programmes and their rejection of the new capitalist spirit are met with strong approval. The Islamists' position is not that the material fruits of capitalism are bad in and of themselves but that the pain experienced especially by the poor in newly liberalising economies is acute and the outcome is far from clear or promising.

The issue of a more equitable distribution of wealth appears with increasing frequency on the agenda of Islamist gatherings.[6] The question also emerged as one of the concerns of a beleaguered Saddam Hussein, and was identified by the Western members of the coalition as a principal issue requiring attention in the post-war Middle East. Little progress, however, has been achieved on this matter that lies at the very heart of fundamental change in the Middle East.

---

[6] Islamic Council of Europe, "The Muslim World and the Future Economic Order", Islamic Information Services, 1979.

The Islamist position on economic policy embraces a wide spectrum of views ranging from advocacy of certain dimensions of the free-market system to a number of aspects of socialism. Whether issuing from Islamist or secularist circles, these viewpoints will continue to conflict with one another, particularly in light of the extensive poverty suffered in most countries of the region. Given the constraints imposed by international financial institutions, such as the World Bank and the International Monetary Fund, however, as well as the prevailing predisposition towards market economies, Islamists in power are likely to adopt a capitalist path of development. This policy is likely to be accompanied, however, by a rhetoric of social justice and an Islamic banking system. The latter, however, would entail little more than restrictions on the domestic use of interest rates, which might even lead to a process of greater equitisation. Nevertheless, the need to participate in the world economic system will require Islamic countries to accept the use of interest rates as part of international banking.

Central to Islamist ideology is the concept of the *Umma*, defined as a unity of the community of believers. This ideological emphasis on unity could possibly serve as a credible basis for cooperation and integration in the region. A natural reluctance by those in power to yield personal and sovereign power will clearly limit the integrative process, but the concept of *Umma* might make regional cooperation or integration more attractive. However, the Islamists will have to come to power in more that one state in order to be able to seriously promote integration in the region.

The West has generally been viewed in the Middle East as seeking to divide the region rather than encouraging cooperation and integration. There is likely to be continued suspicion of Western policy, particularly among opposition groups in the Middle East. Clearly, anti-Western sentiment at a popular level is likely to manifest itself in the context of either anti-regime activities or a democratisation process that will unleash Islamist and nationalist fervour. Nevertheless, encouragement by the EC of regional cooperation, which does not explicitly include Israel's integration into the region, would meet with ready political acceptance on both a popular and official level. This acceptance would give the EC greater room for manoeuvre in the future given possible changes in the existing regimes.

III. Implications of Major Regional and International Issues

The rise of the Islamists needs to be considered in the broad context of long-term security and stability in the region. In the same way that regimes in the Middle East today maintain different political, economic and security ties with the EC as a whole and with its member states separately, so the Islamist groups, if they rise to a position of power, may also pursue different policies that are dictated by the particular interests of the nation state.

Among the attitudes shared by Islamist groups is an animosity towards the West which is primarily directed at the United States because of its support for Israel and other regimes in the region and its principal role in the Gulf war. Despite its resentment of the British and French, which lingers from the colonial experience and was rekindled over their involvement in the war, the Muslim world remains open to improved relations with the EC, if it perceives the Community to be genuinely pursuing alternative policies vis-à-vis the Muslims. There are a number of areas in which the EC can still be seen as pursuing an even-handed policy, such as taking firm action on the question of a Palestinian homeland and protection of the Bosnian Muslims. It could also encourage cooperation and eventual integration between states in the Middle East not just on the basis of security arrangements, but eventually on the basis of wider cooperation. The EC as a whole has the potential to establish a degree of credibility not only at an official level but at a popular level as well. In light of the diminishing popularity of the US, there is clearly room for the EC to play a more dynamic role in the region.

Member states of the European Community have expressed some concern over the Muslim presence in Europe. There are two main aspects to this issue, the first being the fear that the number of immigrants seeking refuge from Islamist regimes in North Africa will increase significantly. The second issue relates to Muslims settled in Europe and their response to calls from Islamists in Muslim countries to act in ways that are detrimental to the interests of their adopted countries. There is a fear that the increase in Islamist activity or the coming to power of an Islamic group, especially in the case of Algeria, would result in increased migration to Southern Europe due to political instability and economic hardship.

A significant number of professionals and other secularists from the middle class who fear that they cannot live in an Islamic society will immigrate, although it is unlikely that there would be a mass exodus of this group. Clearly, the majority of those migrating would be motivated by economic considerations. The poorest members of these populations, however, for whom the political and economic system has long been a source of disillusionment, may be attracted to stay and participate in a new political order. The ideological content of the Islamist message, combined with a leadership that is perceived to have the political will to take difficult decisions, could provide an incentive for people to remain in the country. A great deal depends on the nature of the transition to power of an Islamist group, whether it is peaceful or violent. Hence, the EC has an interest in urging non-interference and allowing the process of political change to take its course.

The Muslim presence in Europe raises questions concerning the issues of identity and integration. Despite the differences in the nature and experience of the Muslim populations in different European countries, they all share the desire to have a decent standard of living in their host countries -- whether or not they plan to return to their countries of origin. The assertion of a distinct cultural and/or religious identity results from a combination of the following factors:

- The very fact that Muslims practice a different religion and observe special traditions often makes them uncomfortable with the values of their adopted country and unable to accept them in their entirety for themselves and their children. The difficulties of integration and the pressure to assimilate can be substantial.

- As a result of experiencing either the disappointment of economic failure or possibly even the elation of economic success, the immigrant Muslim may desperately wish to have a place in society that respects and accommodates his own value system.

- An immigrant Muslim may be encouraged by his country of origin or another Muslim country (Iran, for example, in the Salman Rushdie case)[7] to take action that is detrimental to the host countries.

- There is also the perception that Western policies towards causes related to the Muslim world are often unjust (Muslims in Bosnia, Kashmir, the Occupied Territories, etc.) and do not receive the serious attention they merit.

Hence the question of the Muslim presence in Europe has both a domestic and international dimension. At present the latter affects the former dimension more frequently than the reverse. Muslim grievances need to be paid serious attention such as, for example, their demands in Britain for separate schools. These demands will not go away and represent the aspirations of a group that has lived in a democratic society to which they feel they have contributed and in which they wish to have their way of life protected.

Another aspect which needs to be addressed is the question of democracy and human rights. All shades of non-governmental political opinion not only in the Middle East and the Muslim world, but in most of the Third World as well, assert that the West applies a double standard on the question of democracy and human rights. Among the Islamists, there is a growing disillusionment with the West regarding what is perceived as its lack of effort in putting pressure on regimes in relation to the issue of human rights or its attempts to safeguard Muslim lives. There is a danger that with the growing rejection of secularism and the concomitant

---

[7] J.S. Nielsen (ed.), *The "Rushdie Affair": A Documentation*, Research Paper No. 42, Centre for the Study of Islam and Christian-Muslim Relations, Birmingham, June 1989.

antagonism towards the West, there will also develop a rejection of democracy.

The issue of human rights is of particular importance, and greater pressure needs to be placed on regimes to engage in a democratisation process. There is an ever-growing need for the EC to take a stronger stance on human-rights abuses in the Middle East and to call for wider political participation throughout the region. Contact should be encouraged between the EC and non-governmental organisations. The EC should accept generally the notion of conditionality in its trade/aid packages, linking awards to improvements in a country's human rights record.[8]

Middle Eastern societies are demanding a say in the way in which their people are ruled and their economies managed. The demand for greater accountability and development is likely to increase rather than diminish even if the economic situation improves. Hence, the EC will increasingly find itself under pressure to justify its support for regimes that do not observe democratic principles and practices and that tolerate a high level of corruption.

The European response to Israel's expulsion of over 400 Palestinians by Israel was a test case for future relations between the EC and the Palestinians, especially the Hamas and other Islamic groups. If the EC had been seen to be taking positive action in pressuring Israel, through, for example, the imposition of sanctions, it would have done much to enhance its credibility and attained an important starting point for improved relations between the Islamists and the West. Failure to act not only is seen as a continuation of unfair treatment of Palestinians but also as an anti-Muslim stance.

The position of Islamists towards Israel is one of the areas where there is a major difference between them and the regimes in the region.

---

[8] C. Mallat, "Human Rights in the Middle East", in G. Nonneman (ed.), *The Middle East and Europe: An Integrated Communities Approach* (Federal Trust for Education and Research, 1992), pp. 239-245.

Nationalist forces in the Arab world, particularly in the 1950s and 1960s, were vehemently opposed to Israeli statehood. The Islamist stance of no compromise and their call for the liberation of the whole of Palestine represent in part a continuation of this position within a religious framework. However, the refusal to compromise on the part of the Islamists, if there is a change to an Islamic system of government, would manifest itself mainly in anti-Israeli rhetoric without posing any real threat to Israel's security. The real problem for Israel is related to the increasing socio-economic and political polarisation in Palestinian society as represented by the growing influence of Hamas, the main Islamist group in the Occupied Territories.

Islamists look upon the general question of security structures for the region with suspicion. Existing structures, such as the GCC (Gulf Cooperation Council), are seen as limited to protecting unpopular regimes. There is little hope that new regional security structures can offer genuine stability, given that once they are sanctioned by foreign powers (particularly in the aftermath of the Gulf war), they will be tarnished in the eyes of popular opinion. It would seem unlikely to many in the Middle East that those who destroyed the main Arab military power would wish to see the creation of a structure that fully served their interests.

The question of arms control is viewed by opposition forces as a conspiratorial scheme to undermine the power of Arabs and Muslims. There is also criticism of the Gulf states for "wasting the wealth of the *Umma*" on military hardware that is seen as primarily used to defend regimes from internal threats and which in the context of the Gulf war proved obsolete. In addition, there is the conviction that Muslim countries need to resist Western moves to weaken them by disarming or neutralising their military capability.

The Gulf crisis has sharpened the Muslim world's focus on Israeli military capability. This capability is seen by those in opposition, particularly the Islamists, as one that should ultimately be matched by a strong and united opposition. Islamists associate the destruction of Iraq as a military power with a broader Western and Zionist scheme to weaken and neutralise Israel's enemies, Egypt having been formally neutralised with the signing of the Camp David accords in 1978.

The dismantling of Iraq's chemical and nuclear capabilities was an act that especially antagonised groups opposed to the West. One hears repeated reference to the double standard of an international community that allows Israel to possess nuclear war-heads for self-defence and security. In order for arms control to make any serious headway in the region, strong pressure needs to be put on Israel to sign the Nuclear Non-Proliferation Treaty and to submit its nuclear installations to international supervision.

As a major state in the region as a whole and in the Gulf in particular, Iran will continue to assert its influence and attempt to dominate the region in the medium to long term. The development of better relations and economic links with Europe would mean a more amenable Iran, whose interests are linked with the West.

One of the main concerns of the West is access to a secure and stable supply of oil. There is a fear that if the Islamists come to power they may jeopardise or place conditions on the free flow of oil. The economic dependency of the oil-producing states on imports, however, obliges any regime in power to freely trade its oil with the West.

It is important to make a distinction between on the one hand, the forceful and militant rhetoric of the Islamists in their present position of opposition and, on the other, their attitudes should they succeed in attaining a position of power. The challenge the Islamists pose is primarily directed towards the domestic scene. Although disillusionment with and opposition to individual domestic situations and certain aspects of the international order are not new phenomena in the region, these forces are, nevertheless, rapidly growing and need to be addressed if the threat to security and stability in the region is to be minimised.

4 Europe and the Mediterranean: The Security Dimension

Edward Mortimer

I. Trans-Mediterranean Threats to Security

Background

Until 1990, the problem of "European security" was generally seen as an intra-European phenomenon. European states saw threats to their security arising primarily from one another. Although several of them acquired overseas empires, they still regarded each other's activities as the principal threat to these. The Americas, Asia and Africa were secondary theatres of European conflict. Of course, Europeans operating in these theatres did from time to time encounter local resistance. Occasionally they convinced themselves that such resistance constituted a threat to their national security, but it was hardly considered a threat to the security or peace of Europe as such.

The attitude was carried over into the period of the cold war. The new European powers -- the US and the Soviet Union -- regarded Europe as the primary area of confrontation between them. The rest of the world was viewed as the scene of "regional conflicts", significant beyond their respective regions only insofar as they might affect the East-West balance, and thus the outcome of the primary struggle for control of Europe. North America and the Asiatic part of the Soviet Union were treated as extensions of Europe. Everything else was, in NATO jargon, "out of area".

How much these attitudes have changed since the end of the cold war depends, in part at least, on the geographical perspective of the people holding them. For those in the east and centre of Europe the consequences within Europe of the collapse of Soviet power constitute the main, if not exclusive security concern. For those on the western and southern perimeter of Europe, however, the removal of the old-fashioned Soviet threat, coinciding with the Gulf war, has allowed problems pressing on Europe from the south to seem, for the first time, at least as threatening to its security as those arising from internal conflicts.

In some ways the difficulty in dealing with Europe's southern neighbours is similar to that in dealing with Russia: Europe has to anticipate possible hostility without provoking it. Moreover, the identification of potential military threats to Europe's security from the south, and the making of military preparations to counter them, seem in one sense more gratuitous, and therefore more provocative, than does the same attitude towards potential threats from the east. The peoples of Eastern Europe, including the Russians themselves, are well aware of the enormous effort that the Soviet Union put into building up its military power. They feel themselves to have been, in different ways, the victims of that power. They do not reproach the West for having built up defences against it. On the contrary, many of them are profoundly grateful that the West did so; and while their new leaders naturally hope to benefit from a quite different Western attitude, they accept and even welcome the fact that the West remains in some sense on its guard against a revival of Soviet or Russian expansionism. Most of them, for instance, not only accept but advocate the continuance of NATO, albeit wishing themselves to be more closely associated with it.

Most Third World peoples, by contrast, including notably those of North Africa, feel that their own countries have an almost impeccable record of non-aggression towards Europe in recent centuries. Their historical memory is of being victims of aggression and conquest by European powers. Moreover, many of them are aware that those aggressions and conquests, and especially the maintenance of the European domination which followed, were accompanied by a formidable ideological offensive vilifying the Muslim religion. Islam as a religion, and above all as a culture, was in truth more stubbornly resistant to European colonial penetration than most other non-European cultures and beliefs. Christian missionaries in the colonial era made very few converts from Islam; and the leaders of military resistance to colonial rule in Muslim countries not only appealed to religious sentiment but often regarded themselves, and were regarded by their followers, as religious as well as political leaders. Europeans reacted by depicting all such resistance as fanaticism, and Islam itself as a peculiarly violent and aggressive faith. This is an unfortunate historical legacy, since Islam remains the dominant faith and culture of the whole belt of Africa and Asia which is Europe's immediate neighbour: if a European travels south, whether his starting-point is Moscow or Madrid, the first non-European society he encounters will be a Muslim one.

Potentially Malevolent States

Whatever historical judgement they make on the colonial era, few Europeans today wish to return to it. Equally it seems safe to say that few, if any, Muslim leaders -- even including President Saddam Hussein at the height of his power -- harbour any ambition of using military force to conquer or dominate Europe. Their ambitions usually focus on their own regions and on their co-religionists, or on combating external interference in their own regions and, at best, putting themselves in a position to conduct business with Europe and the United States on equal terms. Their main rivalries are with each other, and the chances of them forming a cohesive power bloc, comparable to the late unlamented communist bloc, seem very remote.

Indeed in one sense the Muslim world is an exact inversion of the Soviet bloc. The latter was essentially an affair of governments and parties, which proclaimed a phoney internationalism not shared by their peoples. Muslim peoples, by contrast, do feel a certain instinctive sympathy or solidarity when they see other Muslims in conflict with non-Muslims; but Muslim governments are usually happy, so long as they can get away with it, to make common cause with foreigners in order to strengthen their own local positions and undermine that of their rivals. That being so, statements or insinuations from European leaders or commentators to the effect that "Islam" (or "fundamentalism", a term sometimes used almost synonymously) has replaced communism as the main threat to or enemy of the West are not merely baseless (since there seems little or no prospect that this phenomenon could take the form of a concentration of military power sufficient to threaten Europe with invasion or domination) but dangerous and even potentially self-fulfilling.   They encourage Muslims to believe that the West is planning a new aggression against the Islamic world; and they make life more difficult for those Muslim leaders who are seeking to cooperate with Europe -- and whose cooperation Europe may well need.

Hardly less implausible and remote is the contingency of a single nation state uniting the peoples of the Arab world, marrying the mineral resources of the Arabian peninsula and the Sahara with the human resources of North Africa and the Fertile Crescent, and using them to build a military machine large and sophisticated enough to overpower Europe.

None of the above needs to be taken as implying that there are no threats of any sort to Europe from the south, or that some military contingencies should not be identified and appropriate preparations made. Clearly there is a danger that an existing state in the vicinity of Europe (which almost inevitably means a Muslim, and in most cases an Arab, state) might, without being strong enough or indeed desiring to attempt any actual seizure of European territory, nonetheless be in a position to threaten Europe with long-range missiles.   Iraq already is (or was) in such a position with regard to Turkey, as also presumably are Syria and Iran; Libya is similarly well situated to threaten Italy and Malta, while France, Italy and Spain could come within reach of Algerian missiles.   The danger becomes more serious, of course, if the missiles can be equipped with nuclear (or biological or chemical) warheads; and the longer the range of the missile, the broader the field of potential aggressors or blackmailers.

Such contingencies have to be taken seriously even if their probability is low. But European leaders need to be very clear in their own minds, and very explicit in their public statements, about what those contingencies are and what they are not. A useful mental exercise, to be undertaken before any public pronouncement is made on such subjects, would be to try to hear how it would sound in reverse.   For instance, before advocating the development of a European "rapid deployment force" for use mainly in Africa or the Middle East, one should think how European public opinion would react to the announcement of an African, or Arab or "Islamic" force to be used mainly for contingencies in Europe. The parallel is of course not an exact one, but the ways in which it is inexact may not be immediately obvious to the non-European observer.

The Danger of Disorder

Less apocalyptic, but more probable, are threats to European security arising not from malevolent state power but rather from a complete or partial breakdown of state authority on the other side of the Mediterranean. There is every sign that the economic and political crises affecting most parts of the Middle East and North Africa are deepening in the wake of the Gulf war.

The rise of terrorism originating in the Middle East, even if partially state-sponsored, has generally, and rightly been seen as reflecting the political instability and social dislocation increasingly prevalent in that part of the world. The displacement of the Palestinians; the disintegration of the Lebanese state into warring factions; the rapidly expanding populations of underemployed and culturally-disoriented people in so many Middle Eastern cities; the revolution in Iran and the repression of Shiite communities in neighbouring Arab states: all have combined to provide a fertile breeding ground of grievance from which terrorist groups and their sponsors can recruit. It is certainly no coincidence that the European state which suffered most from domestic violence in the three decades before 1991, reverting twice to military rule, is the one that is also a Middle Eastern state afflicted by many of the problems just mentioned, namely Turkey.[1]

---

[1] Turkey is in many ways a special problem, both for policy-makers and for analysts. It is a Muslim country located in the Middle East, and the country of origin of one of the largest Muslim communities in the EC. At the same time, it is on the north side of the Mediterranean, belongs to NATO, and considers itself part of Europe. Indeed it has long been accepted as such, at least in a formal sense. Yet there are real problems about its full integration in the EC, given the size and rate of growth

The Arab-Israeli conflict remains, probably, the single most dangerous one on the world scene, not least in the sense that it is the one in which one can most easily imagine a nuclear weapon being used; and for Europeans it is uncomfortably close. The peace process which began in Madrid in October 1991, is in itself a hopeful sign, and certainly a remarkable achievement of US diplomacy, but it is far from certain to lead to a solution of the conflict even in the long term; while in the short term one of its main effects is to exacerbate political divisions within the Arab and Islamic worlds (and indeed within Israel). Islamic militancy continues in any case to feed on the deep political, economic and social

---

of its population and the wide cultural and economic differences between it and the present EC members. Up to now the general European attitude has been to use these problems as a pretence for delaying consideration of its membership application. Turkey has been regarded as an insoluble problem, which could be left on one side - - especially as, with the end of the cold war, its strategic importance has appeared to decline.

The Gulf war and the breakup of the Soviet Union have changed that. It now seems likely that Turkey will play an important part in future both in relations between Europe and the Middle East and as a model and guide, if not a protector, for the Turkish-speaking peoples of Azerbaijan and central Asia, whom it aspires to lead along the path of secular democracy. In this region it has embarked, with US encouragement, on an active quest for influence, in competition with Iran. (It has also taken the initiative in establishing a regional forum for states bordering the Black Sea.) This new importance was implicitly recognised by Western Europe in the decision reached during the Maastricht summit to offer Turkey, along with other European member states of NATO, the chance "to participate fully" in the activities of the Western European Union (WEU).

In these circumstances, Turks may well question whether the problems involved in their EC candidature are really greater than those involved in expanding the Community to include East abd Central Europe and the Balkans. Perhaps the EC needs to consider more carefully whether it is really in its interests to carry on ignoring or shelving Turkey's application indefinitely. Not that the problems involved -- which of course include the Cyprus issue -- can simply be set aside. But instead of accepting these problems with secret gratitude as reasons for postponing consideration of Turkey's case, it would be wiser for the EC and the Turkish government together to make a determined effort to deal with them (if they really can be overcome), and keeping the door open to full membership.

tensions which exist in many Arab countries -- as was spectacularly demonstrated by the success of the Front Islamique du Salut (FIS) in the first ballot of the Algerian legislative elections in December 1991.

Population Movements

Mass immigration, from both the east and the south, is now one of the most widely perceived "threats" to Western Europe. Whether it should be so perceived is questionable, given that there is a "pull" as well as a "push" factor. Many economists argue that Western Europe, with its aging population and falling birthrate, should welcome rather than fear the injection of able-bodied and relatively cheap labour offered by immigration from less prosperous neighbouring countries. That argument lies outside the scope of this paper. Political leaders are convinced, in any case, that whatever the economic pros and cons, mass immigration will have dangerous social and political consequences.

Yet it has proved increasingly difficult to control, and will probably prove even more so in the future, given the economic and political conditions to be expected both in Eastern Europe and in North Africa. There are already some 6 million people of North African origin in the EC -- one-half of them in France and possibly 800,000 (mainly illegal immigrants) in Italy -- as well as large Muslim communities in Britain and Germany, of mainly South Asian and Turkish origin, respectively. That this renders Western Europe vulnerable to domestic violence prompted by conflicts within the Islamic world was seen on a small scale in Britain during the Rushdie affair, and was an obvious source of anxiety to many European governments before and during the Gulf war. The Muslim communities in Western Europe are, to put it at its best, imperfectly integrated into European society. Hostility to them, and especially to the idea of further immigration from their countries of origin, has become a highly charged political issue.

The governments of France, Spain, Portugal and Italy in particular are worried at the possibility of further waves of emigration from the Maghreb, propelled by declining living standards and rising

111

unemployment. (North Africa's population is growing at a rate of around 2.7% annually, and is expected to increase from 61 million in 1989 to around 127 million in 2025.) If this influx is accompanied, as it might well be, by political upheaval, widespread violence and/or the rise of outspokenly anti-European leaders in one or more of the Maghreb countries, both the flow of migrants across the Mediterranean and the reaction of the receiving populations in Europe might become very difficult to control. This scenario has become all the more plausible in the light of the December 1991 Algerian elections and the crisis that followed. The risk that political upheaval in the Maghreb could lead to a massive influx of refugees directly into Southern Europe, which in turn would exacerbate existing social and political tensions there, is clearly greater than ever. And passions would, of course, be even further inflamed if European hostages were seized during a domestic conflict in the Maghreb, or if there were a wave of terrorist incidents in Europe attributable to Arab or Islamic groups.

II. Elements of a European Response

Just as much as in Eastern and Central Europe, the security problems arising on Europe's southern perimeter have economic, social and political roots, and in the long term, effective action in these areas will produce more security for Europe than any amount of military preparations. Unfortunately the long-term results of such action cannot be guaranteed, and even if they could some problems would certainly arise before the long term is reached. But in the absence of an appropriate political framework, some of the necessary short-term measures could actually do more harm than good. To emphasise this point, I shall discuss the "soft" security aspects first.

1. Political and Economic Cooperation

Democracy and Islam

Like Eastern Europe, the Arab world -- and the Maghreb especially -- is going through an economic and political crisis. There is pressure for the introduction of democratic institutions and processes, but democracy may not make economic problems any easier in the short term. There is a large surplus labour force eager to emigrate to Western Europe. There is a return to traditional values, especially those of religion.

Yet, religious and cultural traditions being Islamic rather than Christian, the return to them tends to widen the affective gap with Western Europe rather than bridge it; and the Gulf war, with the great outpouring of pro-Saddam feeling that it produced in the Maghreb, has made matters much worse, at least in the short term. The European Community/Union cannot expect, and does not wish to embrace or absorb the Maghreb in the way it hopes (rhetorically at least) to embrace East and Central Europe. It does, however, have an interest in promoting successful economic, political and social development in the Arab world as an alternative to violence, polarisation and vastly increased levels of emigration. Economic aid is indicated if governments and policies develop that are able to make use of it.

Should democracy be encouraged even if it seems likely to bring to power Islamic parties that at most pay lip service to democracy while they themselves are in opposition, and often not even that? Many Europeans will recognise this dilemma which in the past confronted them in dealing with communist parties. They should not be too glib in dismissing the reasons why some genuine advocates of democracy in the Islamic world are reluctant to extend its benefits to Islamic parties. Yet in the last resort the same arguments which led to the legalisation of communist parties in Western Europe -- in West Germany in the 1960s, for instance, and in Greece and Spain in the 1970s -- must surely apply also to Islamic ones. Once a party agrees to abide by the law and participate in the democratic process it is ultimately self-defeating to exclude it purely on the grounds of its ideology. If it enjoys only minority support, its exclusion endows it with a valid grievance against the authorities, which may even legitimise violence not only in the eyes of its committed supporters but also among a much wider swathe of potential sympathisers. In that case it is surely preferable to insist that it compete on equal terms with other parties so that its arguments can be judged on their merits and the true dimensions of its support established. If on the other hand a party of this type does in fact enjoy majority support, governments which seek to disguise or suppress that fact have little chance of establishing their own legitimacy in the eyes of the population, and therefore little chance of winning support for the hard decisions needed to resolve their countries' economic and social problems.

If Islamic parties do come to power on the other side of the Mediterranean, European governments should certainly not adopt an attitude of a priori hostility to them. The fact that they proclaim their wish to reduce or even eradicate what they see as corrupting Western moral or cultural influences within their own societies does not mean there is an inevitable conflict of interest between them and Europe. On the contrary, once in government they would have reasons of self-interest for wishing to maintain close economic ties with Europe, since if the European market were closed to them they would find themselves presiding over an economic crisis even more acute than the one that brought them to power. In fact, they would share with Europe an interest in maintaining confidence, stimulating growth and providing employment at home, thereby both strengthening their own political position and reducing the pressure to emigrate. European leaders should build on this common interest to establish a dialogue, and should use that dialogue to seek to convince the Islamic leaders that their own interests would be best served by not resorting to violent or coercive methods, since these would certainly drive much of the qualified technical elite to emigrate, and at worst might even provoke civil war.

Economic Issues and Migration

In North Africa as in Central and Eastern Europe, the issues of trade, economic assistance and population movement are closely interrelated. Sir Ralf Dahrendorf has made the point with brutal clarity: "If we do not want the people from the poor countries of our neighbourhood, we have to take the goods which they produce at home."[2]   No doubt that is something of an oversimplification.   Free trade will not guarantee economic growth, nor will economic growth, however spectacular, absorb all of North Africa's galloping demographic surplus. Put negatively, however, the point can hardly be disputed: without access to the European market North Africa has no hope of economic progress, and without economic progress there is no hope of containing the population explosion or preventing a large part of the surplus work force from finding its way across the Mediterranean. No matter how ruthless and efficient the controls on immigration, the incentive to evade them (for employers as well as for the emigrants themselves) will be so great that large-scale illegal immigration will undoubtedly continue.

The US, facing an analogous problem with Mexico, responded not only with the short-term remedy of large-scale financial assistance to help Mexico cope with its debt problem without sacrificing its political stability, but also by negotiating and signing the North American Free Trade Agreement (NAFTA), which could give Mexico a real chance of solving its economic problems in the longer term. President Bush was willing to risk the accusation that in so doing he was "exporting American jobs", while Mexico on its side embarked on a very bold liberalisation of its domestic economy.   The EC and its southern neighbours need to show comparable political courage and imagination. At present the trend on the EC side is in the opposite direction: although North African industrial exports are supposed to benefit from unlimited access to EC markets, the arrival of the single European market in 1993 will have the effect of creating a series of non-tariff barriers.   North Africa really needs to be part of the European Economic Area (EEA) and to be allowed to compete in the sector where it is most competitive, namely agricultural products. Only if it concedes these or similar terms can Europe hope to arrive at an immigration policy that will work.

---

[2] *Financial Times*, 12 December 1991.

Reform of Immigration Policy

Even so, it will still need such a policy. In a unified labour market, national immigration policies are no longer workable. The EC and its partners in the European Economic Area will have to agree on common standards and procedures for the policing of their external coasts and frontiers, common criteria for deciding whom to admit and whom to turn back, and for identifying genuine asylum-seekers from war or persecution.

There should be a joint and continuing effort to establish Europe's probable economic need for, and capacity to absorb immigrant labour. (It has been estimated, for instance, that by 2025, there will be a 30% shortfall in European labour supply for the type of work usually undertaken by North African migrants.) On the basis of that estimate, a North American-style point system of qualifications for would-be immigrants could be established, weighted by regional origin; and the cooperation of the "exporting" countries in limiting or managing migration should be enlisted, in return for guarantees about the treatment which legal immigrants would receive after their arrival in Europe. The housing and absorption of immigrant populations should also be planned on an EC-wide basis, so as to minimise adverse social consequences and to equitably shared the cost among the recipient countries.

All of this may smack unfashionably of *dirigisme* and state intervention in economic matters, and will certainly be resisted by Northern European states (such as the UK) which are not "in the front line" as recipients of migrants from the south. Yet no European political leader is prepared to advocate a pure free-market solution to this problem, which would be to let living standards be evened out between rich and poor countries by allowing completely free movement of goods, capital and labour. That being so, intervention should not only take the form of imposing controls, but also of taking positive steps to secure humane treatment for immigrants while allaying the fears of the host populations and combating the prejudices which feed on those fears. And if the EC is to realise its goal of being a unified economic space with free internal movement of labour, many of these measures will have to be coordinated on an EC-wide basis. Providing the framework for such coordination is, of course, a prime objective of Title VI of the Treaty on European Union.

Integration of Muslim Communities

Europeans should also recognise that their security can be affected by the attitudes of the large Arab and Muslim communities already established in Europe, and therefore by those communities' relationships with their neighbours in European societies. Before and during the Gulf war, anxiety was expressed in both France and Britain about the effect it would have on intercommunal relations, and possibly even on public order. In the event these fears proved exaggerated. The point remains valid, nonetheless, that it will be an element of national weakness, and a possible constraint on foreign policy, if members of these communities do not feel that they are accepted as part of the body politic and therefore do not feel the same loyalty to the state as their fellow citizens. Such communities could then become fertile recruiting grounds for violence and terrorism, and their attitudes could negatively affect relations between Europe and its Muslim neighbours, making more difficult a cooperative approach to all the problems discussed in this paper. Conversely, if they are successfully integrated with the rest of European society, they can provide a very useful channel of communication between Europe and their countries of origin, and indeed with the Islamic world as a whole.

It should therefore be a high priority for European governments, and for the EC, to ensure that second- and third-generation Muslim immigrants are accepted as fellow citizens and feel more, not less, at home in Europe than their parents. On their side, leaders of Muslim communities also need to make every effort, in their constituents' own interests, to set an example of good citizenship, presenting their views and asserting their collective identity in a constructive rather than confrontational way, so that cultural differences -- in themselves something to be valued in a pluralistic society -- do not become impenetrable social barriers. Muslim communities will be better able to play this role as they develop genuinely representative institutions of their own, to conduct the dialogue with the authorities in each European country (and perhaps with those of the EC/EU itself), as well as with non-governmental bodies including representatives of other faiths.

Institutional Framework

The EC has a "Mediterranean policy" and bilateral agreements with the main Maghreb countries, but there is no overall political framework for dialogue comparable to the Conference on Security and Cooperation in Europe (CSCE). A limited but useful dialogue has been established at the western end of the Mediterranean in the so-called "five plus five" process, bringing together France, Italy, Malta, Portugal and Spain on the European side and the five members of the UMA (Arab Maghreb Union: Algeria, Libya, Mauritania, Morocco and Tunisia) on the North African side. There is also the Euro-Arab Dialogue, between the League of Arab States on one side and the twelve members of the EC on the other, but this has been a vapid affair, vitiated above all by the divisions within the Arab world, which the Kuwaiti crisis and Gulf war of 1990-91 have thrown into even deeper and more acrimonious turmoil than that produced by the Camp David accords and the Iranian revolution a decade earlier.

Yet that crisis also lead to Arab and European troops fighting alongside each other in the US-led Operation Desert Storm. This demonstrated spectacularly that at least some West European and some Middle Eastern Arab states could have a common, or at any rate an overlapping, security perspective; while at the same time the crisis revealed and exacerbated sharply antagonistic feelings between the Arab and European populations that face each other directly across the Mediterranean -- precisely those whose governments had established the "five plus five" dialogue. This strengthened the desire of some of the participants in that dialogue for a wider framework -- a Conference on Security and Cooperation in the Mediterranean and the Middle East (CSCM). According to its leading advocate, the then Italian Foreign Minister Gianni De Michelis, such a conference was:

planned as a long-term exercise which must involve all the countries from Morocco to Iran, as well as the European Community countries, the Soviet Union, the United States and Canada, precisely along the lines of the Helsinki rationale. It would have to codify a set of rules and principles governing security, economic cooperation, and respect for human rights.[3]

The proposal, modelled of course on CSCE, might be worth pursuing, but the process envisaged could only be extremely slow. The Italian Foreign Ministry itself admits that "it could take several years before the CSCM process manages to draft a set of principles comparable with those drawn up by the CSCE (a 'Mediterranean Act' or something similar)".[4] The tentative list of participants already ran to 41 states and one "UN-recognised entity" (Palestine -- itself likely to be highly problematic) even before the break-up of Yugoslavia and the Soviet Union. Presumably all the successor states of Yugoslavia would have to be involved, and at least Ukraine, Russia and Georgia among the ex-Soviet republics (and probably Moldova, Armenia and Azerbaijan as well).

Whether such a body could make any significant contribution to solving deeply entrenched issues like the Arab-Israeli conflict must be doubted. Probably, on the contrary, continued progress in the Arab-Israeli peace process is a necessary condition for it to get off the ground. Otherwise the preparatory work could well be stymied by failure to agree on Palestinian representation. To win Arab confidence Europeans need to be seen to be doing something about the Palestinian problem, but in the past their attempts to do so, however tentative (the 1980 Venice Declaration, for example), have looked like second-guessing a US-sponsored process and have led to tensions not only with Israel but between Europe and the US.

---

[3] Italian Foreign Ministry, "The Mediterranean and the Middle East after the War in the Gulf: The CSCM", Rome, March 1991, p. 3.

[4] *Ibid.*, p. 144.

Europe should not wait for a CSCM to be established before addressing its specific problems with the Arab world, and especially with the Maghreb. Useful as the "five plus five" forum is, it would be wrong for Northern European powers such as Britain and Germany to believe that relations with the Maghreb are a matter that concerns only the southern members of the EC -- just as it would be unwise for France and Spain to think that the problems of Central Europe can be left to the Germans to sort out. The most useful framework in the immediate future would be an expansion of the "five plus five" to include all EC members on the European side (plus representation of the EC as such by the Commission).

An informal meeting on this basis (UMA-EC) was held at foreign minister level in November 1990, precisely to discuss such issues as visas and migrant rights in Europe. A second one, scheduled a year later, was abandoned as a result of the alleged involvement of Libya in the Lockerbie air disaster. Unfortunately the UMA itself has been almost moribund since then, owing to divisions between its members and internal political turmoil in at least one of them (Algeria).[5] But the need for a regular framework of Euro-Maghreb dialogue is not diminished by such difficulties: on the contrary, they make it all the more compelling. High priority should be given to finding a way around them.

2. Arms Control and Non-Proliferation

Regional Arms Control

As in the case of the proposed CSCM (on whose agenda, if such a body existed, it would figure prominently), regional arms control is more likely to accompany progress towards an Arab-Israeli peace settlement than to precede it. This applies both to weapons of mass destruction and to conventional weapons.

---

[5] See Francis Ghiles, "The Arab Maghreb Union: Impending Demise?" in *Middle East International*, 9 October 1992.

Israel is unlikely to forego its nuclear deterrent so long as it feels itself surrounded by hostile Arab states. But Arab states are equally unlikely to concede to Israel a *de jure* nuclear monopoly in the region. They may do so *de facto*, after the destruction of Iraq's nuclear programme, but so long as Israel's nuclear monopoly persists Arab states will be very loathe to sign, and still more so to implement the 1992 Geneva Convention banning the production and possession of chemical weapons.

In conventional weaponry, as European experience has shown, arms control is even more difficult to achieve in the absence of a minimal degree of trust between the two sides, since definitions of balance are even harder to agree. In the Arab-Israeli context, Israel only feels secure so long as it has a "quantitative edge" in military technology, to offset the Arabs' numerical superiority. The Arabs cannot accept as "balance" what they see as entrenched Israeli superiority, especially as in their own eyes they are the aggrieved party (because of Israel's occupation of Arab territory), which means that they regard any military balance as fundamentally flawed if it tends to perpetuate the political status quo. In addition, Arab states feel the need to arm against each other, and against third parties such as Iran. But a weapon acquired by, say, Saudi Arabia with a view to maintaining a balance against Iran or Iraq will still be seen by Israel as affecting the balance between itself and the aggregate military power of all Arab states.

Global Arms Control

Probably the single most effective way in which Europe could enhance its security against attack from the south would be to maintain and strengthen the global taboo against the use, and as far as possible, the possession of weapons of mass destruction. To this end, European governments should do what they can to:

• expedite the ratification and implementation of the draft treaty banning the manufacture, possession and use of chemical weapons, concluded after many years of negotiations in Geneva in September 1992;

- develop effective methods of verifying the existing ban on biological weapons; and above all

- work for renewal and strengthening of the Nuclear Non-Proliferation Treaty (NPT) at the extension conference due in 1995.

Supplier Restraint

Since Europe is well ahead of its southern neighbours in weaponry design and production, its security vis-à-vis them would be significantly enhanced by restraint on arms sales in general, or on sales to the Middle East in particular. This is an interest it shares with other advanced industrial regions of the world ("the North"), a category that for this purpose still includes Russia as well as North America and Japan. The Gulf war brought this common interest into sharper focus, and 1991 saw a number of efforts to translate it into policy. Presidents Bush and Mitterrand and Prime Minister John Major all announced initiatives of one kind or another aimed at restricting arms supplies. The five permanent members of the UN Security Council held a series of meetings on the issue, and even the General Assembly passed a resolution calling for a register of arms transfers, while the Japanese government announced that it would take account (inversely) of recipient states' military expenditures when deciding how much economic aid to give them. These are all steps in the right direction, but they have been insufficient to prevent the development of a new arms race in the Middle East.[6]

Perhaps this is not surprising, given the political arguments that can usually be marshalled in favour of any particular arms sale, as redressing rather than destabilising a regional balance, reassuring an insecure state which might otherwise resort to preemptive action, or allowing a friendly state to defend itself rather than rely on foreign forces; and given also the strong private interests, usually wielding considerable political influence,

---

[6] See Edward Mortimer, "Race towards Instability", in *Financial Times*, 14 October 1992.

that rely on arms exports for their well-being -- especially at a time when domestic defence expenditures in most industrialised countries are being sharply reduced, as the end of the cold war has increased the pressure on governments to switch resources from defence to social services and civilian infrastructural projects. Ironically, insofar as arms sales have been restrained, the main factor has probably been similar downward pressure on defence budgets in the would-be importing countries.

There is perhaps more room for optimism about supplier restraint when it comes to technology and materials (including "dual-capable" products) for nuclear, chemical and biological weapons, and for long-range missiles. The ease with which Iraq had circumvented such restraints was a real shock to all the industrial powers, and even to some newly industrialising suppliers such as Brazil and Argentina. Efforts have been made to tighten the procedures and expand the membership of the Nuclear Suppliers' Group, the Australia Group (for chemicals) and the Missile Technology Control Regime. In Europe and North America it is reasonable to suppose that the private sector has also become more aware of its responsibilities in this area -- helped by groups such as Business Executives for National Security in the US. In the former Soviet Union, however, it is to be feared that an opposite process has occurred. That is, while public authorities there may be much more amenable than they were in the days of the cold war to close "North-North" cooperation in such matters, the disintegration of the political, social and economic system has left many individuals and even enterprises with possession or knowledge of the relevant technology, but with few economic prospects other than to market it in the Third World, and little or no feeling of civic restraint about doing so.

3. The Role of Military Force

Power Projection

Since the success of the above precautions cannot be taken for granted, European states will also need to maintain military forces capable of being deployed overseas in an emergency -- preferably with UN authority, but it would be unwise to count on this in all circumstances -- to reassure and protect friends, deter and if necessary correct aggression, undertake peacekeeping duties and respond to threats against trade routes or vital natural resources.

Up to now, such forces have been essentially national in character, although the WEU has played a part in coordinating European contributions to the protection of Gulf shipping (1987-88) and to the enforcement of sanctions against Iraq (1990-92). In April 1991, the WEU was asked by the European Council to study the military aspects of the proposed operation to save the Kurds. But in the event, as in the coalition which carried out Operation Desert Storm, national contingents from European states were placed under American command and related to US forces as much as, or more than, to each other.[7] (Since then, the monitoring of UN sanctions against Yugoslavia in the Adriatic has been carried out partly under joint WEU command. Technically the Adriatic is part of the Mediterranean, but this paper is concerned only with trans-Mediterranean relations.)

Many European leaders, while satisfied with the immediate outcome of the Gulf war and acknowledging the indispensability of US leadership in the specific circumstances of 1990-91, feel uneasy about Europe's inability to act collectively, and hence if need be independently, in such crises. Spanish Prime Minister Felipe Gonzalez put it succinctly:

> The Gulf crisis was a graphic illustration of what could happen to a common foreign policy without a common defence policy. When the peace was being negotiated, Europe did not exist. The US and the Soviet Union would be at the table. But Israel and other countries in the region do 70% of their trade with the EC.[8]

---

[7] It should be noted that the WEU has also been seeking to develop political contacts with Morocco, Algeria and Tunisia. But in these discussions the Maghreb side has preferred to focus on social and economic issues, even though these are outside the WEU's normal remit, rather than on military security.

[8] Interview with the *Financial Times*, 9 May 1991.

The reference to Israel is significant, given that the issue is one on which European views (and perhaps interest, though where US interests really lie in this matter is a much debated question) do differ from those of the US. Not that Europe and the US should ever intervene militarily on opposite sides in the Middle East, but an independent European interventionist capability would certainly strengthen European influence in the region. The Middle East is after all much closer and of more direct interest to Europe than it is to the US. The ability or willingness of the US to mount operations on the Desert Storm scale in defence of international order in the Middle East cannot be taken for granted as a permanent phenomenon. There might be contexts in which Europe would wish to project power there and the US would either disagree with the policies pursued or simply not accord the issue such a high priority - - just as Europe generally feels less concerned than the US by events in the western hemisphere.

Such considerations are, as Gonzalez's remark illustrates, an important stimulus to debate about Europe's defence identity -- although it is doubtful whether, or at any rate how soon Europe will be able to deploy forces "out of area" on any significant scale without at least logistical assistance from the US.

Defence/Deterrence

What should not be in doubt, however, is that European states, or at any rate those which belong to the WEU and NATO, are prepared to defend themselves, and each other, if their own territory is attacked, from whatever quarter. NATO has never been formally directed against any particular adversary, but rather against any state that might launch an armed attack on any of its members. The phrase "out of area", so often used in a NATO context, refers to the location of the attack, not to its origin. There is nothing in the North Atlantic Treaty, nor in the Brussels Treaty which gave birth to the WEU, that could be taken to absolve the signatories from their obligations if the attack comes from a quarter other than the east. Thus it was accepted in January 1991 (not without considerable heart-searching, particularly in Germany), that an Iraqi armed attack on Turkey would trigger Article 5 of the North Atlantic Treaty, obliging all NATO members to consider it an attack against themselves. Similarly, an armed attack by, say, Libya against Italy, or by Morocco against Spain, would trigger Article V of the modified Brussels Treaty, obliging all other WEU members to "afford the Party so attacked all the military and other aid and assistance in their power". Even an act of state-sponsored terrorism, perpetrated in Europe, could theoretically qualify as such an attack, although the likelihood of the treaties being invoked in such a case seems fairly remote.

Whether individually or collectively, European states have to envisage what kind of attack could conceivably be directed against them, and how they would respond to it. In this context they cannot afford to assume that their efforts to head off nuclear proliferation in the Third World will succeed. The author of this paper hesitates to recommend preemptive military action as a method of nuclear disarmament, but it is an uncomfortable thought that Iraq might well now be a nuclear power, had not the invasion of Kuwait provided an unassailable pretext for such action. Be that as it may, consideration should certainly be given, in the new strategic context, to anti-missile defences -- which could now be less comprehensive, and therefore simpler and cheaper, than those envisaged in Ronald Reagan's Strategic Defence Initiative, given that the putative aggressor would not be the Soviet Union but a novice nuclear power in the Third World; and also to the concept of nuclear deterrence "from the strong to the weak", which may perhaps be more credible in the form of smaller nuclear warheads, though not necessarily shorter-range missiles. If such deterrence is held to be necessary, Europe will need to consider whether it can rely on the US to provide it; whether Britain and/or France should provide it (implicitly or explicitly) to their European partners; or whether it should come under some form of collective European command.

5 Europe and the Maghreb: Towards a Common Space

Bernabé López Garcia and
Jesús A. Nuñez Villaverde

I. The Maghreb Colonised: An Extension of Metropolitan Territory

The history of the Maghreb, encompassing both its myths and realities, is inscribed in a broader context that arises from its geographical circumstances. On the one hand, the Maghreb has woven networks of economic and human interdependence with the Western Mediterranean since antiquity, developing a relationship which reached its peak in the 19th and 20th centuries with the establishment of ties of dependency and which made a Maghreb without a Mediterranean Europe unthinkable. On the other hand, the Maghreb became inserted in the Arab-Islamic world as early as the seventh century and has maintained an extended human and cultural -- as well as economic -- relationship with this culture ever since. The intensity of the latter relationship, however, has diminished in proportion to the strengthening of the Maghreb's ties with its European perimeter, which received a new impetus following political independence achieved in the second half of the 20th century.

But so that the current history of the Maghreb has meaning, it will also be necessary to contextualise that history in time and likewise to indicate the key moments that will permit us to understand it. It is evident, without presenting the Maghreb as an ideal world destroyed by colonisation, that this process destabilised the culture that had historically preserved an internal logic and that could have evolved towards its own modernisation -- as had occurred in Japan in the 19th and early 20th centuries. This is not to say that colonisation has not brought to these same societies a kind of modernisation. Some authors do subscribe to that view, including Samir Amin for whom "this type of colonial option has determined, in spite of the broad nature of these efforts, the mediocrity of the results", and have left "difficult social and economic problems to the independent Maghreb states that succeeded French North Africa".[1]

The fact is that the colonial model was imposed, at distinct moments in the 19th century in Algeria and Tunisia and from the beginning of the 20th century in Morocco, with the primary objective of satisfying the metropole's needs (the case of Spain as the colonising power in the north of Morocco is purely marginal, and the same could be said of the Italian domination of Libya) and, consequently, the subordination of these economies[2] and societies. There is no doubt that there emerged in the 1930s the existence of a common economic space, characterised by a pronounced disequilibrium in relations. In the case of Algeria, it was also a common administrative space, since from the beginning, the country was assimilated into metropolitan territory and necessitated the creation of various departments. The differentiation between the indigenous and French societies clearly marked a diversity in other spaces (social, juridical and cultural) as well.

This precarious common space became especially vulnerable to ideological disruption with the exacerbation of nationalist sentiment. This sentiment became radicalised when France refused to understand the underlying message of the manifestos proclaimed by the liberation movements during the Second World War. The Algerian manifestos of Ferhat Abbas in 1942-43 -- like the one entitled "For a French-Tunisian Bloc" written by Habib Bourguiba in May 1943, or that of Morocco's Istiqlal party of January 1944 -- insisted on the idea that the participation of the Maghreb masses in the allied effort demanded parallel political compensation in the form of recognition of various rights and liberties,

---

[1] Samir Amin, *Le Maghreb Moderne* (Paris: Editions de Minuit, 1970), p. 23.

[2] As will be seen later in this paper in the concrete case of agriculture.

including independence.[3]

Ignoring these kinds of proposals, France promoted the idea of a French Union which in reality was nothing more than an idealised version of the common space but which was based on the same assumptions as the colonial plans -- assumptions that condemned it to failure from the start.

II. The Maghreb Independent: The Difficult Search for an Autonomous Space

The transition to independence generated a new idea that attempted, from the metropole's viewpoint, to prolong the common space, at least in its economic dimensions: the idea of "independence in interdependence". Early on, the "internal autonomy" granted to Tunisia in 1954, as in the negotiations concerning independence for Morocco, contemplated the idea of a union with France "by permanent ties of a freely consented and defined interdependence".[4] In reality, this has been the economic model followed, even if the Algerian war of liberation inhibited Maghreb nationalists from putting the scheme into general practice, on ideological grounds. A particular case is that of Algeria whose bilateral relations with France have followed a peculiar course.

III. The Permanence of Verticality

If one word had to be chosen to define the present character of relations between the European Community and the Maghreb, *asymmetry* would be the one which best fits the reality. In effect, this characteristic, which implies relations of a vertical nature, clearly stands out in any analysis

---

[3] An extensive treatment of these manifestos can be found in the classic work of Roger Le Tourneau, *Évolution politique de l'Afrique du Nord Musulmane, 1920-1961* (Paris: Armand Colin, 1962).

[4] Announced jointly by Mohammed V and French Foreign Minister M. Pinay after their meeting on 6 November 1955. *Ibid.*, p. 247.

of the topic, not only in the economic field but also in terms of culture, politics and security. And this verticality applies not only in the character of domination that these kinds of relations imply, but also in the sense of space: narrow North-South ties in the absence of the same ties in a horizontal direction between Europe and its Maghreb neighbours.

Although this fact is widely recognised on both shores of the Mediterranean, the same is not true when attempts are made to identify the causes that have produced it or to present solutions to the current problems. At this point, if it is convenient, and before entering into the terrain of proposals for the future, let us briefly review the distinct mutual perceptions on the part of the two sides.

1. The Maghreb for Europe

Leaving aside considerations of a strategic nature which played a fundamental role in the colonisation of the Maghreb countries and which obeyed the dynamics of confrontation and domination between the regional European powers of the period (France, Spain and Italy), European presence in the area was oriented towards economic objectives which sought to satisfy the needs of their own markets without attending to the implications for the development of the territories. There was nothing novel in this mentality and, to some extent, it cannot have been hoped that the European leaders would have possessed at this time in history the necessary vision to foresee the consequences of their policies.

From an economic point of view, they were presented with an extensive territory from which they could extract minerals and which, above all, provided arable lands that would contribute to meeting the demand for products vital to the European diet (fruit and other horticultural products). In this way, a process was started which, even if it saw the appearance of modern agriculture in North Africa, abruptly departed from the traditional agricultural model that had sustained the habits of consumption of the indigenous population and contributed in great measure to the emergence of a problem which continues today: the insufficiency of foodstuffs.[5]

The existing equilibrium in the region, before the arrival of the Europeans, was based on a subsistence economy characterised by a form of life adapted to the conditions of the natural environment. In the humid zones, the use of land for agriculture was combined with raising livestock. The most extensively used system in the plains was the biannual rotation of crops, leaving part of the land fallow for feeding livestock. Sheep predominated in the driest plains and cattle in the humid zones. Pastoral nomadism was characteristic of the steppe and the desert. In summary, it was a traditional agricultural system oriented towards a level of production sufficient for a farmer and his family's consumption.

The arrival of the Europeans -- the French in Algeria (1830), Tunisia (1881) and Morocco (1912), the Spanish in Morocco (1912), and the Italians in Libya (1911) -- interrupted that model. Thus began the sustained expropriation and purchase of lands with the objective of putting them in the hands of European colonists (to the extent of 40% of all arable land in Algeria, 18% in Tunisia and 12% in Morocco).[6] Beginning around this time, modern agriculture was initiated and oriented towards meeting the needs of the metropoles, which can basically be summarised by a strong expansion in vineyards (especially in Algeria), fruit and early vegetable plantations (Morocco) and olives (Tunisia). Among the more serious and immediate repercussions of this process was the displacement of cereals in the south, substituted by new products, and with the consequent reduction in production; the disappearance of fallow lands that had served as pastures for livestock; and migration towards the new areas of agriculture in need of labour (which started the process of uncontrolled urbanisation).

---

[5] The development of this section follows the analysis contained in José M. Jordán, "La agricultura de los países del Norte de Africa: Situación y perspectivas," *Revista Valenciana d'Estudis Autonómics*, No. 14, October 1992, pp. 123-145.

[6] *Ibid.*, p. 133.

The independence of the Maghreb countries has not served to end the dual character of its agriculture. Each of the countries attempted to face its new situation by adopting distinctive economic policies as follows:

- Morocco adopted a decisive line of support for its agriculture, although tipped clearly towards the modern export sector, with successive plans for agricultural reform which have not gone much beyond the unequal parcelling out of land and displaying a strong inclination towards irrigation (necessary to strengthen commercial agriculture) through the construction of a large number of reservoirs.

- Algeria opted for a completely different route based on a wager for industrialisation in which agriculture occupies a lowly position. The central planning development model led to the nationalisation of the great landed properties in the countryside which had previously been in French hands and were now converted into self-managed state farms. The results have been extremely poor, and Algeria now suffers from a greater food dependency than its neighbours.

- Tunisia followed a middle-of-the-road plan, which changed course in 1969 from an initial phase of collectivisation (in which private lands were absorbed into large collectives managed in common) to a regime of private initiative which has found better results.

Alongside agriculture, there exist other factors that complete the panorama of the Maghreb's significance from a European point of view over the last few decades. It is enough to highlight the following:

- The succession of crises and conflicts that have arisen in the Persian Gulf region, the traditional source of the majority of the energy consumed by the European countries, has triggered a search for alternative suppliers. In this sense, the importance of Algeria, Tunisia and Libya as suppliers to Europe has increased over the last decade.[7]

- The only reference to EC-Maghreb relations in the Treaty of Rome appears in the annexes, which mention the existence of several special regimes with Morocco, Libya and Tunisia. It was not until 1969, however, that the first commercial agreements were signed with Morocco and Tunisia.

The bilateral focus that the EC applied to the countries in the region was a constant that was maintained until the summit of the Heads of State in Paris (October 1972). It was here that the Global Mediterranean Policy (GMP) was put in motion, implying treatment of the area as a whole, and the negotiations of cooperation agreements began with Algeria, Morocco and Tunisia (signed in 1976).

The GMP now implies not only talk of commercial exchanges, but also includes issues of economic and financial cooperation (through the Financial Protocols), social questions, political dialogue and scientific and technical cooperation. The formula for free access of industrial goods and the regime of preferences for Maghreb agricultural products in Community markets, as opposed to the most-favoured-nation (MFN) status enjoyed by EC member states, has proven to be clearly insufficient in meeting its stated objectives (to contribute to the economic development and social and political stability of the Maghreb).

In 1985, before Spain and Portugal's imminent entry into the EC, the southern countries again forcefully presented their protests against the negative effects of the GMP. This led to a redefinition of the norms of application, but did not serve to reverse the negative tendencies which had prevailed up to that time.

As a last step in EC-Maghreb relations, we have to remember the

---

[7] To illustrate this point, it is sufficient to note that Spain buys 65% of the gas that it currently consumes from Algeria.

Renewed Mediterranean Policy (RMP), approved in December 1990.[8] In addition to reinforcing the existing provisions of the GMP, this policy presented new proposals, such as assisting the countries to realise their plans for structural reform, implementing regional projects and creating a link between these countries and the process of European construction.

In reviewing the results of the various formulas of EC-Maghreb relations, one clearly sees that qualitative and quantitative gains have been made in the importance that Brussels attaches to its southern neighbours: the perspective has evolved from a bilateral one to a regional one and is not solely circumscribed to commercial issues. However, none of these formulas has effectively attended to the ever more serious problems that afflict the region. The continuous succession of proposals, the majority of which emanate from the southern EC countries, makes it clear that along with a major interest in and preoccupation with events in the region, there exists an evident misorientation concerning the best way of finding real solutions.

In the area of economic and financial cooperation, successive generations of financial protocols have been negotiated with all of the Mediterranean Non-Community Member Countries (MNMCs) since the advent of the Global Mediterranean Policy. These protocols translate into contributions from the Community budget and loans from the European Investment Bank (EIB). Negotiations are presently underway for the Fourth Protocols (operative for the period 1992-96), which at an estimated total of 4,405 million ECUs, represent a tripling of the volumes granted under the Third Protocols.

Table 1 presents the actual flow of funds officially committed by the EC since 1977 to the Maghreb countries, which for this purpose refer to Algeria, Morocco and Tunisia, inasmuch as Mauritania is included within

---

[8] The relationship of the characteristics and results of the GMP and the RMP are dealt with in Alejandro V. Lorca, and Jesús A. Nuñez, "España y la cooperación euromagrebí: ¿un motor de desarollo?", paper published in seminar proceedings entitled *El Magreb tras la crisis del Golfo: transformaciones políticas y orden internacional* (Granada, 1991).

the framework of the Lomé Convention,[9] and no agreement has been negotiated with Libya. Funds have been transferred in the framework of 4-year Financial Protocols.

Table 1
EC Financial Protocols with Maghreb Countries (millions of ECUs)

Protocol	Algeria	Morocco	Tunisia	Total
I (1977-81)	114	130	195	339
II (1982-86)	151	199	139	489
III (1987-91)	239	324	221	784
IV (1992-96)	350	438	284	1,072
Total	854	1,091	739	2,684

When these figures are compared with those that represent commercial deficits or levels of existing external debt in the region, it can be immediately deduced that the EC has not yet decided to play an important role in the search for solutions to the challenges posed on its most immediate borders. In this regard, the future is also not very optimistic, if we consider the climate of international economic crisis in which we find ourselves and the competing claims from Central and Eastern Europe. Since the fall of the Berlin wall, attention to the East is an evident fact of Community foreign policy.

In the allocation of official development assistance, of which the EC is among the world's primary donors, Europe has not assigned high priority to the Maghreb: of the total development aid provided by the EC in the

---

[9] According to Bichara Khader in his book *Europa y el Gran Magreb* (Barcelona, 1992), p. 280, Mauritania received a total of 237.2 million ECUs during the period 1975-90.

last decade, only 12% has been destined for NCMCs, compared to 67% to ACP (African, Caribbean and Pacific) countries and 21% to Latin America and Asia.

In any event, it is necessary to understand that solutions to Maghreb problems will never come from the hand of public capital. Only if capital and technology in private hands are directed towards the area can a more positive picture be drawn. Unfortunately, there have not even been important initiatives in this area.

In purely commercial terms, the EC[10] only conducts 4% of its external trade with the Maghreb (the entire Mediterranean accounts for 8% of Community commerce, while EFTA absorbs 25% and the United States accounts for 18%) and records an annual surplus of 7,000 million ECUs with the entire group of NCMCs. In reality, the Community is passing through an introspective phase in which its member countries are reorienting a large part of their trade towards intra-Community exchanges at the expense of trade maintained with other regions. Faced with a continuation of this phase combined with the prospect of a European Economic Area (EEA) that foresees incorporation of several Central and Eastern European countries, it cannot be hoped that European commercial interests in the Maghreb will experience a positive change.

The picture of European interests in the Maghreb could not be complete without at least brief reference to geo-strategic questions. Among permanent European interests is the fact that the principal lanes of maritime traffic in the Atlantic as well as the Mediterranean that serve to supply Europe with all kinds of goods pass under the gaze of our southern neighbours; thus, there exists the possibility, although currently improbable, that this traffic could be significantly disturbed. Concern over the growing volume of weapons that is being detected in the region, the acquisition of which is motivated more by existing rivalries between those countries than by the desire to directly threaten Europe, also presents a serious preoccupation for Community leaders. In this respect, the appearance of weapons of mass destruction -- especially in Algeria and Libya -- chemical and nuclear, does not at all contribute to a climate of tranquillity that favours cooperation.

---

[10] Among the member states, France, Germany, Spain and Italy have the largest commercial interests in the Maghreb.

In addition to these factors, there exist others of a circumstantial nature that also explain the growing preoccupation of EC member-state governments with events in the region: the Libyan situation, Algeria's evolution since the coup d'état at the beginning of 1992, the Saharan conflict, the rise of radical Islamist movements, the recurring waves of immigrants heading towards the EC, etc. Collectively, these pose a set of problems which, beyond the economic interest any of the European countries might have in the area, may be the real cause of the growing attention being paid to the Maghreb in Brussels.

2. Europe for the Maghreb

Beginning with the initial idea of the asymmetrical character of the relations between both areas, it is enough to say, even with the risk of exaggerating, that "Europe is everything for the Maghreb". With a reiterative reference to the neocolonial character of EC-Maghreb relations, which indicates among other things the profound mark that this period left on Maghreb societies and many times has served to conceal the responsibility of their own leaders for addressing the problems of their countries even now that more than thirty years have passed, Europe continues to be an omnipresent force in the life of these people, if only as a negative referent.

Seen both as a model to follow -- exemplified by the creation of the Arab Maghreb Union (AMU) along similar lines as the EC and the Moroccan application for admission to the Community in 1987 -- and a danger to avoid (rejection of the Western lifestyle; fear of new forms of colonialism), the European presence is easily discernible in the region. And this is the case in cultural life (elites educated according to European patterns and in French) as in economic (with the persistence of colonial models of the international division of labour established by the metropoles at the time) and political life (with attempts at organisation following outlines elaborated on the Old Continent).

From a more concrete point of view, the importance of the EC for the Maghreb can be graphically illustrated by the following points:

- In the area of commerce, the Community is the principal partner and provider for the five Maghreb countries, representing 65% of their total trade with the rest of the world. The character of this trade responds to the classic scheme of North-South relations, in which the EC sells manufactured products and equipment and acquires raw materials and energy (from Algeria, gas and oil; from Morocco, phosphates, fruit and horticultural products; and from Tunisia, olive oil, petroleum and phosphates), from which can be deduced a commercial surplus favourable to the North, except in the case of its commerce with Algeria.

- Of all products entering the EC from the Maghreb at the end of the 1980s, 55% came from Algeria, while Morocco (25%) and Tunisia (18%) remained well behind.

Maghreb countries have pursued privileged relations with Brussels since their independence. Proposals to this end[11] have reflected a changing perspective over time, which has seen an almost exclusive focus on commercial questions in the earlier phase pass more recently to a global orientation in both geographical terms and in the scope of issues. See, for example, the GMP and the RMP.

From the point of view of the Maghreb countries, the results show undeniable growth in their sale of industrial and agricultural goods to Community markets. At the same time, however, there has not been any qualitative improvement in their position as commercial partners with the EC. Each new expansion of the Brussels club has translated into negative effects for Maghreb interests. According to Maghreb spokesmen, the following areas represent the chief sources of disappointment in their relations with the EC:

- *Freedom of access for industrial products.* Each time the Community has seen one of its industrial sectors threatened by competition that could arise from this provision, it has imposed penalising restrictions. (The textile sector is a good example of this phenomenon.) In all fairness, responsibility for the Maghreb's disappointing export record should also be attributed to its own inadequate economic policies (unbalanced rates of exchange, failure to take advantage of export markets, and inexperience in opening up channels for export).

---

[11] Morocco and Tunisia were pursuing the creation of a free-trade zone as early as their first round of bilateral negotiations with the EC in 1969.

- *System of preferences for agricultural goods.* The increase in Maghreb exports of agricultural goods has been less than that experienced by its industrial products. The explanation can be found in a combination of factors: the efficiency of the protectionist mechanisms of the ACP countries, stagnation in demand for Mediterranean products in the EC, the increase in the index of self-sufficiency after Spain and Portugal's entry and the inability of Maghreb exporters to create competitive distribution channels conditioned to meet the rigorous quality norms and terms of payment demanded by importers.

- *Equitable treatment in the social sphere.* There have been constant complaints of what are considered discriminating measures against Maghreb nationals in EC member states in such areas as equal treatment and social security.

- *Cooperation.* Actions in this area are regarded as sporadic and limited in character as perhaps best illustrated by the scarcity of financial flows dedicated to the Maghreb.

Although still in its early phases of implementation, it is evident that the RMP does not contain an effective formula for realising its stated objectives. To date there has been a steady stream of proposals reflecting a diverse set of ambitions, which only goes to show that the search continues without results while the economic and social inequities between the two shores of the Mediterranean continue to increase.

IV. Cultural Prejudices in the Mediterranean

But Euro-Maghreb relations are not confined to ties of an economic nature, however broad these may be. Other problems exist: those arising from demography, the distribution of scarce resources, human migratory patterns, the integration of minorities and human rights violations. These qualify as *real* problems, in comparison to another set which, from our standpoint, should be considered *false* and which poison relations on both shores of the Mediterranean. The latter are the fabricated "dangers", "ghosts" and "challenges". Among them, two in particular stand out today and directly contribute to what we might call "misencounters" between the two regions: the manipulation of migratory patterns and the incomprehension of the political dimension of Islam, that other civilisation that exists on the southern shore of the Mediterranean. The first of these problems can contribute, against the background of the *myth of invasion*, to the growth of racism and xenophobia and make the integration of foreign minorities in recipient countries difficult. It may also exacerbate a deep-rooted mistrust towards people who have suffered colonisation. The second problem can also lead, on European shores, to the rise of another *myth that associates Islam with fanaticism* and asserts a fundamental incompatibility between Islam and democracy. On the southern shore, this myth can contribute to the distortion of Islam in order to convert it into a narrow form of nationalism, an element of affirmation and rejection of other models of civilisation and conduct.

1. The Myth of Invasion

The Mediterranean is a political border and above all an economic barrier which separates the population on its two banks. The European alcazar, "Fortress Europe", has erected this barrier in order to protect itself from the danger of "invasion" from the South.

The *myth of invasion* is supported by arguments based purely on demographic projections: currently, the European states on the northern shore account for 51% (190 million) of the total Mediterranean population, compared to the Arab states of the southern and eastern shores which add up to around 34% (129 million). Turkey represents around 15% (with 56.7 million) and Israel-Palestine only 1% (hardly 4 million). But over a span of three decades, today's total of 380 million will have increased by 170 million persons, 68% of them in Arab countries, 22% in Turkey and only 10% in Europe. These figures, unfortunately, have come to be cited with disturbing frequency as constituting a threat to Europe.

We say "unfortunately" because of the enormously pessimistic assumption behind the argument that everything will remain the same after 30 years, whereas some indicators are highly encouraging. For example, demographic studies show an anticipated reduction by one-half the present fertility rate in the Maghreb countries.[12] Furthermore, although population growth in the Mediterranean basin tends to diminish the human weight of the North and to increase that of the South, the density remains, as a consequence of North Africa's greater territory, lower in North Africa and the Arab-Islamic Levant than in southern Europe. The 76 inhabitants per square kilometre in Spain or Greece (not to mention the 191 in Italy) are greater than the 50 in Tunisia, Morocco or Egypt and, of course, the 10 in Algeria or the 2,5 of Libya. The South will continue to be less dense than the North for a long time, although, even so, without sufficient resources to provide for its population.

Europe has passed through a period of euphoria in its internal economic construction and is currently living through a crisis which is leading it to revise its model. It is feeling the pressure of different domestic circumstances and the challenges of its eastern and southern neighbours: contribute to their development or face recurring waves of immigration. But it is in this context that there is revealed more than one Europe: one that looks to the East, one that which looks to the South and one that which remains estranged from and/or indifferent to what are considered the interests and problems of others.

Southern Europe is reacting by trying to make other EC countries aware of these realities. A report written by the Spanish government and directed at its fellow European members concludes that "the Maghreb today is a time bomb that Europe is able to deactivate."[13] Political leaders in the Maghreb are conscious of this possibility and hope to derive their own benefit by leveraging the "powder keg" as a bargaining chip. In an interview last autumn, King Hassan II expressed the strategy in this way: "I think Europe has the right to preserve itself, but it is a

---

[12] See Abdelhamid Bouraoui, "La población magrebí ante el siglo XXI: una mirada de futuro," in Bernabé López, et al. (eds.), *España-Magreb, siglo XXI*, p. 150.

[13] "Europa ante el Magreb", report by the Directorate General of Foreign Affairs for Africa and the Middle East, 26 February 1992.

right which it will have to revise soon, because it needs a strategic area on its southern flank".[14]

Meanwhile, European public opinion perceives of the Maghreb primarily as the source of an immigrant "invasion" that threatens to jeopardise its current *status*, which is already insecure in today's world economic climate. In countries like France, immigration becomes the scapegoat even when, as indicated by Sami Nair, there doesn't really exist an immigration problem, except in the minds and fears of the public.[15] In countries like Spain, the feeling of "invasion" grows in accordance with the frequency with which references to "wet backs" from the Strait of Gibraltar appear in the headlines. Scant consideration is paid to the actually modest number of immigrants among us and even less to the interdependence between our two worlds that argues persuasively for the North's indisputable need for a South that supplies labour and raw materials. And all this overlooks the fact that immigrant labour in Europe is typically not performing tasks in competition with the national work force, and businessmen have a stake in being able to rely on this source of labour to get the work done.

2. Islam, an Ingredient of Western Culture

Another problem, mentioned earlier, arises from the *West's inability to comprehend Islam as a civilisation and a political culture*. In order that the entire Mediterranean region becomes an operative space of intercultural coexistence and harmony, it seems necessary to add to the concrete provisions intended to eliminate the profound iniquities other measures which are designed to overcome the prejudices that separate the populations.

One of the greatest sources of prejudice in the Mediterranean basin and which incites immense distrust is an ideological world view that

---

[14] *Le Monde*, 2 September 1992.

[15] *Le regards des vainqueurs* (Paris, 1992), p. 69.

fallaciously places two worlds in opposition. There is the world of the West that implies the ethnocentric concept of what in the 19th century was called "Civilization". The other, perceived as "near in threat and far in its human and cultural morphology",[16] corresponds to the other shore comprising the "barbaric and Third World" and which now forms a part of another religious-cultural aggregate (such as Islam) and political-linguistic grouping (such as the Arab world). These two worlds find themselves *deceptively confronting* one another. The former is at its peak in terms of cohesion and identity -- although this should not be exaggerated or taken for granted, in light of recent setbacks and confusion -- and the latter is experiencing its usual state of crisis, although still capable of mobilising large sectors of the population as was seen during the days of the Gulf war.

We use the word *fallacious* to characterise the opposition between these two worlds, the dividing line between the northern and southern shores, because it is too frequently forgotten that Islam, in the words of one of the Arab world's greatest thinkers, Muhammad Arkoun, although "rejected by Western ideology as a nebulous Orient, an obscurantist Middle Ages, an underdeveloped mentality, ... forms an integral part of the axes, of the categories and of the constitutive themes of all 'Western' Christian thought".[17] This same author questions "the legitimacy of the tenacious distinction between a dreaming, mystic, archaic, superstitious 'Orient' (with which Islam is always associated) and a realistic, rational, emancipated 'West' (with which Christianity is always connected and, more recently, Judaism)".[18] Perhaps the decisive and healthy influence of Islam on the culture of the Western world has not been sufficiently remembered. As the great Spanish Arabist and historian of science, Juan Vernet, pointedly asks: Five centuries after the discovery of America, are we still not conscious that "one of the greatest services done by the

---

[16] See Samir Amin, *op. cit.*, p. 171.

[17] Muhammad Arkoun, "L'Islam devant la crítica moderna i l'hegemonía de l'Occident", *L'Avenc*, No. 146, March 1991.

[18] Mohammad Arkoun, *L'Islam. Hier. Demain* (Paris, 1978), p. 124.

Arabs for culture was the transmission to the West of diverse technical elements, naval architecture (the Latin sail and the wheel), and astronomic (determination of coordinates) and geographical knowledge (nautical maps) which were to permit navigation across the Atlantic"?[19]

A final and distinct observation we wish to make on this subject is that the ideology of combat for hegemony converts concepts such as the "West" or the "Orient" into necessarily opposing terms and imbues them with a certain tension. This is precisely the point so brilliantly made by Fernand Braudel in describing "the great game in the Mediterranean".[20] To translate influence into an expression of superiority and dominion has been, in summary, the history of humanity; nevertheless, its unhappy consequences -- exploitation on the one side and humiliation and resentment on the other -- are too well known.

V. Conclusions and Proposals

The history of EC-Maghreb relations, which we have attempted to present in the preceding pages, makes evident the asymmetric character of that relationship that was noted at the beginning of the paper. In economic terms, the Community has felt little need for the Maghreb until now and believes that it can operate in the future under the same hypothesis; our southern neighbours, however, see their dependency on Brussels increasing not only in the commercial field, but also in other areas such as finance and technology.

Despite recent obstacles, the European Community marches towards a European Union and promises to become one of the primary centres of power within a multipolar world. Meanwhile, the Arab Maghreb Union,

---

[19] Juan Vernet, *La cultura hispano árabe en Oriente y Occidente* (Barcelona: Ariel Historia, 1978), p. 234. French translation entitled *Ce que l'Europe doit aux arabes de l'Espagne*.

[20] Fernand Braudel, *La Méditerranée et le monde méditerranéen à l'époque de Philippe II* (Paris: A. Colin, 1966), Volume 2, p. 131.

which merits support as offering one of the few means of escape from the current situation, struggles under the burden of indifference on the part of the international community and inability on its own part to put into effect its ambitious plans.

At the same time, the countries of Central and Eastern Europe appear to be moving towards a more advantageous position for attracting the attention of Brussels: scenarios of future integration seem quite feasible in several cases; financial institutions are being created to focus on the problems of the region, such as the European Bank for Reconstruction and Development (EBRD); and aid projects are already on the move which command considerably greater sums than have until now been dedicated to the South (e.g. Operation PHARE). In this sense, time runs against the Maghreb. Its leaders cannot ask for longer terms to initiate the necessary processes of political and economic reform, because they run the risk that by the time that these reforms are finally achieved, they may find that they have been overtaken by events.

Considerations of security and stability in the Mediterranean are assuming a significance that is far greater than any accomplishments in the areas of political, economic or social development. Democracy and human rights should rightfully be associated with the concepts of stability and collective security. "Political realism", however, frequently leads European governments to tolerate, if not openly support, the dictatorial regimes in the Mediterranean which are the true powder kegs of instability -- not only on a national but regional level as well. Furthermore, it appears increasingly necessary to instrumentalise formulas at the national level in the coastal states that have the effect of violating human rights.

We conclude that there is the possibility to accommodate the aspirations espoused on both shores of the Mediterranean. When we assert that the EC does not have economic interests of high priority in the region, we are only stating an objective fact which is confirmed in the available statistics on trade and aid. However, this reality is characterised by a narrow vision and does not recognise that the economy is an element -- and a very important one -- of security, and cannot conceal the fact that there exist other more profound interests which affect the stability of the region.

The future of the EC does not lie in the creation of a fortress out of the belief that we will thereby be able to insulate ourselves against the prevailing difficulties of the outside world. A strategic discussion of the future obliges the EC to include this economic and political periphery among the variables it considers in finding the necessary stability which will permit concentration on previous plans. In that context, European leaders should be conscious that integration of their peripheries (both East and South) should be a primary and unconditional objective for their own project of European integration.

6 EC-Middle East Relations:
The Peace Process and Revisions to the Community's Mediterranean Policy

Paul Clairet

Introductory Observations

The current peace process taking place in the Middle East has served as a useful device for evaluating the general impact of the European Community's actions in the region, and particularly its Renewed Mediterranean Policy (RMP).

The peace process has revealed:

• the growing importance of the political dimension of agreements and other actions taken by the European Community in the Middle East; and

• the need to coordinate Community policy with individual member state policies to create the political "critical mass" necessary to allow the full economic influence of the Community to be exerted in the region.

The recognition of these developments and their transformation into principles of action have created a concept of "common action", which has been inscribed in the Maastricht Treaty and is increasingly being invoked in the Community's relations with the Middle East, as well as other parts of the world.

I. The Line-Up on the Eve of the Negotiations

The *peace process* that was inaugurated in Madrid in October of 1991, arose naturally from the fortuitous coincidence of two important international events: the end of the East/West rivalry and the crisis in the Gulf. Fortuitous, because it takes for granted the fact that Saddam Hussein failed to understand the full implications of the end of the Cold War. That is, the unravelling of the USSR meant that the only power capable of dissuading the United States from intervening in the name of a timely "new world order" had suddenly vanished from the world scene.

By contrast, the *end of the Cold War* made Israel's most resolute adversaries (Syria and the PLO, in particular) acutely aware that they could no longer depend on the support of their former protector, the USSR. At the same time, the government of Mr. Shamir also did not realise that the end of the Cold War greatly diminished the strategic value of Israel, in the same manner experienced by South Africa, Zaire and Afghanistan. The Rabin government elected in June 1992, realised, however, that Israel's new trump would henceforth lie in its own capacity to act as a *pole of stability* in the region.

The end of the Cold War permitted Americans and Europeans to envisage the elimination of several sources of regional instability, one of the most important being the Arab-Israeli conflict (see Annex I).

For many interested parties, the Gulf crisis acted both to speed up events and clarified certain issues. The participation of a number of Arab countries, for example, in the anti-Iraq coalition demonstrated that Israel was no longer the single cause of their differences and alliances. And for Israel, whose territory was being protected for the first time in its history by armies other than those of Tsahal, the reality of having been the target of Iraqi SCUDs diminished considerably the "strategic importance" that had historically attached to the Occupied Territories.

In the eyes of the Americans, direct intervention had the effect of reducing the significance formerly attributed to Israel. However, for Europeans as well as for Americans, the need to avoid the accusation of applying a *"double standard"* was the major motivation for initiating a Middle East peace conference. At the same time, it was important to challenge the link suggested by Mr. Hussein between Iraqi occupation of

Kuwait on the one hand, and control of the Occupied Territories by Israel and of Lebanon by the Syrians on the other hand.

The former USSR viewed the prospect of a Middle East peace conference as a means of restoring as soon as possible and on new grounds their formerly privileged relations with the Arab-Muslim world, especially after having recently renewed its relations with Israel.

II. Formulation of the Process

Confident of its political and military leadership, which was further bolstered by the Gulf war, the United States was able to organise a peace conference that featured the following characteristics:

- *regional in scope* for the purposes of "reassuring" Israel and for warding off the UN and any claims of international law;

- *an international dimension*, to satisfy the Arab participants: composed of co-sponsorship by the Soviets/Russians (albeit shadows of their former selves) and the presence of the European Community (invited as such), in addition to the participation of a growing number of "extra-regional parties" for a series of meetings in a multilateral framework, including Japan, China, India, Turkey, Canada, EFTA nations, the Gulf countries, etc.; and

- *a marginal role for the United Nations* (a mute observer in Madrid).

These conditions appeared temporarily acceptable to the Arab parties.

The European Community seemed destined to play a marginal role in the negotiations, beginning in Madrid in October 1991, to the end of the first session of the working groups within the multilateral framework (finalised by the Lisbon Steering Committee in May 1992) including the launching of this framework in Moscow in January 1992. At the suggestion of the ruling Israeli government -- believed by some to be a puppet of US authorities and which had been hostile to the equitable and balanced attitudes and principal positions of the Community since 1980 (see Annex II) -- the Community and its member states were viewed as a source of funding for the process but without enjoying any decision-making power or even influence.

Given this unsatisfactory situation, certain individual member states began to work towards a real international conference under the aegis of the UN, while the Community and its member states continued to demonstrate support for the US "regional" formula (see Annexes III and IV).

III. A Renewed Mediterranean Policy in the Region

These efforts to marginalise the Community conflicted with the important role -- largely economic until now -- played by the Community in the Mediterranean. This role derived not only from its geographical proximity and the intricate links woven by history, but also by virtue of its being the principal economic and commercial partner of the region. And, with the adoption of a Renewed Mediterranean Policy (RMP) by the Council of Ministers in December 1990, the Community became by far the main supplier of aid and development assistance to the region.

The EC's RMP carries a total budget for the period 1992-96 of 4.400 million ECU. Of this total, 1.300 million ECU consists of grants from the EC's budget and the remaining 3.100 million ECU are loans from the European Investment Bank (EIB). The new policy included the following specific elements.

- A 47% increase in the resources provided in the *Financial Protocols* to bilateral agreements between the EC and Maghreb and Mashreq countries for the period 1992-96: 2.375 million ECU (compared to 1.618 million ECU in the previous protocols) of which 1.075 million ECU were a grant (including 300 million ECU devoted to dealing with the social effects of *structural adjustment*) and 1.300 million ECU were loans from the EIB. (See Table 1.)

Table 1
4th Financial Protocols to EC Bilateral Agreements
with Maghreb and Mashreq Countries, 1992-96

	4th Protocol (millions of ECU)				3rd Protocol (millions of ECU)				Percent Increase between 3rd and 4th		
	EC Budgetary Funds	a	EIB Resources	Total	EC Budgetary Funds	a	EIB Resources	Total	EC Budgetary Funds	EIB Resources	Total
Maghreb											
Morocco	218	25	220	438	173	11	151	324	26%	46%	35%
Algeria	70	18	280	350	56	4	183	239	25%	53%	46%
Tunisia	116	15	168	284	93	6	131	224	25%	28%	27%
Subtotal	404	58	668	1,072	322	21	465	787	25%	44%	36%
Mashreq											
Egypt	258	16	310	568	200	11	249	449	29%	24%	27%
Jordan	46	2	80	126	37	2	63	100	24%	27%	26%
Syria	43	2	115	158	36	2	110	146	19%	5%	8%
Lebanon	24	2	45	69	20	1	53	73	20%	-15%	-5%
Subtotal	371	22	550	921	293	16	475	768	27%	16%	20%
Israel	-		82	82	-		63	63	-	30%	30%
Total	775	80	1,300	2,075	615	37	1,003	1,618	26%	30%	28%

a Share stipulated for risk capital.

151

- Support for *"horizontal cooperation"*, i.e. regional and environmental projects: 230 million ECU in grants and 1.800 million ECU in loans from the EIB (500 million ECU earmarked specifically for environmental protection).

- A *special aid package* of 600 million ECU to palliate the adverse effects of the Gulf war on Jordan, Egypt, Turkey, Israel and the Occupied Territories; an additional 150 million ECU in "urgent aid" to assist displaced Iraqis.

This new policy, which introduced both a qualitative (represented by the horizontal cooperation) and quantitative leap in the Community's involvement in the Mediterranean, was supplemented by EC accords with individual countries as characterised below.

- *Association agreements*, aiming towards a Customs Union, were negotiated with Turkey (1963), Cyprus and Malta, all three of which have applied for membership in the Community.

- A *free trade agreement* had been reached with Israel (1975); cooperation began to "intensify" in parallel with the peace process, a development made possible by the position of the Israeli government elected in June 1992.

- *Preferential agreements*, which are non-reciprocal and allow free access to the EC market for industrial and certain agricultural products, were concluded with Morocco, Tunisia, Algeria, Syria, Jordan and Lebanon. A *partnership* with Morocco and Tunisia is in the making, awaiting the addition of Algeria with a view towards creating a Maghreb "economic space".

In addition to these accords negotiated within the framework of the Renewed Mediterranean Policy, other initiatives have had a distinct bearing on the Community's influence in the region. These are outlined below.

- *Cooperation with Yugoslavia* (1980), which has been unilaterally denounced and will be replaced at the first opportune moment by individual accords with the former Yugoslav republics, beginning with Slovenia.

- *Non-preferential cooperation with Yemen* was extended (1985) with the political objective of encompassing the entire new republic with this policy, in order to safeguard the democratic know-how of the southern part and to prevent territorial claims by Saudi Arabia.

- *Twelve years of cooperation with the Gulf Cooperation Council (GCC)* is leading towards the creation of a free trade zone which is presently under negotiation. There again, beyond bilateral economic questions (such as equal access, environmental protection, taxes on chemical products imported from the Gulf, industrial cooperation, etc.), the Community needs to become more aware of the political dimensions of its policies in the region. These might include, for example, adherence to the basic requirements of successful peace negotiations (an end to financial support of Islamic movements), steps designed to ensure the stability of the whole region (withdrawal of support for radical groups such as the FIS -- Front Islamique du Salut -- the Muslim Brothers, etc.) and modulated support to meet Iranian aims according to the nuances and variations of the relations each of these countries has with Iran.

- *Cooperation with Iran* which, while still only in an exploratory phase, has been suspended due to the absence of progress or guarantees in three principal domains: respect for human rights; direct or indirect non-intervention in the region and beyond, e.g. Sudan and Algeria; and a willingness to open nuclear facilities to inspection and to halt their armament efforts.

The RMP did not appear overnight. The necessity of and desire for a "common Mediterranean policy" had been expressed as early as the 1972 EC summit of Heads of State and Government. Between 1975 and 1977, these were couched in accords with the 12 countries (and Yugoslavia in 1980), and complemented by additional protocols in 1986 and 1988.

Thus, the bilateral policy of *aid* which arose from decolonisation has been followed by a policy of common *cooperation* which, when combined with the Renewed Mediterranean Policy, has lead towards a definite *partnership* with the region.

This trend towards forming a partnership, combined with the factors of instability (and of settlement) linked to the end of the Cold War, has revealed the necessity to consider the political as well as economic aspects when formulating a Mediterranean policy. Thus, in the course of the Gulf crisis -- and in the strict framework of its competencies -- the Community initiated embargo measures against Iraq and supplied aid to the front-line countries. To return to my earlier point, the peace process in these circumstances served to *clarify* certain questions and *accelerated* events in the sense that they demonstrated the need to go beyond the role of principal economic partner. What was required of the European Community then was decisive *political* action to exert a stabilising influence over *a region which depended on the "neighbourliness" of the Community in the much the same way and extent as does Central and Eastern Europe.*

IV. The Community and Its Member States in the Peace Process

The peace process served as an *accelerator*. As early as October 1991, at the initiative of the then presiding Council president, M. van den Broek, an ad hoc group known as the "Peace Process" was created within the framework of the European Political Cooperation (EPC). Even before Maastricht, such questions were dealt with according to a *"joint action" approach* [article J.3 of Title V - Provisions on a Common Foreign and Security Policy (CFSP) of the Maastricht Treaty]. Activities falling under both EPC and Community competencies were approached simultaneously -- at the initiative and under the responsibility of the Commission.

An EC troïka issuing from this group went to Washington for each bilateral session. "Behind the stage" and alongside the US and Russian co-sponsors (but clearly in an inferior position), the Community knew how to stir up the *political expectations* of the Arab and Israeli protagonists in order to acquire the status of a legitimate participant in the talks in the eyes of the State Department.

The peace process served as a *revelation*. Confronted by the reality of the situation, the Community and its member states dismissed lofty ideals in the name of pragmatism, without renouncing the principles set forth since 1980 (see Annexes V to VII). As a result, the Community began to play a much more active role in the multilateral framework, both in the Steering Committee and in the working groups. The positions it has held include:

* Main organiser/"gavel holder" for the Economic Regional Development Group;

* Co-organiser for the "Water", "Environment" and "Refugee" Groups; and

* Contributor (intermediary between "extra-regional observer" and "participant" -- reserved for parties and co-sponsors) to the Arms Control Group. This latter role conferred on the Community access not only to plenary sessions ("improved" formula of Madrid: 2 + 12), but also henceforth to regional meetings where it is represented by the Presidency of the Council.

The Community's pragmatic approach also advanced the participation of other interested parties, as illustrated by the fact that the United Nations henceforth has the right to participate in the talks in the capacity of an "extra-regional party". Additionally, the Palestinians, including those of the diaspora, will finally take part in five working groups (initially, Economic Development and Refugees). It was only the Israeli restrictions that were maintained with regard to members of the PLO or residents of East Jerusalem.

The principal influence of the Community has to be relativised due to the architecture of the process. The bilateral track remains the heart and the motor of the talks. The multilateral track,[1] which is organised into five working groups coordinated by a Steering Committee, continues to serve to reinforce the bilateral track. For the moment indeed, the process is not sufficiently advanced to apply Minister of Foreign Affairs Peres' formula: "Bilateral relations regulate past litigation, multilateral relations prepare future cooperation."

V. Beyond the Renewed Mediterranean Policy and the Peace Process: The European Challenge in the 1990s

The Report of the European Council of Lisbon on the probable evolution of the Common Foreign and Security Policy (CFSP) suggests two important roles for the Maghreb and the Middle East (see Annex VIII):

- The Mediterranean region, and in particular the Middle East (the CCG, Iraq, Iran and Yemen), is *one of the most sensitive regions of the world with regard to the Community's CFSP*, especially as long as the region remains the principal energy supplier in the world.

- Europe has a *vital interest* in avoiding any interruption in the supply of petroleum -- and, in a growing manner, gas -- coming from the Maghreb as well as from the Middle East. In addition, securing a market position in the Middle East (ranking at present number two behind the US but before Japan) remains one of Europe's major goals.

One can identify four potential challenges facing Europe from the Middle East:

---

[1] Consisting at first, in Moscow, of the five permanent members of the UN Security Council and the international community, without the UN, i.e. "the UN without the UN". Subsequently, the UN has been progressively introduced in the process -- not as a framework actor but as an extra-regional actor. In any event, the international community serves as a "witness" to the will of each protagonist to progress, the prospect of which some of them actually dread.

- *Risk of military conflict between the three principal rivals* (the GCG, Iran, and Iraq) as they attempt to exert their supremacy in the region. For example, the Iranian armament effort ($6 billion in 1992 -- four times greater than it was during the 1979 war with Iraq) is aimed at establishing a dominant economic and military position in the region. Nevertheless, there is little risk for Europe as long as none of the three becomes the dominant supplier of gas or petroleum. The Gulf crisis showed that problems with any single nation will not provoke major supply disruptions.

- *Concerted action of these three regional powers* to break off Europe's petroleum supply, a highly inconceivable prospect.

- *Political instability of one of the regional powers*, leading to the collapse of a regime or government. If any one of these countries does not adhere to Western standards of behaviour, their ensuing instability would constitute a major challenge to Europe. There is little risk, however, of lasting disruption to the supply of oil or gas in that they constitute the major, and in some case only source of national income for the countries of the region, such as was the case in Iran in 1979.

- *Nuclear proliferation.* Iraq, Iran, Syria, Pakistan and others are in the process of attaining -- or have already attained -- a nuclear capacity. Primarily a tool in their regional power game, this capacity is not presently directed against Europe. None of these powers, in fact, is capable of mounting a menacing force like that of the former USSR within the next ten years; nevertheless, this possibility should become a factor in the strategy of the European Community and its member states.

None of the challenges presented above appears to pose an immediate and significant threat to Europe. On the contrary, it is the *structural factors of destabilisation*, which the Renewed Mediterranean Policy is designed to relieve, that require more immediate attention. The most pressing among these factors are economic and social degradation/ destabilisation and the resulting *migratory pressures* (Maghreb residents towards Europe and Mashrek inhabitants to the Gulf and Balkan states). There is expected to be a near-doubling of population on the southern shore of the Mediterranean over the next 20 years. Many of these people will seek refuge in a *religious activism* that can take any one of various forms (integration of church and state, fundamentalism, etc.). This development also poses the risk of widespread political disturbance.

In the context of the Middle East peace process, I would propose that the European Community focus on the following "hierarchy" of priorities. First, "economic" questions should receive the greatest attention, especially for the "core countries" (Israel, Occupied Territories, Jordan, and Libya and even Syria and Egypt) -- which, in a sense, comprise the "operational" region. Secondly, eventually enlarge the region to include the "second circle" of countries (Iran, Iraq, Pakistan, Turkey) to which Israel attaches increasing importance.

In short, the importance of the region for Europe and its geographic definition should not be confused with or limited to its Arab-Israeli dimension. The creation of a pole of stability with the "core countries" only will only have a lasting viability or impact if it is part of a larger vision. I urge the exploration of international institutional mechanisms, such as exist between the EC and the Organisation for Economic Cooperation and Development (OECD) or the EC and the Group of 24, that hold the promise of creating a "leading effect" and, for the moment, can neutralise the hostile reactions of certain second-circle countries.

Annex I

Israeli-Palestinian Conflict
(Arab-Israeli Dimension)

I. Present Situation -- Historical References

A. After the PLO programme was adopted in November 1988, several *peace initiatives* have punctuated the diplomatic process:

1. The PLO Programme (15 November 1988)

Proclaims the birth of the Palestinian state. The diplomacy of the PLO will henceforth be based on the *implicit recognition* of Israel's right to exist as a state defined by its 1967 frontiers, alongside a Palestinian state, in compliance with United Nations Assembly Resolution 181 (29 November 1947) on the division of Palestine. This programme calls for an *international conference* on the basis of UNSC Resolutions 242 and 338 (Israeli withdrawal from the Occupied Territories and the right of each nation to live peacefully and securely within safe and recognised borders).

2. The Shamir Plan (14 May 1989)

Allows the commencement of *elections* in the Occupied Territories, in accordance with the main lines of the Camp David agreements. These elections are to take place in ten districts, each one electing a representative to the autonomous Council, which will serve as the sole spokesperson for the Israeli nation and will be able to negotiate a five-year *law of temporary autonomy*. At the end of the first three years, *discussion on the final status* will begin. All of the Palestinians living outside of the West Bank and Gaza will be excluded from voting, including the Palestinians of East Jerusalem.

3. President Mubarak's Ten Points (August 1989)

- Israel will have to commit to honour the outcome of free and democratic elections held in Gaza and the West Bank.
- Voting will be performed under the supervision of occidental observers.
- The Israeli army must withdraw in advance from the regions where elections will be held.
- Israeli nationals will be forbidden access to the Occupied Territories on the day of the elections.
- The Palestinian residents of *East Jerusalem* will have the right to participate in the elections.
- The candidates will enjoy complete freedom of expression.
- Those elected will be protected by a form of immunity, sheltering them from all judicial action.
- Israel will have to commit to participate in *talks on the final status* of the territories within three to five years (considered as an *intermediary period* before being bound by a common agreement).
- All Israeli activity in the Occupied Territories will have to be suspended.
- Israel must accept *the principle of the "exchange of territories for peace"* as an integral part of any final settlement.

4. The Five-Point Baker Plan (December 1989)

- After the Israeli and Egyptian initiatives, the United States feels the situation is ripe to hold a dialogue between an Israeli delegation and a Palestinian delegation in Cairo.
- Egypt cannot take the place of the Palestinians, but conferences between Egypt and the other parties will be necessary.
- Israel will only take part in the dialogue if all of the Palestinian delegation complies with its requirements.
- Israel will participate in these talks *on the basis of the Shamir plan*, and the Palestinians will be free to express their opinions concerning the election arrangements (based on the Shamir plan) as well as the negotiation process.

- In order to facilitate the whole of this process, the United States recommends the arrangement of a meeting between Israeli, Egyptian and American ministers of foreign affairs.

The PLO has announced that it is ready to endorse this plan on the condition that it can contribute certain amendments. As for the Israelis, this condition is precisely the stake in the Baker plan that provoked the rise of the Shamir-Peres national union government.

B. These four plans are an improvement over both the Reagan plans (1 September 1982) and the Fez plans (6-9 September 1982). The former provided for autonomy of Gaza and the West Bank, in association with Jordan, after the conclusion of negotiations between Israel and Jordan, which certain Palestinian representatives were party to ("*Jordanian option*"). The Fez plan gave implicit recognition of Israel, offset on the one hand by the reaffirmation of the right of the Palestinian people to self-determination and their ability to exercise inalienable and indivisible national rights under the direction of the PLO (*their sole and legitimate representative*), and the call for Israel's withdrawal from the territories occupied (including East Jerusalem) in 1967 on the other hand.

The success of the Reagan plan (and of all those which followed it) resulted from the so-called "Kissinger clause" which refused any recognition of the PLO, until it *explicitly* recognised Israel. Now, the Arab countries and the PLO can only give up their sole trump in exchange for all the concessions that Israel must accept (withdrawal from the Arab territories occupied in 1967, recognition of the PLO as the representative of the Palestinians and the right of the Palestinians to self-determination). The Israeli guarantee was symmetrically opposite; the question seemed irresolvable, and therein lies the *Arab dimension* of the *Israeli-Palestinian problem*.

It is in this context that President Anwar Sadat's trip to Israel in November 1977, seemed especially noteworthy. In the course of that visit, he renounced the negotiations with Israel which placed that country in the position of negotiating for its very existence.

161

C. The Arab dimension of the Israeli-Palestinian problem has also contained several instances of territorial litigation, as follows:

1. With Syria for the conquest of Golan, annexed 14 December 1980;
2. With Lebanon for an official establishment of a "security belt" in the southern region of that country, in June 1985; and
3. In East Jerusalem, annexed 28 June 1967, and proclaimed by the Knesset on 30 July 1980, as "the eternal and indivisible capital" of Israel. There again, beyond the Israeli-Palestinian dimension, the fact that Jerusalem is the "third sacred city of Islam" brings an Arab-Israeli significance to this decision.

D. Historical Reference Points

1. Successive Palestinian Territorial Laws

- 1948-1949: The territory of Gaza comes under Egyptian control. 25 February 1958, President Nasser acknowledges Gaza's status as *autonomous, without Egyptian supervision.*
- 24 January 1949: The kingdom of Transjordan becomes the kingdom of Jordan with the annexation of the West Bank and East Jerusalem. The Jordanian Parliament, where prominent Palestinians were sitting for the first time, ratifies the annexation on 24 April 1950.
- 4 February 1960: Jordanian nationality is granted to all Palestinians living in the kingdom and abroad.
- 26-29 October 1974: At the Arab summit of Rabat, King Hussein renounces, to the PLO's advantage, Jordan's rights to the West Bank and East Jerusalem.
- June 1988: Six months after the beginning of the Intifada, King Hussein *breaks all legal and administrative links between Jordan and the West Bank.*

2. The PLO Rise to Power: Fifteen Years to Obtain Arab Support

- September 1964: The second Arab summit in Alexandria

recognises the PLO (formed in June 1964) as the representative of the Palestinian people.

- 26-28 November 1973: The Arab summit in Algiers recognises the PLO as the "only" representative of the Palestinian people.
- 6 September 1976: Palestine is admitted as the 21st member of the Arab League.
- March 1979: The Israeli-Egyptian treaty of Washington (following the agreement at Camp David, 17 September 1978), which foresees one *autonomous* government for the West Bank and Gaza, is rejected by almost all of the Arab nations.

3. International Recognition of the PLO

- 22 November 1967: the UNSC passes Resolution 242, calling for an Israeli evacuation of the *Occupied Territories* and the right of all the nations in the region to live within safe and recognised borders.
- 10 December 1969: The UN General Assembly admits the *existence of a Palestinian people*. It recognised, on 14 October 1974 by 105 votes (including France), the PLO as the *representative* of the Palestinian people, and underlined on the 22 November 1974, Palestinian rights for *self-determination, sovereignty, and national independence*. The PLO is admitted to the UN General Assembly as an *observer*.
- 13 November 1974: Speech by Yasser Arafat before the United Nations General Assembly.
- 16 March 1977: US President, Jimmy Carter, declares that "a *homeland* will have to be provided for Palestinian refugees".
- 13 June 1980: In a declaration, the European Council (Venice) calls for *PLO association in the negotiations*.

4. Widespread Support of the PLO in the Occupied Territories

In 1986, there were 1,502,000 Palestinians in the Occupied Territories (835,000 in the West Bank, 542,000 in Gaza and 125,000 in East

Jerusalem). Their solidarity with the PLO was demonstrated on several occasions:

- 15 August 1975: PLO creation, 11 years after its own formation, of the PNF (Palestinian National Front), based in the Occupied Territories.
- 12 April 1976: PLO sympathisers lead the polls at the municipal elections in the West Bank.
- 9 December 1987: Beginning of the Intifada ("war of stones") uprising which, over the months, would be renewed and sometimes animated by the Hamas Islamic movement.
- 15 November 1988: Proclamation of the Palestinian State, recognised by several countries, at the Palestinian National Council (PNC) in Algiers.

II. Treatment in the United Nations

A. Three Basic Resolutions

1. UN General Assembly Resolution 181 (29 September 1947) dealing with the *division* of Palestine: two states, Arab and Jewish, which would allow for an international administration of Jerusalem.

2. UNSC Resolution 242 (22 November 1967), five months after the "six-day war". The resolution affirms that "the foundation of a fair and lasting peace" will include:

- The "withdrawal of Israeli forces from the territories occupied during the recent conflict" for the United States, it is the original English text (the draft of the Resolution was British) which speaks "of territories", which make law.
- The "cessation of all assertions and statements of belligerence", implicitly implicating border incidents and *terrorist* acts.
- "Respect and recognition of sovereignty, the territorial integrity and independence of *each state in the region* and of their right to live in peace within safe and recognised borders protected from threats

or acts of force."

Moreover, Resolution 242 affirms the necessity of:

- Guaranteeing freedom of navigation on the region's international waterways: coming closer to holding back access (rent of the islands?) to the sea of Iraq.
- Realising a fair settlement on the *refugee* problem.
- Guaranteeing the territorial inviolability and political independence of the region through such measures as the creation of *demilitarised zones* (constituting the first plan for a regional system of security and arms control).

3. UNSC Resolution 338 (22 October 1973), to which the PNC refers in its proclamation of 15 November 1988. Passed during the "Yom Kippur" war, the resolution contents itself with calling the conflicting parties "to begin to apply the resolution immediately after the cease-fire in all arrangements." Therefore, the Palestinian question continues to be perceived as a "refugee problem".

B. Other Resolutions, coming from the General Assembly, are also worth referencing.

1. Resolution 194 (11 December 1948): After the first Arab-Israeli war, confirms the right "of refugees who desire to go back to their homeland to return as soon as possible" or, in default of this, to "receive allowances as compensation". This and other rights will be recalled by 20 subsequent General Assembly resolutions adopted between 1949 and 1967.

2. Resolution 273 (11 May 1949): By a large majority, admits Israel as a *member of the UN*.

3. Resolution 2442 (19 December 1968): Concerned with "Israel's human rights violations in the Occupied Territories", denounced

throughout the 1970s and 1980s, by numerous texts.

4. Resolution 2525B (10 December 1969): Recalls for the first time since 1948 the "inalienable *rights* of the *Palestinian people*." Confirmed by Resolution 2628 (4 November 1970) which assures that "the respect of Palestinian rights is an indispensable element in the establishment of a fair and lasting peace".

5. Resolution 2649/70 (30 November 1970): Explicitly mentions the Palestinian people's "right to self-determination".

6. Resolution 2649/72 (8 December 1972): Regards the "*changes enacted* by Israel in the Occupied Arab Territories" as "*null and void*." Perspective which will later be surpassed by a condemnation of population transfers and construction of settlements. Thus, Resolution 32/5 (28 October 1979) stipulates that "all the measures and decisions taken by the Israeli government. . .in order to modify the *geographic law and the demographic composition* in the Palestinian and other Arab territories occupied since 1967 do not have legal validity and will not pose a serious barrier to the peace efforts".

7. Resolutions 3236 and 3237 (22 November 1974): In the presence of Arafat, who had addressed the General Assembly, recognises "the Palestinian people's right to *sovereignty and national independence*" (3236) and invites the PLO "to participate in the work of the General Assembly as an *observer*" (3237).

8. Resolution 3379 (10 November 1975): Likens Zionism to a form of racism.

9. Resolution 3161 (9 December 1976): Calls for "the *Middle East Peace Conference with the participation of the PLO*," a move reaffirmed by Resolution 3320 (25 November 1977). This explains Resolution 3465 (29 November 1979) with regard to the Camp David agreements reached "outside of the scope of the United Nations and without the participation of the *PLO which represents the Palestinian people," and "condemns all the partial and distinct accords* which

constitute a flagrant violation of the rights of the Palestinian people, of the precepts of the United Nations Charter and of resolutions adopted concerning the Palestinian question."

C.   The resolutions adopted since have remained faithful to these concepts. A fundamental contradiction persists therefore between UNSC Resolutions 242 and 338 and the rest of the texts adopted by the General Assembly.   This contradiction is responsible for the US and Israel's insistence on the former two versus the PLO's insistence on accepting the "ensemble" of UN resolutions.   The Palestinian National Council in Algiers overcame this supreme obstacle on 15 November 1988 by recognising Resolutions 181, 242 and 338.

This time, Israel found itself up against a wall: the United Nations General Assembly concluded its session of December 1988, in Geneva, demanding (by a vote of 138 to 2 -- Israel and the United States -- with 2 abstentions -- Canada and Costa Rica) "an immediate start on the organisation of an international conference," on the basis of Arafat's proposals.

Annex II

European Positions on the Arab-Israeli Dimension of the Palestinian Question

What have been the accomplishments of European Political Cooperation (EPC) in the Middle East?   In a privileged position to make "its own contribution to the preservation of international peace and security" (preamble of the Single European Act), the Community has not yet reached a high level of efficacy in the region.

In statements of increasingly precise principles (Venice Declaration-June 1980, Brussels Declaration-February 1987, and Madrid Declaration-June

1989) the European Community has insisted equally on Israeli and Palestinian rights, and has pursued (following an initiative by the Spanish Presidency) an active diplomacy based on face-to-face dialogue with the interested parties. These discussions have been aimed at reconciling the different points of view and promoting an election procedure in the Occupied Territories as well as securing international guarantees -- including those of Europe -- for a lasting settlement of the conflict. Principal elements of the three declarations are outlined below.

1. Venice Declaration (European Council, June 1980)

- Traditional links with the Middle East call Europe to play a special role.
- Europe, on the basis of UNSC Resolutions 242 and 338, proclaims "the right for the security and the existence of all the nations in the region, including Israel, and for justice for all peoples, which implies the recognition of the legitimate rights of the Palestinian people".
- The Palestinian people must be able to exercise their right to self-determination; the PLO must be *party to* the negotiations.
- The settlements, as well as the demographic and territorial modifications, in the Arab Occupied Territories are a violation of international law.

2. Brussels Declaration (European Council, February 1987)

- Reminder of Venice 1980.
- The twelve favour an international peace conference under the aegis of the United Nations with the participation of interested parties as well as all parties in a position to contribute to the establishment of peace and security in the region.
- Mention of direct Community aid and preferential access to the European market for certain Palestinian products.

3. Madrid Declaration (European Council, June 1989)

- Reminder of Venice 1980.

- Recognition of the right of the Palestinian people to self-determination *with all that implies*.
- The PLO should *participate* in the negotiation process in the framework of an international conference.

Annex III

Statement on Israeli Settlement Policy in the Occupied Territories

European Political Cooperation Press Release (P. 41/91) Brussels, 3 May 1991

The Community and its member states are gravely concerned at the recent establishment of two new Israeli settlements in the Occupied Territories, at Revava on 15 and 16 April and at Talmon Keva on 22 April.

They deplore the fact that the Israeli government has given permission for these new settlements.

The Community and its member states reaffirm their long-standing position that Jewish settlements in the territories occupied by Israel since 1967, including East Jerusalem, are illegal under international law and under the 4th Geneva Convention in particular.

The Community and its member states consider that the initiative of the American Secretary of State, Mr. Baker, now offers genuine prospects of progress towards peace in the region. They fully support this initiative and the process envisaged, which should enable the necessary dialogue between the parties concerned to get underway. They also consider that any establishment of new settlements in the Occupied Territories, which is in any case illegal, is especially harmful at a time when all parties should show flexibility and realism so as to bring about a climate of

169

confidence favourable to the starting of negotiations.

The Community and its member states strongly urge the Israeli government neither to allow nor encourage the establishment of settlements in the Occupied Territories.

European Political Cooperation Press Release (P. 65/91)
Brussels, 17 July 1991

The Presidency recalls the Declaration of the European Council at Luxembourg (28-29 June 1991) on the peace process, which confirmed the support of the Community and its member states for the current initiative, launched by the United States, and which urgently called on all parties to overcome final difficulties so that a peace conference could be convened.

The recent positive evolution in the attitude of the government of Syria is welcomed.

Noting the forthcoming visit of Secretary Baker to Israel and the region, the Community and its member states consider that the peace process has entered a crucial stage. They are hopeful that the conference may now soon be convened. The Community and its member states call upon the parties concerned to refrain from any actions which could jeopardise the peace efforts, to which they will continue to contribute.

Declaration on the Middle East

European Political Cooperation Press Release (P. 68/91)
Brussels, 29 July 1991

The Community and its member states reviewed the present developments in the peace process. They noted with satisfaction the emerging consensus on the current initiative, launched by the United States, to convene a peace conference leading to the beginning of negotiations between the parties.

The Community and its member states welcome the fact that a number of Arab countries have responded positively to the call in the London G-7 Summit Declaration by offering a suspension of the Arab boycott in return for a freeze by Israel of its settlement policy. They stress how important it is that this positive gesture be reciprocated.

They stress again the importance of overcoming final difficulties, including the question of Palestinian representation, so that a conference to which they will make their full contribution as a participant, may now be convened shortly. They are convinced that with the necessary political will and courage of the parties concerned a solution to those difficulties can be found.

Annex IV

Declaration of the European Council on the Peace Process in the Middle East

European Council in Luxembourg, 28-29 June 1991

The European Council has examined the state of play on the Middle East peace process. While reaffirming its well known positions of principle, it emphasised the necessity of setting in train without delay a process, on the basis of UN Security Council Resolutions 242 and 338, leading to a just and comprehensive solution to the Arab-Israeli conflict and the Palestinian question.

To this end, the European Council believes the current initiative, launched by the United States offers real prospects of peace in the region. It confirms its firm support for this initiative and calls urgently on all parties to overcome final difficulties so that a peace conference can be convened. As a participant in the peace conference, the Community and its member states aim to make their full contribution to its success and to the negotiations between the parties.

Besides a settlement of the Palestinian question through the exercise of the Palestinian people's right to self-determination, lasting peace and the stability of the region should involve the end of the state of belligerence among all states in the region, the commitment not to resort to force and to the peaceful settlement of disputes, and respect for the territorial integrity of all states, including Israel.

The European Council confirms the determination of the Community and its member states to contribute to the economic and social development of all peoples in the region once the prospect of peace is clear. To this end, the Community and its member states will work to promote intraregional solidarity and relations of friendship and cooperation with all countries in the region. The Community and its member states emphasise their interest in a political dialogue with regional groupings.

The European Council once again underlines the need for all parties to adopt reciprocal and balanced measures to establish a climate of confidence to get the negotiations going, and to avoid all measures that might hinder the process. It believes specifically that the policy of establishing settlements in the territories occupied by Israel, which is in any case illegal, is incompatible with the will expressed to make progress with the peace process.

Annex V

Declaration on the Peace Process in the Middle East

Extracted from the Conclusions of the Presidency of the European Council in Maastricht, 9-10 December 1991

The European Council attaches great significance to the Middle East Peace Conference in Madrid, which has launched a process of negotiations on the basis of UN Security Council Resolutions 242 and 338 which should lead to a just and comprehensive solution to the Arab-Israeli conflict and the Palestinian question. On the basis of the principles which have long governed their position, the Community and its member states are determined to continue to undertake all possible efforts alongside the United States and the Soviet Union to support this process. In Madrid they pledged their constructive partnership in all phases of the negotiations.

The European Council considers it of vital importance that the momentum gained at Madrid is not dissipated on procedural matters. It noted that the second round of bilateral negotiations has been convened in Washington. These negotiations should be pursued in good faith by all parties. Only then may the way be opened to movement on substance and meaningful confidence-building measures. The European Council considers a halt to Israel's settlement activity in the Occupied Territories an essential contribution to creating the stable environment which progress in the negotiations requires. Renunciation of the Arab trade boycott is another.

With regard to the situation in the Occupied Territories, it is important that both sides show restraint and that Israel abide by the provisions of the Fourth Geneva Convention. The European Council looks forward to a tangible improvement in the situation in these territories, even before the putting in place of interim or other arrangements. In this respect it noted reports indicating that since the Conference in Madrid, the level of violence there has diminished. Indeed, this conference has led to an atmosphere of hope, both in the Occupied Territories and elsewhere, which should not be disappointed.

The European Council reaffirms the commitment of the Community and its member states to make an active practical contribution to progress in the multilateral phase of the negotiations on regional cooperation. It expresses the hope that all parties in the region will participate in these negotiations. The European Council considers that the bilateral and multilateral agenda should go hand in hand, each one reinforcing the other. However, regional cooperation cannot progress faster than

173

movement towards a political settlement. Given its close ties with all the parties involved, the Community and its member states are determined to remain in close contact with all participants and to do all they can to promote significant steps in the direction of a comprehensive, just and lasting settlement.

Annex VI

Declaration on the Middle East Peace Process

European Political Cooperation Press Release (P. 23/92)
Brussels, 17 February 1992

The Community and its member states are following closely the developments in the Middle East peace process in both its bilateral and multilateral tracks.

The achievement of lasting peace in the region is of vital importance for Europe. This is why the Community and its member states are fully committed to playing a consistent role in this process, bearing in mind that the Middle East is a neighbouring region, with which Europe has long-standing political, historical, cultural, economic and commercial ties, and whose stability and security are essential to Europe's own stability and security.

The Community and its member states have maintained regular contacts with the parties to the bilateral negotiations as well as with the co-sponsors and other participants. The Community and its member states will not spare any efforts to provide their good offices if requested by the parties involved themselves.

The inception of the multilateral phase of the Middle East peace process in Moscow has the potential to reinforce the bilateral talks. It is in itself a concrete confidence-building measure, enabling peace to become a reality and genuine regional cooperation to develop. However, substantive progress in the multilaterals can only be attained if the central issues of the bilaterals also register some progress.

The Community and its member states reiterate their commitment to play a constructive and active role in the multilateral negotiations. To this end, some obstacles should be overcome. First of all, the presence of all the parties directly involved is essential in the next phases of the multilateral process. Secondly, a formula allowing for a broader Palestinian participation should be sought. Thirdly, the United Nations and their specialised agencies should participate and contribute to the building up of regional cooperation. Fourthly, the Community and its member states should participate, preferably as co-organiser, in all working groups established for the multilateral negotiations. They believe it is necessary to be fully engaged in working groups of a clearly political nature, such as "Arms Control and Regional Security", besides their full involvement in working groups of an economic nature.

Annex VII

Declaration of the European Council on the Middle East Peace Process

Extracted from the Conclusions of the Presidency of the European Council in Lisbon, 26-27 June 1992

The European Council reaffirms its support for the peace process launched in Madrid in October 1991 which provides a unique opportunity for peace. It is of paramount importance for the world and Europe in particular, which has an essential role to play in the political and economic stability of the region. The European Council pays tribute to the commitment and perseverance of the co-sponsors as well as to the wisdom and courage displayed by the parties directly involved.

The European Council has taken note of the results of the election in

Israel. It believes that these results, which are an illustration of the democratic tradition in Israel, will reinforce the peace process and the commitment to a just and lasting settlement. It hopes that the new Israeli government, as well as the Arab parties involved, will seize the opportunity to negotiate a comprehensive peace.

The European Council recognises that it is for the parties to the dispute to establish the terms of a settlement, which, to be effective, must be freely negotiated and agreed among them. But the European Council reiterates its belief that for an agreement to prove just and lasting it will have to be based on United Nations Security Council Resolutions 242 and 338, which enshrine the principle of land for peace. It should provide for the security of all States in the region, including Israel, within recognised and guaranteed borders, and for the Palestinian people to exercise their right to self-determination.

The European Council reiterates the need for all parties to commit themselves to the peace process, to refrain from all acts of violence and to avoid any action likely to endanger the negotiations, or to threaten the climate of confidence. It hopes that the new Israeli government and the Arab parties will act quickly to implement confidence-building measures. It looks forward to a halt to the building and expansion of Israeli settlements in the Occupied Territories, including East Jerusalem, which are illegal under international law, and to full application of the provisions of the Fourth Geneva Convention. The European Council also calls upon the members of the Arab League to lift the boycott of trade to Israel, which is incompatible with the spirit of the peace process.

The European Council reiterates the commitment of the Community and its member states to play a constructive and active role in the peace process, in both its bilateral and multilateral tracks, based on the Community's well known positions of principles. Both Israel and her Arab neighbours can rely on Europe's commitment to building a future of peace and prosperity in the region in the light of progress achieved in the peace process.

The European Council reiterates the Community's wish for full implementation of Security Council Resolution 425. It reaffirms its support for Lebanon's independence, sovereignty, unity and territorial integrity. It calls for the withdrawal of all foreign forces from Lebanon and for cooperation by the parties with the United Nations forces serving there. The European Council believes that the Lebanese people should be permitted to make their views known in elections which are held under conditions guaranteed to be free and fair.

Annex VIII

Extracts from the Report to the European Council Meeting on the Probable Evolution of a Common Foreign and Security Policy Lisbon, 27-28 June 1992

Maghreb and Middle East

The southern and eastern shores of the Mediterranean as well as the Middle East are geographical areas in relation to which the Union has strong interests both in terms of security and social stability.

The Union has therefore an interest in establishing with the countries of the area a relationship of good neighbourliness. The goal should be to avoid a deepening of the North-South gap in the region by favouring economic development and promoting full respect for human rights and fundamental freedoms and the development and consolidation of democracy and the rule of law.

1. Maghreb

The Maghreb is the Union's southern frontier. Its stability is of important common interest to the Union. Population growth, recurrent social crises, large-scale migration, and the growth of religious fundamentalism and integration are problems which threaten that stability.

Without prejudice to the necessary differences in approach concerning the region's various countries, attention might be given in priority to the following:

(i)   promoting a constructive dialogue, aimed at creating an area of peace, security and prosperity, in which respect of the fundamental principles of international law is assured;

(ii) establishing a framework of cooperation in all fields, which should gradually lead to an upgraded partnership between the Union and its member states and the Maghreb countries;

(iii) strengthening of existing cooperation measures on the foreign policy aspects of the fight against terrorism and illicit traffic in drugs;

(iv) ensuring full compliance by the countries of the region with the relevant treaties and agreements on disarmament and arms control, including those on non-proliferation;

(v) supporting the current moves towards regional integration.

2. Middle East

The Middle East has been one of the constant preoccupations of the Community and its member states. The instability which has been a permanent feature of this region affects international security and the interests of the Union, the most important of which are to ensure the stability of the area and a relationship of cooperation and dialogue.

Within the framework of the objectives set by the Union, the following domains are potentially open to joint action:

(i)   development of systematic action to support the process of negotiations launched by the Middle East Conference in Madrid on the basis of the relevant resolutions of the United Nations Security Council which should lead to a just and comprehensive solution to the Arab-Israeli conflict and the Palestinian question;

(ii)   ensure the Union's active involvement in the peace process;

(iii) making efforts to persuade Israel to change its policy regarding settlements in the Occupied Territories and to persuade Arab countries to renounce their trade boycott;

(iv)   support moves towards regional integration;

(v)   ensure the full compliance by the countries of the region with the relevant treaties and agreements on disarmament and arms control, including those on non-proliferation, and with the relevant resolutions of the United Nations Security Council;

(vi)   the foreign policy aspects of the fight against terrorism and the illicit traffic in drugs.

Annex IX

Chronology of Key Events

I. Preparatory Phase

1. At the United Nations

08/10/90
Shootings in Jerusalem (22 Palestinians killed by Israeli forces on the Esplanade of the Mosques), followed by several days of confrontation in the Occupied Territories.

13/10/90
Adoption of a UNSC resolution condemning these "acts of violence", which the United States finally agreed to in order to maintain the anti-Iraq coalition.

20/12/90
UNSC Resolution 681 on the Gulf crisis implicitly calls for a peace conference for the Middle East. The preamble refers to a decision by the President of the Security Council (20/12) to the effect that "an international conference, when the time comes and if *accurately designed*, should facilitate" the resolution of the Arab-Israeli conflict.

2. In the Region

02-03/05/90
President Mubarak's visit to Damascus confirms the Syro-Egyptian reconciliation.

28-30/05/90
The Arab summit in Baghdad, convened to address the *"challenge" of the massive immigration of Soviet Jews to Israel*, revealed the Arab disunity, confirmed also by the absence of the Moroccan king, the Algerian president and, particularly, the Syrian president.

10/08/90
Extraordinary summit of the Arab League (Cairo) confirms the *division within the Arab world*. Iraq is condemned and the league decides, by a weak majority, to send a pan-Arab force to protect Saudi Arabia. The countries of the GCC, Egypt, Syria and Morocco take part in the anti-Iraqi coalition.

12/08/90
The Iraqi president, Saddam Hussein, "associates" the resolution of the Iraq-Kuwait crisis with an Israeli withdrawal from the Occupied Territories and Syrian withdrawal from Lebanon.

18/01/91
Israel is hit by the first Iraqi SCUD. At the request of the United States, it does not strike back, and the departure of the Arab countries from the anti-Iraq coalition is prevented.

06/03/91
While the Americans start to pull out of the Gulf, the six GCC nations as well as Egypt and Syria sign a cooperation agreement ("Damascus Declaration"), aiming towards the creation of a peace-keeping force to ensure the *security of the region.*

10/03/91
Agreement between the US Secretary of State and the signatories of the Damascus Declaration on *regional security arrangements.*

18/03/91
In an interview with the *Figaro*, Yasser Arafat says he is ready to agree to a *"direct dialogue" with Israel* on the condition that it take place *"under the flag of the United Nations."*

01/04/91
After meeting with President Assad in Damascus, President Mubarak calls for a *peace conference on the Israeli-Palestinian conflict.*

22/05/91
In Damascus, President Assad (Syria) and President Hraoui (Lebanon) sign a treaty of "fraternity, cooperation and coordination," which sanctions *Syrian hegemony in Lebanon.*

01/06/91
In response to King Hussein of Jordan's proposition to begin *direct contacts*, Israel "invites" him.

14/07/91
In a letter to President Bush, Syrian President H. El Assad accepts US proposals for a Near East peace settlement -- which envisions a *regional conference* under the aegis of the United States and the USSR

-- deemed "balanced and positive" and naturally able to serve as a foundation for a *global solution* based on UNSC Resolutions 242 and 338.

01/08/91

Conditional Israeli acceptance (observer role for the Community and the UN, no negotiations concerning the status of the Golan Heights or East Jerusalem, and refusal of any presence of the PLO) of US peace conference proposals.

28/09/91

In Algiers, Palestinian National Council (PNC) acceptance, by a vote of 256 to 68 with 12 abstentions, of *the start of Palestinian participation in the peace conference* proposed by the United States and the USSR. PNC mandates the executive committee to negotiate the terms of this participation, which symbolises a victory for Yasser Arafat.

17/10/91

The PLO approves the formation of a *Jordanian-Palestinian delegation.*

19/10/91

Reconciliation between Syria and the PLO, following a meeting in Damascus between H. El Assad and Y. Arafat.

3. The US and Soviet Co-Sponsors

06/03/91

Before the US Congress, President Bush cited the lessons of the Gulf war: "It is time to put an end to the Arab-Israeli conflict." His statement was followed by four trips to the region over a period of ten weeks by Secretary of State Baker, all of which failed to form a consensus on the *organisation* of a peace conference. This unsuccessful period, however, was followed by four rounds of eventually profitable sessions.

08/03/91

First Baker trip: Saudi Arabia (8th and 9th of March), Egypt (10th and 11th), Israel (11th and 12th), Syria (13th), USSR (14th and 15th), Turkey (16th). Baker reports that he is "encouraged" by the "signs of good will" he encountered. Meeting on the 12th, in Jerusalem, is the *first meeting* of a US secretary of state with ten Palestinian "insiders".

08-11/04/91

Second Baker trip: Jerusalem matches its "yes" to a *regional* conference with numerous conditions and guarantees. Although Baker announces "progress" towards peace (on the 11th of April), the PLO refuses to hold a "regional" conference (on the 14th).

18-20/04/91

Third Baker trip: In Jerusalem, second interview with Palestinians from the Occupied Territories (20/04). In Cairo, *first explicit commitment by an Arab country to participate in the peace conference*.

26/04/91

Baker trip interrupted due to the failure of mediation efforts.

10/05/91

First visit to Israel of a Soviet Minister of Foreign Affairs, A. Bessmertnykh, which he follows with a trip throughout the region, in particular to Cairo (on the 12th and 13th of May) where he speaks with Mr. Baker about *US and USSR "collective efforts"* to organise a conference on the Near East.

11-16/05/91

Fourth Baker trip: Fruitless (involving visits to Syria, Egypt, Israel).

23/05/91

J. Baker affirms that "the largest obstacle to peace" is the continuing Israeli presence in the Occupied Territories.

29/05/91

President Bush proposes an *arms control plan for weapons of mass destruction* in the Near East.

18-22/07/91
Fifth Baker trip: To Syria (where he salutes "this large political change" -- referring to M. Assad's acceptance of the conference plan), Egypt, Jordan, Saudi Arabia, and Israel.

01-05/08/91
Sixth Baker trip: Conditional agreement of Israel (1 August), Palestinian agreement matching the conditions and guarantees in East Jerusalem (on the 2nd). Visit to Jordan, Morocco, Tunisia and Algeria in order to resolve the problem of the *Palestinian representation*.

16-20/09/91
Seventh Baker trip: To Jerusalem, Cairo, Damascus and Amman where delivery of *individualised* "letters of assurance" detailed the US position.

13-18/10/91
Eighth Baker trip: To Jerusalem, Cairo and Amman; PLO approves the formation of a *Jordanian-Palestinian delegation* (on 17 October).

18/10/91
In Jerusalem, in the course of a joint conference with Soviet Minister of Foreign Affairs (B. Pankine), Mr. Baker announces the peace conference will open in Madrid in the presence of Presidents Bush and Gorbachev.

29/10/91
In Madrid, Presidents Bush and Gorbachev emphasise that the United States and the USSR, co-sponsors of the conference, want to serve as "catalysts" but refuse to "impose a settlement" in the Near East.

4. The Community and Its Member States

The Community position, especially with regard to the "*regional*" character of the envisaged conference, is developed and asserted within the framework of the EPC (see Annexes III and IV). Four ministerial declarations are issued:

03/05/91
Reminder of the "illegal" character of the Israeli presence in the Occupied Territories and of the obstacle this poses to the "initiative and the envisaged process" which, themselves, are "fully" supported.

17/07/91
Confirmation of support and satisfaction with regard to Syria's positive attitude and reminder that the Community and its member states "will continue to provide their support" for the efforts under way.

29/07/91
Reference to the G-7 (Group of 7) appeal on the Arab trade freeze because of the Israeli presence, satisfaction with the positive attitude of "several Arab countries," appeal to "overcome ... the Palestinian representation question."

10/10/91
Reaffirmation of "their well-known principal positions" and of their "determination to provide all possible support ... and to play an *active role as a participant ... alongside the co-sponsors*," satisfaction with regard to the attitude of the PNC and appeal for "a speedy resolution of the question of an *authentic* Palestinian representation." For the rest, reiteration of the points raised in the former declarations (boycott, Israeli presence ...).

The European Council of Luxembourg (28-29/6/92):

- Implicitly makes reference to its former declarations -- on Palestinian self-determination, respect for the territorial integrity of all the states in the region, etc. (see Annex II) -- and explicitly to

UNSC Resolutions 242 and 338;

- Confirms its support for "the initiative under way" and makes a statement expressing the will of the Community and its member states to "provide their *full* contribution to its success and to the *negotiations* between the parties," as well as to "the conference *participants*"; and
- Defines at the same time the role of the Community and its concept of the finalities of the process: "to contribute to *the economic and social development of all the inhabitants of the region*"; to work for the "promotion of *intraregional* solidarity and for relations with *the whole* of the countries in the region", to establish and develop a "*political dialogue* with the *regional groupings*".

II. After the Formulation of the Process

1. The Peace Conference: Dates and Key Stages

30/10/91

Three-day *inaugural plenary session* of the "Conference for Peace in the Middle East" in Madrid. George Bush calls for "territorial compromises" for a "genuine peace," and Mikhail Gorbachev, for "respect for the rights of Palestinians". I. Shamir puts the Arabs on guard against negotiations "focused on the Palestinian question". *Invited "as such,"* the European Community, represented by the Dutch President of the Council and President of the Commission, places an emphasis on the parallelism between the bilateral and multilateral frameworks in the search for a global, balanced and equitable solution. The UN is in the corridor in its capacity as an "observer".

03/11/91

First series of *bilateral* meetings between Israelis on one hand, and Syrians, Lebanese and Jordo-Palestinians on the other hand. Tense climate between the Syrians, Lebanese, Israelis and Palestinians emphasises the "good atmosphere" of their first meetings.

10-18/12/91
Second round of *bilateral* meetings in Washington: procedural quarrel on fundamental questions prevents the Israelis and the Jordo-Palestinians from opening negotiations and causes a complete blockage. Opening delayed from 04/12 to 10/12, with Israel wishing to show its discontent that the meetings were not held "in the region." These meetings continue to be held *in Washington* at the rate of one week out of every five to six. After September 1992, always in Washington (and *not in Rome* as initially anticipated in July 1992) on a permanent weekly basis, punctuated by interruptions lasting several days, as arranged between the protagonists.

28-29/01/92
Commencement of multilateral negotiations in Moscow. In addition to member states participating individually, the European Community is present as a "co-organiser" in three working groups (Refugees, Water, and Environment), "principal organiser" for Regional Economic Development, and "extra-regional party" for Arms Control. Absence of Syrians, Lebanese and Palestinians and of the UN. The *Steering Committee* meeting allows the reaffirmation of the central character of the bilateral meetings.

27/05/92
First operational Steering Committee meeting draws on a haphazard balance of the five working groups: Water (Vienna, 13-14/05), Refugees (Ottawa 13-15/05), Environment (Tokyo, 18-19/05), Arms Control (Washington, 15-16/05), Regional Economic Development (Brussels, 11-12/05). Absence of Syria, Lebanon, and the UN.

Autumn 1992
In the *multilateral framework*, a second series of operational meetings of the working groups is held: Arms Control (Moscow, 15-17/09) where the *Community obtains the status of "contributor";* Water (Washington, 15-16/09); Environment (The Hague, 26-27/10); Regional Economic Development (Paris, 29-30/10); and Refugees (Ottawa, 11-12/11).

2. At the United Nations

16/12/91
In Washington, the UN General Assembly *repeals*, by a large majority, its resolution of 10/11/75 *likening Zionism to "a form of racism* and racial discrimination."

06/01/92
Unanimous UNSC adoption of Resolution 726, which *"firmly condemns"* the Israeli deportation of Palestinians, on the basis of the protection of civilians during a time of war, and makes explicit reference to the Geneva Convention of August 1949. Strictest text ever written with regard to Israel: The six resolutions since 1987 are limited to "regret", the resolution of 13/10/90 only implicates "Israeli security forces".

3. The Community and Its Member States

30/10/91
Creation, at the initiative of the acting Presidency of the Council (NL), of a working group, known as the "Peace Process", which is put in charge of directing Community participation (in the framework of the EPC) in the Conference and helping to define its role. Apart from their contribution to work on the *multilateral* front (see above), the Community and its member states send a troika coming from the EPC "Peace Process" Working Group as an extra to each *bilateral* session in Washington.

26/03 to 03/04/92
Visit of the troika, coming from the special group of coordination in the region. Meeting with all of the principal actors in the peace process in the countries concerned: Egypt (and the Arab League), Occupied Territories, Israel, Jordan (and the PLO), Syria, Lebanon (and, in Beirut, the four Ministers of Foreign Affairs from Syria, Jordan, Lebanon and the PLO).

Annexes V to VIII specify the former positions:

09-10/12/91
The European Council of Maastricht stresses the former positions (*cessation* of the Israeli presence, *end* of the Arab boycott, appeal for a "lasting, global and fair" settlement), reiterates the commitment to *"contribute actively and in a practical manner"* to the multilateral activities, while bearing in mind the central character of the bilateral negotiations whereby the Community intends "to maintain direct contact with all of the participants".

17/02/92
At the Council of Ministers in Lisbon, emphasis placed on the participation of the Community, "as organiser of *all* the working groups," and, beyond, on the participation of all the parties and of the United Nations as well as a "wider participation of Palestinians". Reaffirmation of the central character of the bilateral negotiations, which are the only ones that evidence the position of "a genuine regional cooperation".

26-27/06/92
The European Council of Lisbon implicitly recalls the principal Community positions and, in light of the results of the Israeli elections, reiterates the desire to "play an active and constructive role" in both frameworks (bilateral and multilateral) after having reaffirmed that "Europe ... has an essential role to play in the political and economic *stability* of the region".

26-27/06/92
The European Council, in the report on "The Probable Evolution of the CFSP," identifies the areas where *"common actions"* (art. J.3, Title V of the Maastricht Treaty) are feasible with regard to Maghreb and the Middle East.

7 EC-Turkish Relations: Unfinished Forever?

Heinz Kramer

For obvious reasons it seems appropriate to include EC-Turkish relations in any discussion about the European Community and the Mediterranean. Unquestionably Turkey (also) is a Mediterranean country. The Commission of the EC, too, assigns the operative responsibility for its relations with Turkey to that part of its general directorate for "external relations" (DG I) that deals with "North-South relations and Mediterranean policy, relations with Latin America and Asia" and not to that part which deals with, among other things, "co-operation with other European countries". Without exaggerating the significance of such administrative arrangements, however, it should be obvious that such a way of putting things would not coincide with Turkey's view of the basic character of the relationship. Nor can it be regarded as satisfactory in terms of political analysis.

This does not mean that there is no overlap between the issues of EC-Turkish relations and the Community's Mediterranean policy. And, of course, there are topics common to both areas of the EC's external relations such as, for instance, immigration, "Islam", and problems of political and economic stability. However, without going into the details of the debate about Turkey's "Europeanness", one can generally state that EC-Turkish relations have been conducted in the past outside the Community's Mediterranean affairs and, most likely, will continue to be so. For Turkey, without a doubt, these relations have been part of its "European policy". The public debate in the member states about the issue of an eventual Turkish EC membership also indicates that the issue is widely regarded as an "internal" European affair, although in a somewhat "inverted" sense. Hence, this paper will deal with the issue from that perspective as well, but will not address related aspects of "classical" EC-Mediterranean relations.

190

Unfortunately, public debate in Western Europe about EC-Turkish relations is highly stereotyped, focusing on one or two issues at best and widely neglecting or distorting the historical development of that relationship.[1] By contrast, an attempt will be made to achieve a more comprehensive coverage in this paper. We start by briefly sketching the motives and interests that guided Turkey and the EC in conducting their respective foreign relations, followed by a description of approaches and attitudes that have been brought to the relationship by the Community and its member states. The first part of the general background of the relationship will be complemented by a second part that deals mainly with the basic texts and their implementation over the history of EC-Turkish association to date, culminating in the fate of Ankara's application for membership in the Community. Part III focuses on the major issues in the relationship in light of the debate over Turkish accession to the Community. The final part of the paper considers perspectives for the future of EC-Turkish relations taking into account the fundamental changes that have taken place in Europe over the last three years.

I. The Background: A Relationship with Limited Common Perspectives

Security interests, economic considerations, and foreign policy requirements resulting from past agreements have collectively formed the

---

[1] This remark may be illustrated, for example, by the fact that one can read in a recent publication of the Royal Institute of International Affairs that "(i)n 1996, Turkey's association agreement with the Community will come to an end." See Anna Michalski and Helen Wallace, *The European Community: The Challenge of Enlargement*, European Programme Special Paper (London: Royal Institute for International Affairs, 1992), p. 50. Here, the authors are most likely confusing the end of the "transition period" for the establishment of a customs union between the EC and Turkey as stipulated in the Additional Protocol to the Association Agreement with the end of the agreement itself, which legally will be concluded at an unspecified date in the future.

191

basis for the relationship between the EC and Turkey over the last three decades. While it has never been entirely clear how intensive the Western Europeans wanted the alliance to be, Turkey has always demonstrated its interest in maintaining as close a relationship as possible. In this way, the process of "Westernisation", which was launched in the last century and later enforced by Atatürk after the founding of the Turkish Republic, should finally be brought to a successful conclusion. By contrast, the members of the EC seemed increasingly prepared to invest only the minimum amount of mutuality and "closeness" in the relationship as was regarded absolutely essential to ensure their interests. They seemed to harbour reservations about taking any steps in the direction of a lasting and irreversible integration of Turkey into the EC.

EC-Turkish relations, and especially implementation of the Association Agreement, which the EC and Turkey entered into in 1964 in order to institutionalise their relationship, has always suffered from this discrepancy in the respective aspirations of the partners. Turkey often attempted to go beyond the day-to-day business and to bring its more basic goals and interests into play in order to more fully benefit from the Community. Each time, however, this strategy led to political problems, because the Community was not ready to give Turkey all that it wanted. Finally Turkey's disappointment at what it perceived as insufficient political acknowledgment by the EC of the goals of the partnership led the government in Ankara to change its strategy. The association was no longer considered workable, and instead the Turks set their sights on EC membership as the means of realising their ambitions.

1. Motives and Interests

Hence, a close look at the motives and interests of both sides regarding their relationship seems appropriate in order to obtain a better understanding of the past and the present situation and its problems.[2]

On the Turkish Side

Relations with the European Community were seen by a majority of the political and business elites in Turkey in a context which goes far beyond foreign-policy considerations. They perceived the existence and identity of the Turkish nation as being directly affected by these relations. For them, it was a matter of Turkey being recognised as a member of the West and as a European state. EC membership, in their view, was synonymous with the definitive acknowledgement that Turkey met contemporary standards of Western civilisation. Simultaneously, the ultimate success of the Kemalist "revolution" would thereby be confirmed.[3]

This attitude continues to dominate the approach of a considerable part of the Turkish elite with regard to the question of EC membership. It has, however, come under attack more recently by those who argue that, given the past experience of EC-Turkish relations, the Community will never accept Turkey as a member, and that, furthermore, under the new

---

[2] This issue is dealt with in greater detail in an earlier publication by the author; see Heinz Kramer, *Die Europäische Gemeinschaft und die Türkei. Entwicklung, Probleme und Perspektiven einer schwierigen Partnerschaft*, Internationale Politik und Sicherheit, Vol. 21 (Baden-Baden: Nomos Verlagsgesellschaft, 1988), especially pp. 13-28.

[3] For a general survey of the Western orientation of Turkish foreign policy, see Oral Sander, "Turkish Foreign Policy: Forces of Continuity and Change", in Ahmet Evin (ed.), *Modern Turkey: Continuity and Change* (Opladen: Leske Verlag, 1984), pp. 115-130. The "Kemalist" origins of this orientation are especially dealt with by Mehmet Gönlübol, "Atatürk's Foreign Policy: Goals and Principles", in Turhan Feyzioglu (ed.), *Atatürk's Way* (Istanbul: Otomarsan, 1982), pp. 255-302 (including numerous direct quotations from Mustafa Kemal's works). A contemporary version of Turkey's *vocation européenne* can be found in Turgut Özal, *La Turquie en Europe* (Paris: Plon, 1988); this book, which obviously was not written by the then Turkish Prime Minister, can be best understood as a pleading for overcoming West European doubts about Turkey's "Europeanness".

international constellation after the end of the East/West conflict, a wide range of alternative orientations is offered to Turkey which are equally apt for fulfilling the country's historical mission and political aspirations. The *vocation européenne*, nevertheless, remains at the top of Turkey's hierarchy of interests concerning the establishment of the closest bond possible with Western Europe.

Next to this, there are other important political motivations. One concerns the political rivalry with Greece. In view of the deep conflicts between the riparian states of the Aegean Sea reaching far back into history, Turkey takes particular care to see that it enjoys the same status as Greece does in its relations with third countries. Thus, after the Greek application for association with the EEC in 1959, the Turkish application was to some extent, a "logical" consequence.[4]

An important and, as can be realised today, consequential departure from this standard conduct of Turkish foreign policy was the quiet toleration of the Greek application for membership of the EC in 1975. Turkey reacted to this attempt by its rival to develop closer ties with Western Europe only after 1976, and in a completely unexpected manner, by embarking on a policy of clear dissociation from Europe that culminated, in 1978, in a move for a five-year "moratorium" of the association regime.[5] The lasting negative consequences of this temporary change in its standard foreign policy are felt by Ankara today, as Greece uses its position as a member of the Community in a manner that keeps Turkey apart from Western Europe, without the other members of the EC really

---

[4] See Mehmet Ali Birand, "Turkey and the European Community", *The World Today*, Vol. 34, No. 2, 1978, pp. 52-61 and Tozun Bahceli, "Turkey and the EEC: The Strains of Association", *Revue d'intégration européenne/Journal of European Integration*, Vol. 3, No. 2, 1980, pp. 220-237.

[5] A very good description and analysis of this special period of Turkey's EC policy and its domestic political background can be found in Erol Esen, *Die Beziehungen zwischen der Türkei und der Europäischen Gemeinschaft unter besonderer Berücksichtigung der innertürkischen Kontroversen um die Assoziation, 1973-1980* (Pfaffenweiler: Centaurus Verlagsgesellschaft, 1990), especially pp. 132-166 and 213-236.

being able to effectively prevent Greece from doing so.

Another motive consisted of Turkey's security interests, which constituted its chief reason for accepting the offer of the "Truman Doctrine" after the Second World War. As a consequence, Turkey became incorporated into the Western security system.[6] This move led, as a consequence of developing East/West antagonism and the superpower rivalry, to its integration into the Western economic system as well. Turkey's development was dependent on these ties, which initially were concentrated exclusively on the United States.

As Turkey's disappointment with the United States grew -- above all in response to the American position during the different stages of the Cyprus crisis ("Johnson letter" of 1964, arms embargo after 1975) and its neglect of Turkish security interests in the course of the détente process in the late 1960s and early 1970s -- Turkey turned more toward Western Europe. It began to see itself more clearly as a member of the European component of NATO and, at the same time, looked for compensation for the reduced aid from the US.

In addition to these political motives one may add a number of Turkish economic interests which played a certain role in the relations with Western Europe. Primarily, it has been a question of safeguarding trade relations. The EC is the major export market for the agricultural and industrial products of the country. Additionally, investment capital from Western Europe has been necessary for the Turkish economic development and modernisation. The possibility of free movement of Turkish workers in the EC, which has in principle been established in the Association Agreement, is seen by Turkey as an important instrument for

---

[6] For details, see Bruce R. Kuniholm, *The Origins of the Cold War in the Near East. Great Power Conflict and Diplomacy in Iran, Turkey and Greece* (Princeton: Princeton University Press, 1980); for a Turkish view, see also Metin Tamkoç, "The Impact of the Truman Doctrine on the National Security Interests of Turkey", *Dis Politika/Foreign Policy*, Vol. 6, Nos. 3-4, 1977, pp. 18-40 and Yulug Tekin Kurat, "Turkey's Entry to the North Atlantic Treaty Organization", *Dis Politika/Foreign Policy*, Vol. 10, Nos. 3-4, 1983, pp. 50-77.

relieving the pressure off its own labour market which suffers under structural unemployment. As a by-product, labour-force migration would also secure a certain inflow of foreign exchange in the form of guest-worker remittances.

What is more important under the present circumstances, however, is guaranteeing a constant and high flow of direct foreign investment from Western European firms. This would compensate for the still insufficient national rate of savings, and it would assist in obtaining modern know-how and technology that Turkey needs for the continued modernisation of its economy. In contrast to the early period of association relations, the financial aid granted by the EC in the framework of the association's financial protocols is no longer of special significance. Due to the development of a negative political climate between the Community and Turkey, however, its political significance has grown completely out of proportion.

On the Community Side

From the Community's perspective, security and military interests prevail in its relations with Turkey. The country has been seen as the "southern pillar of NATO", and its ties with the Western system were, for the sake of ensuring Western European security, were not considered renounceable.[7] Thereby was not only its function as a "barrier" against a Soviet advance to the South emphasised, but also its function as a "bridge" between Europe and crisis areas in the Near and Middle East.

After the end of the East/West conflict and the associated breakdown of communism and the Soviet Union, the importance of Turkey's "classical" security policy role in the Western context diminished tremendously. But it has been restored almost overnight. Today, the country is seen by its

---

[7] See, for example, Albert Wohlstetter, "Die Türkei und die Sicherung der Interessen der NATO", *Europa-Archiv*, Vol. 40, No. 16, 1985, pp. 507-514 and Maurizio Cremasco, "The Strategic Relevance of Turkey-EC Relations", *The International Spectator*, Vol. 18, Nos. 1-2, 1983, pp. 47-61.

Western allies in Europe and the US in a new strategic position. This new position is characterised by a two- or threefold function which Turkey is expected to fulfil in the context of the "new world order". First, it has to continue its role as a very important strategic ally with regard to Western political interests in the Middle East after the Gulf war. Second, and perhaps more important, it has to function as a secular "model" for the newly emerging republics of Central Asia in order to prevent them from adopting the fundamentalist Islamic system. A third issue, which sometimes is considered to be of strategic importance as well, concerns Turkey's role in the process of re-ordering the Balkans. Turkey, on the other hand, continues to show a strong interest in close military and security relations with the West in view of its unstable and violence-prone regional environment.[8]

The Community's economic interest in its relations with Turkey are clearly of less importance than its security-policy considerations. The country is not ranked among the EC's top economic partners either in trade or direct foreign investment. Yet, even at this relatively modest level, the EC members were able to achieve a leading position in the Turkish market. The position of the West Europeans is additionally strengthened by the fact that the EC continues to be the most important market for Turkish products in the OECD area. Hence, Turkey is already deeply integrated into the Community's economy, and the existing net of tight reciprocal economic ties forms a substantial basis for future economic development. Turkey has no reasonable alternative in the near future to these relatively narrow economic relations with Western Europe.

---

[8] See Heinz Kramer, "Die sicherheitspolitische Rolle der Türkei nach dem Ende des Ost-West-Konflikts: Ein Anker Out-of-Area?", in Wolfgang Heydrich, et al. (eds.), *Sicherheitspolitik Deutschlands: Neue Konstellationen, Risiken, Instrumente*, Internationale Politik und Sicherheit, Vol. 32, (Baden-Baden: Nomos Verlagsgesellschaft, 1992), pp. 415-438. For similar arguments, see also Lothar Rühl, "Die Türkei zwischen Europa und dem Orient", *Europa-Archiv*, Vol. 47, No. 11, 10 June 1992, pp. 295-302 and Graham Fuller, "Turkey in the New International Security Environment", in F. Stephen Larrabee (ed.), *The Fragile Powderkeg: Balkan Security After the Cold War* (forthcoming); for a reflection of this new strategic position in the more popular media, see also "Across the Great Divide", *Time*, 19 October 1992, pp. 29-33.

This brief glance at the constellation of interests which underlies the relations between Western Europe and Turkey shows an asymmetrical pattern. Only in the sphere of security policy have there been (and seem to continue to be) parallel, and in part, identical interests on both sides. However, Turkish dependency on the economic and financial relations with the West is met by a much smaller dependency on the part of EC members. The same is true for Turkey's fundamental political interest in a strong orientation towards Western Europe. This, as well, finds hardly any parallels among the countries of the Community or in Brussels.

2. Approaches and Attitudes

It can, therefore, be of no surprise to anyone that the attitudes and approaches of the Community and its member states reflect this situation in their respective relations with Turkey.

The Community

The Community's consistently reluctant reaction to the Turkish demands was a result of both the overall internal situation in the EC and specific concerns of various member states concerning the possible consequences of a Turkish accession and/or the domestic situation in Turkey. Since the early 1970s, the EC has experienced a series of consecutive enlargements, bringing the number of EC members between 1972 and 1986 from six to twelve, accompanied by a general loss of momentum toward integration since the second half of the 1970s. This, in the opinion of the Commission, did not constitute an appropriate environment in which to substantially upgrade Turkey's status in the Community much less to consider Turkish accession. The main arguments of the Commission, in this respect, have been summarised in its "opinion" of December 1989 concerning the Turkish application.[9]

The Member States

This attitude on the question of EC-Turkish relations was backed by the individual member states and was reflected in the general character of their respective bilateral relations with Turkey. Most of the EC members do not have special foreign-policy interests with regard to Turkey and view their bilateral relations primarily in terms of security considerations complemented by general aspects of foreign trade.

The United Kingdom, in principle, advocates close and good relations between the EC and Turkey short of membership. Since the rise to power of the Conservative Party, the British government has generally abstained from harshly criticising Turkish political developments even under the system of military rule between 1980 and 1983. The firm Turkish commitment to NATO and Özal's liberal market-oriented economic policy always counted more than allegations of human-rights violations. The Cyprus question, in addition, constitutes a special link between London and Ankara as both countries are guarantors to the status of the Republic of Cyprus as laid down in the treaties of 1960. This fact accounts for an historical moderation in Britain's policy vis-à-vis Turkey. All of these factors, however, failed to induce London to dissociate itself from the general political line of the Twelve as expressed in the respective declarations which were issued in the context of EPC.[10] Nevertheless, there prevailed a generally hopeful expectation in Turkey with regard to special pro-Turkish activities of British

---

[9] See Commission of the European Communities, *Commission Opinion on Turkey's Request for Accession to the Community*, Brussels, 20 December 1989 [SEC (89) 2290 fin./2](plus Annex).

[10] This generally moderate attitude of the British Conservatives towards Turkey was also displayed in the behaviour of conservative MEPs and members of the Parliamentary Assembly of the Council of Europe. During the recurrent debates on Turkish issues in these parliamentary bodies, conservative representatives generally took a distinctly more pro-Turkish position than the rest of the Assembly.

presidencies in the institutions of the Twelve.

The Italian government has displayed a similar behaviour. It fully subscribed to the EPC declarations but showed a fairly noncommittal attitude in bilateral relations concerning "critical" issues of Turkish politics. This position seemed to be influenced by the Italian economic interests in its relations with Turkey; the country traditionally ranks second in the hierarchy of EC-Turkish trade relations and has no interest in losing this privileged position. This has not, however, prevented the government in Rome from taking a critical position with regard to Turkey's recurring demands for improvement of the association's regulations in the field of agricultural products. This coincides with Italy's scepticism toward a Turkish accession to the Community due to the expectation that Ankara would become a competitor both in the agricultural sector and as a recipient of subsidies from the Community's structural funds. On the other hand, Italy would welcome another Mediterranean member of the EC in order to balance the influence of the more industrialised "North" in Community affairs.

France has displayed a somewhat different attitude in its relations with Turkey. The French government began to show a more critical attitude toward the domestic political events after the 1980 coup. Hence, in 1982, it joined the Scandinavian countries in their case against Turkey before the European Commission of Human Rights, thus, together with Denmark and the Netherlands being the only EC member states to take this step. It is widely believed among the Turkish political elite that this attitude results mainly from an important Armenian influence in the French polity together with a general pro-Greek French attitude, which found its most prominent expression in the hasty and unconditional support for Greece's EC membership application in the late 1970s. All this adds up to a markedly reserved Turkish attitude toward France which seems to be reciprocated by Paris. It does not come as a surprise, then, that Paris never has been an advocate of Turkish EC membership. Over the last few years, however, the political climate between Paris and Ankara seems to have warmed up due to rising French interests in Turkey's economic potential.

Among the "smaller" EC members, Denmark and the Netherlands continually have shown a critical attitude with regard to domestic political developments in Turkey. Both countries have voiced their deep concern about the military coup of 1980 and, after restoration of civilian government, continued to criticise human-rights violations and insufficient democratic institutions in Turkey's domestic political setup. These reservations have diminished in more recent years and today, especially with the present Dutch government, security arguments seem to dominate, leading to a more moderate attitude toward Turkey. Both countries, however, continue to follow the official line of the Community with regard to Turkish accession.

The other Benelux countries, as well as Ireland, and Portugal do not show any significant characteristics in their bilateral relations with Turkey or with regard to EC-Turkey relations. One can, however, fairly plausibly assume that particularly the less industrialised members of the Community, including Spain, do not look very favourably upon the prospect of another semi-developed country entering the EC. Hence, all of them tend to advocate an improvement in relations between the Twelve and Ankara short of membership because this would leave to them full control over Community concessions toward Turkey in the fields of sensitive industries and agriculture. Furthermore, there also would be no new competitor for structural-funds money.[11]

The bilateral relations with the most important impact on the overall relationship continue to be those between Turkey and, respectively, Germany and Greece. As Turkish-Greek relations are directly part of the whole story, they will be dealt with in a later section.

German-Turkish relations, in any respect, are outstanding among the

---

[11] This attitude not only holds true with respect to an eventual Turkish accession to the Community, but is also underlying those countries' line of reasoning regarding the prospects of an EC enlargement in general.

respective bilateral relations between the Twelve and Turkey.[12] This is indicated by the special historical foundation of German-Turkish relations as expressed by the terms of "traditional German-Turkish friendship" and German-Turkish *Waffenbrüderschaft*, which are regularly evoked in official assessments of the bilateral relationship. It is also indicated by the markedly leading position of Germany among the EC trading partners of Turkey and among the foreign investors from the Community. Furthermore, Germany is the only European country which, in the framework of NATO, has provided a considerable amount of military aid to Turkey on a regular basis. The special German position in Turkish society is underlined by the fact that the largest number of Turkish citizens living outside Turkey resides there.

This background to the bilateral relationship creates a special situation which can be described as a mix of myths, complex interdependence, exaggerated expectations, and an excessive use of "double talk" on the level of official gatherings and public media. Furthermore, Turkey and Turks tend to assign to Germany and Germans a special responsibility with regard to Turkish-EC relations thus adding another dimension to an already complicated bilateral situation.

What is hardly realised in Turkey and seldom clearly expressed by the Germans, is the fundamental asymmetry in their bilateral relations. Not only do the Turks seem to invest much more emotion in that the relationship than do Germans, but the objective importance of the bilateral relations is much greater for the Turkish side than vice versa. In almost every respect, Germany constitutes for Turkey one of its most important foreign partners whereas Turkey's ranking in Germany's respective foreign policy hierarchy is much lower.

It is this broad and complex background of German-Turkish bilateral

---

[12] It is interesting to note that despite this fact we do not have, up to now, a comprehensive account and analysis of this bilateral relationship. The years until the early 1960s are covered by Gülüzar Gürbey, *Die Türkei-Politik der Bundesrepublik Deutschland unter Konrad Adenauer (1949-1963)* (Pfaffenweiler: Centaurus-Verlagsgesellschaft, 1990).

relations which one has to keep in mind when looking upon Germany's position in EC-Turkey relations. Here, Bonn has always favoured close ties between the Community and Ankara but also has been very reluctant to expand these ties to include Turkish membership. The main reason behind this German position has been fear of a large and uncontrollable influx of migrant workers from Anatolia which would add to the 1.75 million Turks already living in Germany. For this reason, the German government also has successfully tried to prevent the regulations of the Association Treaty concerning free movement of labour from becoming fully operational in 1986. Added to this is a general feeling in leading German political circles that an eventual Turkish membership in the Community might be a costly affair of which Germany would have to bear the major part in terms of financial contributions. Finally, the German government did not see the Community as being sufficiently strong in terms of its institutional and economic integration to be ready to incorporate such a large country as Turkey.

Hence, Bonn over the years has done nothing to speed up Turkish accession even though Germany, in general, favoured a revival of the association relationship and its continuous development in the direction of customs union and fully established political dialogue. This generally positive attitude of German governments in Turkish eyes, however, has been overshadowed by Bonn's unwillingness to live up to Turkey's particular expectations concerning Germany's role in Turkey's relations with the EC.

3. Membership -- A Fading Aim

Given these general attitudes of the EC member states toward Turkey's accession, it seems to be only "natural" that after the acceptance of the Commission's "opinion" by the Council of Ministers in February 1990, West Europeans almost completely stopped talking about Turkish membership in the Community. This trend was accentuated by the events of 1989-90 in Eastern Europe and the consequential break-up of the Soviet Union in 1991. Since then, the Community's foreign policy is preoccupied by attempts to assist in the establishment of democracy and a market economy in the former Communist countries of Europe. This has led to a fundamental shift in the foreign-policy focus of Western Europe.

As a consequence, when the issue of EC enlargement regained political prominence by entry bids of EFTA member states and similar aspirations of East and Central European states, the public discussion of the issue almost completely neglected Turkey (and other countries which had already put forward applications as well). For the majority of Europeans it seems clear that Turkey will have to wait until after an eventual accession of some former communist countries of Eastern and Central Europe.[13]

This is also substantiated by the fact that the actual debate about reviving EC-Turkish relations which also was at the centre of the most recent meeting of the Association Council on 9 November 1992 in Brussels, does not touch upon the issue of membership. What was debated, rather, were problems of optimising a "second-best approach" which leaves open the issue of accession by concentrating on hammering out a sort of "special relationship" between the EC and Turkey. Thus, Turkey will be put into a prominent position outside the Community, taking into account its newly regained strategic importance for the West. It is unclear, however, if this will finally prove to be an improved stepping-stone for accession or will lead to a definite "singularisation" of the country at the periphery of the Community.[14]

II. The Background: Texts and Reality

What is sometimes striking is the amount of neglect that is given to the

---

[13] See, for example, Hans Arnold, "Die Europäische Gemeinschaft zwischen Vertiefung und Erweiterung", *Europa-Archiv*, Vol. 46, No. 10, 25 May 1991; see also CEPR, *Is Bigger Better? A CEPR Annual Report* (London: CEPR, September 1992).

[14] A good example of this ambiguous approach is Lothar Rühl, *op. cit.*

legal bases of the existing relationship and its problematic implementation over the last two and a half decades. Hence, a short review may be appropriate in order to restore historical consciousness.

1. The Association Agreement of 1964 and Its Implementation

The Association Agreement, which came into effect on the first of December 1964 after long negotiations,[15] provides that after a "preparatory period" lasting at least five years, a customs union for industrial products between the EC and Turkey should next be created during a "transitional period". As is stipulated in the Additional Protocol to the Agreement, which came into effect in 1973,[16] that should be the case for the majority of goods until 1985 and for the rest until the end of 1995. The "transitional period" is followed by the "final period" of the association, which is based on the customs union and should lead to a stronger coordination of the economic policies of both sides. The duration of the "final period" is indeterminate. The EC, in Article 28 of the Agreement, concedes the possibility of a later Turkish entry into the Community, if and when the country is in the position to entirely take over the resulting obligations.

There is, thus, no automatic Turkish entry into the EC in the framework of the Association Agreement. On the other hand, in 1963 the Community had already made clear, through its concession of the option to enter, that Turkey is viewed politically by the West Europeans as being a "European country". This follows from a clause in Article 237 of the EEC Treaty which allows entry only for European countries. Hence, one could fairly reasonably conclude that both sides, Turkey and the Community, are of the opinion that their relationship should not stop at the level of an open-ended customs union but should eventually

---

[15] For the text of the agreement, see *Official Journal of the European Communities*, L 217, 29 December 1964.

[16] For the text of the Additional Protocol, see *Official Journal of the European Communities*, L 293, 29 December 1972.

culminate in Turkey's accession to the EC. Therefore, Turkey believes that it has a certain privileged role in the EC's worldwide net of contractual relations with third countries that emerged mainly in the 1970s. This was repeatedly emphasised in Turkish circles, especially with a view to other Mediterranean countries with which the EC had concluded extensive Cooperation Agreements.[17]

The establishment of the customs union, however, could not be finalised in the scheduled time period, because Turkey was not in the position to keep its obligations in the stepwise reduction of its customs duties vis-à-vis the EC countries, nor in the adoption of the common external tariff of the Community vis-à-vis third countries. A negligible reduction of custom duties for products of the EC was effected only in 1973 and 1976, the adjustment to the EC external tariff was not begun at all, and the reduction of quantitative restrictions on imports from the EC was also stopped in 1976. It was only in January 1988 that Turkey started again to fulfil is obligations with respect to reduction of custom duties with the aim to meet the 1996 deadline in a comprehensive manner.

Thus, since the late 1970s the customs union had mainly been a "one-way street", because the Community had already almost completely opened its market for the import of Turkish industrial goods in 1973. Those exceptions which survived were later eliminated. Only with regard to textile and clothing products did the EC, in the context of the worldwide regulated restrictive trade policies on textile goods since the end of the 1970s, also initiate market-access restrictions vis-à-vis Turkey. They were transferred, in 1987, into an orderly marketing agreement which has been regularly re-negotiated since then. These measures, however, ran up against severe Turkish criticism from the start.[18]

---

[17] See, for an example of the time, Yildirim Keskin, "The Turkey-EC Association and its Problems", in Werner Gumpel (ed.), *Die Türkei auf dem Weg in die EG* (München/Wien: R. Oldenbourg Verlag, 1979), pp. 65-72.

[18] For more details of the "textile dispute", see Heinz Kramer, *Die Europäische Gemeinschaft und die Türkei, op. cit.*, pp. 112-120.

This criticism was also directed at the EC's restraint in opening its markets to Turkish agricultural exports which, at the beginning of the 1970s, still made up the main part of the Turkish export trade. In the meantime, since January 1987, the Community has also abolished custom duties on agricultural produce from Turkey, with only a few exceptions. The Community has, however, adhered to the principle of "Community preference" in agricultural policy and is making full use of its effective system of non-tariff trade barriers vis-à-vis Turkey. The abolition of custom duties can, therefore, hardly contribute to the growth of Turkish agricultural exports. Hence, Turkey is only technically in a better position than other third countries, without being able to really benefit from this advantage. Nevertheless, one can establish that the Community did grant Turkey extensive advantages in the domain of trade, without having received those Turkish returns which were contractually agreed upon.

A special issue of Community criticism regarding the establishment of customs union over the recent years has been the so-called "fund levies" on imports which Turkey introduced in the early 1980s in order to raise money for various extra-budgetary funds. These funds have been established mainly in order to finance large-scale infrastructure projects, state-subsidised housing projects, and the establishment of Turkey's national defence industry. The EC regards these "fund levies" as contravening the stipulations of the Association Agreement which forbid the invention of NTBs (non-tariff barriers) as a replacement for lowered or abolished custom duties.

The recurring and sometimes substantial surplus which the Community, nevertheless, was able to record in its trade balance with Turkey, emphasised the huge difference in the state of economic development between the partners. This also constituted the main reason for the insufficient use Turkey could make of the preferential treatment it had been granted. Only after the 1980 economic reform in Turkey had ripened the fruits of the previous import-substituting industrialisation policy did the situation somewhat improve. Turkey's trade deficit declined and the composition of its exports changed in favour of manufactured goods. The dominant position of only some industrial products (textiles and clothing) among the country's export goods to the EC shows, however, that the Turkish state of development is still too limited to allow Turkey to be able to take full advantage of the preferential trade treatment granted by the EC. In this respect, there are, consequently, doubts as to whether the association's concept of rapidly promoting Turkish development through the implementation of the customs union would have been effective at all.

This situation was also partly foreseen at the time of the conclusion of the agreement. The EC had, therefore, granted Turkey considerable financial aid, which was intended to contribute to covering the foreign-exchange demands resulting from the balance-of-trade deficits. In the course of three consecutive Financial Protocols, each one lasting over a period of five years, the Community, until 1980, granted Turkey loans totalling 705 million European Units of Account (EUA).[19] They were predominantly given on very favourable conditions (30-year term, 10 and 8 free years respectively, and a maximum interest rate of 4.5%). Only 115 million EUA were provided under conventional market conditions. The loans were issued mainly for the development of the infrastructure of firms in the paper, chemicals and metal-working industries. A disadvantage of the allocation of funds was the almost total neglect of projects in the backward regions in the east and southeast of Turkey.

In addition to these sums, Turkey received from the West European states, especially the EC members, since the end of the 1950s, in the framework of the OECD consortium and on bilateral terms, additional considerable sums as balance-of-payments aid and development aid.[20] Taken altogether, Turkey without doubt occupies a prime position among the recipients of West European aid.

---

[19] The EUA was used to establish the annual EC budget. In this sense, it was something like a forerunner to the ECU, but it had a much stronger link to the dollar.

[20] For more details, see Heinz Kramer, *Das wirtschaftliche Element in den Beziehungen der EG zur Türkei -- eine Bestandsaufnahme*, Ebenhausen: SWP, 1987 (unpublished manuscript).

Since 1980, however, Turkey has every reason to complain about the EC's failure to continue with its financial assistance. In that year, the fourth Financial Protocol was concluded. It provided for EC aid of 600 million ECU, from which more than one-half again should be on with very favourable conditions. However, because of the September 1980 military intervention and the subsequent suspension of basic democratic freedoms, the Commission stopped the ratification process of the protocol. Since that date, the Council of Ministers has not been able to pass the protocol due to a repeated Greek veto; since the beginning of the process of democratic normalisation through the parliamentary elections in November 1983, however, the fundamental grounds for delaying ratification have been removed. The fourth Financial Protocol, in a certain sense, has become a political symbol of all problems burdening EC-Turkey relations over the past decade.

The Turkish public suspects that this European behaviour was stimulated by deeply-entrenched anti-Turkish sentiments, which aimed at jeopardising the long-sought membership. This uneasiness was additionally fed by the position of the EC and its member states concerning the question of free movement of Turkish workers. In Article 12 of the Ankara Agreement, it is stipulated: "The contracting Parties agree to be guided by Articles 48, 49 and 50 of the Treaty establishing the Community for the purpose of progressively securing freedom of movement for workers between them." In the 1970 Additional Protocol, it was established that this should happen, "between the end of the twelfth and the end of the twenty-second year after the entry into force of that Agreement" (the Association Agreement). Accordingly, freedom of movement was to be brought about between 1 December 1976 and 1 December 1986.

With the beginning of the year 1973, however, the German government issued a ban on the recruitment of guest workers from non-EC countries, and the other member states soon followed suit. Since then, immigration into the EC, in principle, is possible for Turks only when members of the family join a worker who is already legally settled in a member country. The German government, with the silent agreement of all its EC partners, did its utmost to prevent the terms of the Association Agreement from taking unlimited effect. As a consequence, up to the present, "free movement" resulted only in a marginal improvement of the situation of those Turkish workers and their families who were already living in the EC.

In November 1986, the Community proposed to the Turks a final solution of the freedom-of-movement question, in which the immigration of new workers would be virtually suspended for the duration of the association. For this proposal it followed Bonn's opinion that on the grounds of the wording of Article 12 of the Association Agreement a difference between the EC-freedom of movement and the association-based freedom of movement was possible.[21]

Taking into account the unfavourable developments in the realm of trade relations, financial aid, and free movement of labour, the Turkish leadership by the mid-1980s increasingly came to the conclusion that sticking to the Association Agreement no longer had promise for the future of EC-Turkey relations. Added to this was a growing feeling of being unfairly treated by the constant EC complaints about the insufficient state of democracy and human rights in Turkey. The pressure in the Turkish public grew continuously to supersede the association regime with accession to the Community. It was hoped in this way to reach a solution of those problems and secure those advantages that seemed otherwise unsolvable or unreachable.

2. The Turkish Application for Accession and the Community's Reaction

Openly ignoring a growing number of warnings coming from EC capitals not to put forward an application for entry into the Community under the

---

[21] See Kay Hailbronner, "Die Freizügigkeit türkischer Statsangehöriger nach dem Assoziationsabkommen EWG/Türkei", in *Europarecht*, Vol. 19, No. 1, 1984, pp. 54-84 and Hans Krück, "Die Freizügigkeit der Arbeitnehmer nach dem Assoziierungsabkommen EWG/Türkei", in *Europarecht*, Vol. 19, No. 3, 1984, pp. 289-310.

circumstances of the time,[22] the Turkish government of Prime Minister Turgut Özal, on 14 April 1987, presented its letter of application to the Council of Ministers.[23] In the following months, the Turkish government, with the assistance of the country's unified business community and supported by all large parties, undertook a political campaign in order to convince the EC member states of the advantages of Turkey's EC membership. At the same, the Turkish government intensified its efforts to prepare its administration for coping with the task of EC membership. Administrative units dealing with EC relations were established or extended in almost every ministry and governmental agency. Parallel to this, Turkey tried to speed up the process of aligning its legislation with the respective Community law.

But, in Ankara and Istanbul it was deliberately overlooked that the Turkish side to a large extent shared responsibility with the Europeans for the unsatisfactory situation into which the relationship had run. Neither the Turkish government, nor the country's political and business elites, had, at any time, made it clear through their behaviour in the association that they really were conscious of the reciprocal character of the initiated process of integration with Western Europe. In the foreground of their statements and behaviour had stood, at all times, demands on the Community for one-sided advances and aid, in order to overcome Turkey's underdevelopment in the interest of as early as possible an entry into the Community.

In the 1960s and 1970s, an economic policy was pursued which either repressed or explicitly disregarded the needs for adjustment which resulted from the establishment of the customs union for the Turkish economy.[24] Nor did the economic reform which was initiated after

---

[22] See for details Heinz Kramer, *Die Europäische Gemeinschaft und die Türkei, op. cit.*, pp. 120-150.

[23] For the text, see Turgut Özal, *op. cit.*, p. 255.

[24] This is convincingly argued by Turkish scholars as well; see Osman Okyar, "The Turkish Industrialization Strategies, the Plan Model and the EEC", in Osman Okyar and Okan H. Aktan (eds.), *Economic Relations Between Turkey and the EC* (Ankara:

1980 and enforced under Prime Minister Özal, in any way lead to a greater preparedness to keep up with the contractual obligations for the continuous reduction of customs duties. Taken altogether, Turkey had undertaken since 1963 no real political efforts to improve the prerequisites for entry into the Community in the spirit of an integration-orientated and cooperative relationship.

The integration of the country with the Community, in early 1987, had consequently, contrary to the perspective of the contractual agreements and the respective political declarations of both sides, not risen substantially above the level which had already been reached at the time of the conclusion of the 1973 Additional Protocol. In this situation, the Turkish application, naturally, raised a number of delicate problems. The EC did not see itself in a position of flatly rejecting the application. On the other hand, none of the members really was ready to proceed to the stage of opening entry negotiations. They were even opposed to giving Ankara a concrete date at which, in the opinion of the Twelve, such negotiations could be opened in the future. But it was only Greece that openly expressed its opposition to the Turkish move.[25]

It took the Commission over two and a half years to prepare its "opinion" on the Turkish application. When it was finally published on 18 December 1989, the content did not come as a surprise to anybody. The Commission reaffirmed the principle of Turkey's general eligibility for membership of the Community as had already been stated in the Ankara Treaty of 1964. However, Brussels, at the same time, expressed its

---

Hacettepe Institute for Economic and Social Research on Turkey and the Middle East, 1978), pp. 14-43 and Mükerrem Hiç, "The Importance of Turkey's Development Strategy for her Integration into the EEC", in Werner Gumpel (ed.), *op. cit.*, pp. 19-46; for a description of the situation of the 1980s, see Heinz Kramer, *Das wirtschaftliche Element, op. cit.*

[25] The Greek government even seriously looked into the possibility of asking the Community's European Court of Justice to annul the Council's decision to ask the Commission to prepare an "opinion" on the Turkish request for the reason that the decision had not been taken unanimously. Finally, Athens did not pursue that line of action.

doubts "that the adjustment problems which would confront Turkey if it were to accede to the Community could be overcome in the medium term, despite the positive features of the recent developments in Turkey."[26]

This judgement of the Commission was mainly based on considerations concerning the economic development gap between the two sides. In particular, four kinds of difficulties were stressed:

- very major structural disparities, in both agriculture and industry;
- macroeconomic imbalances, which have worsened this year;
- high levels of industrial protectionism; and
- a low level of social protection.

From these difficulties, the Commission concluded: "As long as these disparities continue to exist, there will be reason to fear that Turkey would experience serious difficulties in taking on the obligations resulting from the Community's economic and social policies."[27]

It was more in passing that the Commission also pointed to concerns prevailing among the Twelve about heavy financial and social burdens which the EC might have to shoulder in case of a Turkish membership. In that context, the issues of rising expenditures for structural funds and of labour migration were mentioned. Political problems of an eventual accession were also not dealt with at length. In a fairly short paragraph the issues of democratic deficiencies, human rights and minorities were mentioned together with the Greek-Turkish disputes and the question of Cyprus.[28]

---

[26] Commission of the European Communities, *Commission Opinion*, point 7.

[27] Commission of the European Communities, *Commission Opinion*, *op. cit.*, point 8.1. This argument was substantiated in a lengthy annex to the "opinion"; see Commission of the European Communities, *The Turkish Economy: Structure and Developments*, Brussels, 18 December 1989 [SEC (89) 2290 final, Annex].

[28] See Commission of the European Communities, *Commission Opinion*, *op.cit.*, point 9.

It was very well foreseen by the Commission that its "opinion" would create open disappointment in the Turkish public and would not be met without resistance by the government. Therefore, and, at the same time, taking into account the firm conviction of the great majority of the member states that relations with Turkey should continue in a positive and cooperative manner short of membership, the Commission suggested an approach for the revitalisation of relations. It outlined a package of various measures that "will focus on the following four aspects corresponding to Turkey's aspirations and needs: completion of the customs union, the resumption and intensification of financial cooperation, the promotion of industrial and technological cooperation, and the strengthening of political and cultural links"[29] and which were to be implemented in the framework of the existing Association Agreement.

Although the Turkish government and the public made clear that they did not accept the Commission's arguments for postponing eventual accession negotiations to an unspecified date,[30] they were not able to prevent the EC member states from accepting the Commission's "opinion" at the EC Council's session on 5 February 1990 without major qualifications. This position of the Council, therefore, also implied the Community's strong interest in improving its relations with Turkey on the existing basis. Hence, the Commission was asked to develop detailed suggestions in that regard on the basis of its respective remarks in the "opinion".

---

[29] *Ibid.*, point 13.

[30] A careful reading of the wording of the "opinion" does not substantiate the view that one could sometimes hear in Turkish circles that the Commission only postponed the opening of negotiations with Turkey until 1993. As is stated in point 4 of the "opinion", that date, in late 1989, was regarded by the Commission as the earliest possible date for starting new entry negotiations in general. Hence, this sentence should be understood more as an abstract argument than a firm commitment regarding negotiations with Turkey. What is expressed, in fact, is that at some point after 1993, a reconsideration of the Turkish application with the aim of opening negotiations is not foreclosed.

3. Unsuccessful Attempts at Improving the Relationship

It took the Commission only a few months until 12 June 1990 to fulfil this task. At that date, it presented to the Council what became known as the "Matutes package" after the member of the Commission in charge of relations with Turkey.[31] Following the line it had already indicated in its "opinion", the Commission offered proposals for measures in the four areas it had mentioned in that paper.

With regard to the finalisation of customs union, its proposal included keeping the deadline already agreed upon in the Association Agreement, i.e. end of 1995, with regard to all industrial products including coal, iron and steel. That would mean for Turkey not only catching up with the schedule established in the Additional Protocol but also abolishing by that date all those measures introduced during the 1980s, the consequences of which are equivalent to custom duties, i.e. the system of special levies for the various funds invented by the Özal administration in order to enhance the economic modernisation of the country. The Community mainly would have to end its practice of enforcing "voluntary" export restraints on Turkish exporters of textile and apparel. Furthermore, it was envisaged to seek ways and means for the inclusion of agricultural produce in the customs union although one could assume that this would not be completed by the end of 1995 as has been originally foreseen in the Additional Protocol (Art. 33-35). Another important issue in this respect would be the alignment of respective Turkish law in order to bring down legal barriers in the field of competition law, tax law, etc. which could prevent the effective and full functioning of the customs union.

As regards the intensification of industrial and technological co-operation, the proposals suggested a large menu of possible measures. Fields mentioned included macroeconomic and monetary policy, industrial cooperation, services (especially financial services), transport,

---

[31] Commission of the European Communities, *Commission Communication to the Council concerning relations with Turkey and a proposal for a Council decision about a fourth financial protocol*, Brussels, 12 June 1990 [SEC (90) 1017 final].

telecommunication, energy, environmental questions, science and technology, social affairs, tourism, education, culture, and audio-visual media. In short, one can conclude that the Commission proposed to incorporate all those activities into the relationship that had already been mentioned in the Ankara Agreement but which had been neglected for one reason or another so far. The Commission's proposals also take into account the progress that Turkey has made in these fields since then, especially during the 1980s.

In order to enable the Community to implement the programme of large-scale cooperation, the Commission proposed the conclusion of a fourth Financial Protocol which, after the 1981 forerunner had been exhausted, had been newly initialled on 26 January 1989. Unless a quick conclusion and ratification of that protocol would take place, Turkey would remain the only Mediterranean country with which the Community would be unable to engage in large-scale economic and technical cooperation due to the lack of respective financial means.

Finally the Commission proposed an intensification of the political dialogue which, up to then, was irregularly conducted at ministerial and Political Committee level according to the "troika formula".[32]

This programme, if vigorously and quickly implemented, could have made a substantial positive impact on EC-Turkish relations. Without precluding an eventual later accession, it could have qualitatively upgraded the relations to a level commensurate with the far-reaching ambitions as laid down in the Ankara Agreement. However, the "Matutes package", to the present, could not be implemented. Greece was not ready to lift its veto against any substantial step into the direction of an improvement in EC-Turkish relations unless parallel progress (in the Greek sense) was made in the Cyprus issue. The other EC members have not been able to overcome the Greek resistance nor have they been willing to engage themselves in the difficult business of

---

[32] For details of EC-Turkish relations in the framework of European Political Cooperation, see Wolfgang Wessels and Wolf von Leipzig (eds.), *European Political Cooperation and Turkey* (Bonn: Europa Union Verlag, 1993), forthcoming.

finding ways and means to circumvent the Greek veto. Turkey, on the other hand, for political reasons, was very reluctant to agree with an unbundling of the package. Hence, a real political breakthrough in relaunching the relationship did not take place.

This even holds true under the radically changed international political constellation which today forms the larger framework for EC-Turkish relations. Although the new situation in the Middle East, in Central Asia, and in the Balkans in the eyes of all Community members has largely upgraded the strategic position of Turkey,[33] the Twelve have been kept victim of Greek EC-membership as regards relations with Turkey. This was very clearly shown by the latest attempt to redress the balance that had been undertaken by the British EC presidency during the summer of 1992. Although fairly modest in wording, the British proposal for implementation of the "Matutes package" did not meet with Greek consent.[34]

A similar situation occurred at the last meeting of the Association Council at ministerial level on 9 November 1992. Greek resistance caused by the failure of the latest Cyprus talks under UN auspices in New York, which Greece (and other EC members) attributed largely to Turkish-Cypriot stubbornness, prevented the passing of a joint political declaration by the Association Council. This declaration was intended to announce the establishment of a regular political dialogue between the two sides at the highest level, i.e. head of states and/or governments. The main points of the declaration were, however, included in the statement of the British presidency of the Community during the meeting, and they have been met with agreement in the statement by Turkey's foreign minister. Hence, the envisaged political dialogue, finally, can be

---

[33] This has also been underlined by the European Council of Lisbon (26/27 June 1992) which stated in the context of its declaration on enlargement, that "the Turkish role in the present European political situation is of the greatest importance ..."; see "Conclusions of the Presidency", *Agence Europe*, No. 5760, 28 June 1992, p. 5.

[34] See *Agence Europe* of 4 May 1992 and 20/21 July 1992 for a summary of the British proposal; see also *Briefing* (Ankara), No. 906 (21.09.92), pp. 9-10 for a Turkish view of the issue.

regarded as being established.[35]   The future practice of the dialogue, however, will most probably depend on the interest and according behaviour of the respective Community's acting presidency.   As in the past, one can expect some irregularity regarding the cycle of political dialogue meetings between the EC and Turkey.

The consistent Greek veto policy could, however, not prevent modest attempts at restarting the association relations on the "technical level", especially after the new Turkish coalition government of December 1991 took a somewhat more pragmatic approach towards EC-Turkish relations. The Association Committee, i.e. the operation-orientated body of the association, resumed its regular meetings. It installed groups of experts in order to establish an inventory of possible and necessary "technical" measures for a relaunching of the association and for possible EC-Turkish cooperation outside the association framework.   This inventory was presented to the meeting of the Association Council of 9 November 1992 and approved by the ministers.[36]

If followed by respective operational activity, measures for the completion of the "transitional period" of the association in areas beyond customs union which had been interrupted for almost twenty years, could finally be taken up again. In addition to that, discussion about modest cooperation between the EC and Turkey in fields such as trans-European networks, aid to the Commonwealth of Independent States (CIS), and science and technology in general has started. The most concrete results, so far, have been reached by including Turkey in the so-called "horizontal activities" of the Community's redirected Mediterranean policy.   In this way it is possible to provide at least some funds for Turkish institutions in areas like environmental protection, scientific

[35] See "Association between the European Economic Community and Turkey", The Association Council, Press Release (CEE-TR 120/9), Brussels, 9 November 1992, point 9.

[36] For the text of this report, see the Annex to document CEE-TR 120/9.

cooperation, or urban affairs.[37]

This progress of late at the "technical level" of EC-Turkish relations cannot, however, generate that momentum which is necessary for overcoming the political blockade. The most one should expect will be a smoothening of the climate between the two sides due to an enhanced frequency of official interactions. There can be no doubt, however, that this type of progress is highly vulnerable to any serious complication that may emerge at the more political level of the relationship.

III. The Main Economic and Political Controversies between the EC and Turkey

On this level, it is not only the Greek policy of veto which renders a revitalisation and upgrading of EC-Turkish relations difficult. There exist other issues which, in the past, have created considerable problems for a smooth conduct of relations and which, to a large extent, seem to continue to do so. All of them also have played a role with respect to formulating the Community's position regarding Turkey's application for membership. Hence, they deserve a closer look as being recurrent political features of EC-Turkish relations.

These issues mainly concern the question of Turkey's level of economic development and its perspectives for bridging the gap with the Community. Additional issues include the state of democratic development in Turkey with a special emphasis on questions of human rights and treatment of the Kurdish minority. A very delicate question concerns Turkey's "cultural" affinity to Western Europe. The problem sometimes is posed in terms of the country's "Europeanness" or, more bluntly, characterised as a religious-based European Christian prejudice against Muslim Turkey. In political terms, however, as has already been

---

[37] For details on this development, especially for the political compromise necessary to overcome Greek reservations about Turkey's inclusion in the "horizontal activities", see *Agence Europe,* 27 June 1992, p. 7 and 30 June 1992, p. 11

indicated, the "Greek factor" is of primordial importance for EC-Turkish relations.

1. The Issue of Economic "Fitness"

In the aftermath of the Turkish application for membership, the issue of the country's economic "fitness" in terms of its ability to shoulder the economic consequences of such a step has been widely debated. This debate cannot even be summarised here.[38] It has, however, calmed down to a considerable extent after the publication of the Commission's "opinion" although its underlying economic analysis was objected to by Turkish specialists.[39] However, as the issue of an eventual Turkish accession cannot be regarded as settled, the question of Turkey's preparedness in economic terms will continue to play a role. In our paper, it will only be tackled in a very general manner.

There can be no doubt that over the last decade the Turkish economy, in many respects, has succeeded in bridging the gap with the Community. The policy changes introduced in the early 1980s under the aegis of Turgut Özal have resulted in another huge step of modernisation of the

---

[38] See, for instance, Heinz Kramer, *Die Europäische Gemeinschaft und die Türkei*, *op. cit.*, pp. 172-264; IKV (ed.), *The Competition Capacity of Turkish Agriculture and Industry within the European Economic Community* (Istanbul: IKV, 1986); SIAR (ed.), *Prospects for Turkey's Accession to the Community* (Istanbul: SIAR, 1987); and State Planning Organization (SPO), *Turkish Agriculture and European Community Policies, Issues, Strategies and Institutional Adaptation. A Report* (Ankara: SPO, December 1990).

[39] See Harun Gümrükcü, "Die Stellungnahme der EG-Kommission zum Antrag der Türkei auf Beitritt zur Gemeinschaft. Eine kritische Darstellung", *Nord-Süd aktuell*, Vol. 4, No. 2, 1990, pp. 243-250. Another attempt at correcting the view of the Commission's economic conclusions can be seen in a publication which exclusively concentrates on what the authors think to be advantages for the EC deriving from Turkish accession; see Zentrum für Türkeistudien (ed.), *Türkei und Europäische Gemeinschaft. Eine Untersuchung zu positiven Aspekten eines potentiellen EG-Beitritts der Türkei zur Europäischen Gemeinschaft*, Studien und Arbeiten des Zentrums für Türkeistudien Band 10 (Opladen: Leske+Budrich, 1992).

economic infrastructure, the production structure and the financial sector of the country's economy. This has been achieved by a consequent policy of outward orientation[40] combined with large state-funded infrastructure projects, especially in the communications sector. In consequence, Turkey during the 1980s, on average, experienced the highest growth rate of all European economies.

This, however, did not lead to a considerable reduction of the gap with the Community with regard to per capita income.[41] This mainly is a consequence of Turkey's still high population-growth rate. Another important qualification which has to be made concerning the impressive overall growth record of the country, is its relatively low figure as regards the average annual growth of gross fixed-capital formation. This is an indication of the fact that the development of the productive basis of Turkey has relatively lagged behind other sectors of the economy.[42]

On the other hand, such general remarks based on overall averages actually do not say very much about likely consequences and developments on e.g. sectoral level. Such developments, however, are more relevant in evaluating the consequences of stronger economic integration in more political terms. Generally speaking, one could assume less problems if the strong and the modernising sectors of the Turkish economy would be "winners". Unfortunately, we do not know very much about this aspect of the issue although some Turkish studies which mainly have been undertaken by the government's State Planning Organisation, have come to a fairly optimistic outlook.

---

[40] For a comprehensive account of this policy, see Anne O. Krueger and Okan H. Aktan, *Swimming against the Tide. Turkish Trade Reform in the 1980s* (San Francisco, CA: ICS Press, 1992).

[41] This is also true if one uses Purchasing Power Parities for the measurement of GDP per capita, although the discrepancy is somewhat reduced in absolute terms.

[42] For details on this and other economic factors mentioned, see the regularly published OECD *Economic Surveys* on Turkey; the most recent covers the years 1991-92.

Anyhow, the remaining questions will be answered in the coming years, if Turkey sticks to its intention to implement the customs union as envisaged by the Association Agreement. This step would lead to a degree of opening of the Turkish market which is almost equivalent to membership in a common market. If Turkey can manage to realise this, its economy has passed an important test in terms of qualification for accession to the single market of the EC.

With regard to other economic problems mentioned in the Commission's "opinion", which may pose an obstacle to early Turkish membership, the situation over the last few years has not changed much. Severe macroeconomic imbalances, structural disparities, and an underdeveloped system of social security continue to be landmarks of the Turkish economy. Chances for a rapid improvement of the situation in these respects are slim.[43]

However, this need not give rise to great concern regarding closer economic integration with the EC as long as the Community does not transgress the limits of a "single-market Community" too far in the direction of economic and monetary union. At least for the EC, financial burdens on the Community resulting from the problematic state, in structural terms, of the Turkish economy need not and, most likely, will not be unbearable.[44] Without going into the details of the debate about which is the most probable figure for a Community financial transfer to Turkey, one should not forget that, in principle, EC contributions to less developed member states are the result of political decisions, as most recently could be amply studied in the debate about the so-called "Delors-2 package" and the resulting decisions of the Edinburgh European Council. Hence, ultimately, Turkey would, more or less, get what its partners were ready to concede.

---

[43] For a review of these issues in the context of Turkey's general economic policy, see Mükerrem Hiç, "Market Economy and Democracy. Turkey as a Case Study for Developing Countries and Eastern Europe", *Orient*, Vol. 33, No. 2, 1992, pp. 205-226.

[44] This will be even more so after another round of EC enlargement in which "rich" EFTA countries will enter the Community.

Even the automatic assumptions behind agricultural spending is open to a certain degree of political manipulation as has been shown by the, though still insufficient, attempts at reforming the Common Agricultural Programme (CAP) in order to make it cheaper. All this leads to the conclusion that the financial argument in the case of Turkish accession has been used and continues to be used by Community and other West European circles not as an "objective" factor but as a sophisticated way of stating that the EC and its members, for whatever reasons, are not (yet) ready to accept Turkish accession.

There are, however, some aspects to the issue that need a closer look. For one, the picture would change dramatically if the EC was to approach the stage of economic and monetary union as envisaged in the Maastricht Treaty. Under such circumstances, the macroeconomic imbalances, especially inflation and public debt, effectively would prevent a Turkish membership in EMU. As this, by all experience, cannot be regarded as a quickly passing phenomenon of the Turkish economy, the realisation of the Maastricht Treaty would erect a large hurdle in the way of a closer economic integration between Turkey and the Community.

Secondly, and this aspect tends to be very much underrated by Turkish authorities and politicians, the existing macroeconomic imbalances in the Turkish economy would, in the case of accession, create severe internal economic and social problems for Turkey. This can be studied to some extent in the Greek case, where the inability of the government to redress macroeconomic imbalances over the last five years has led to huge problems which also affect the country's ability to effectively participate in the EC's economic integration.[45] As, in a "single-market EC", political consequences of national economic mismanagement are still attributed to national authorities, effects in terms of diminishing electoral support have to be borne by national governments without a chance of much relief from Community level.

---

[45] For more details, see Heinz-Jürgen Axt, "Southern Europe Facing the Single Market's Completion", *Intereconomics*, Vol. 26, No. 4, July/August 1991, pp. 192-202.

A third point which needs some consideration is the difference between an "objective" political situation and its "subjective" perception by politicians and public opinion. Concerning the likely costs of Turkish membership, the West European public, especially the German one, is of the firm conviction that they are unbearable. This impression may be created by a wrong idea about the level of development of the Turkish economy which in turn is a result of the experience of large-scale labour migration, because this is regarded as a phenomenon that only occurs in rather underdeveloped countries. More recently, at least in Germany, a general public resistance has been developed against spending more money for the Community. It is generally believed that "Brussels" already gets too much and that, above that, the redistribution is too much in favour of "poor" member states which often are regarded simply as "inefficient". As long as politicians are obliged by electoral circumstances to take such opinions and attitudes seriously, the chances for an "objective" public evaluation of the likely costs of an eventual Turkish accession are slim. Turkey's aspirations for definite integration with Europe, thus, partially tend to become a victim of intra-EC general public dissatisfaction.

2. The Issues of "Democracy" and "Minority"

This situation is even further complicated because many of those groups of Western European societies which may be able to do a more "objective" evaluation of the economic aspect of Turkey's integration with the Community, also have developed a negative attitude toward the country. They mainly have done so for genuinely political reasons which are connected with the state of democratic development and human rights in Turkey. Over the very recent years, the "Kurdish issue" has been added to this.

Hampered Process of "Democratisation"

Over the last decade, the situation of democracy and human rights in Turkey has been a recurring issue complicating EC-Turkish relations.

This contrasts sharply with the situation that prevailed during most of the first fifteen years of the association relationship. Although the respective negotiations leading to the Agreement of 1964 and to the Additional Protocol of 1973 took place in the immediate aftermath of military interventions which were accompanied by restrictions of human and political rights, this did not significantly influence the negotiating climate. Nor did the serious deterioration of the domestic political situation in Turkey during the second half of the 1970s, which was also accompanied by a general loss of personal security for many citizens, create major repercussions for EC-Turkish relations.[46]

This changed almost overnight with the third military intervention in September 1980. Since then, Western Europe's public, especially the German one, the EC's institutions, especially the European Parliament, and other Western European organisations like the Council of Europe have continually monitored the human rights situation in Turkey.[47]

For a long time, they found many reasons for complaints about Turkey's human-rights record even after the return to civilian political rule with the elections of November 1983. These constant complaints seriously hampered a rapid normalisation of EC-Turkish relations during the 1980s. Many in the Turkish political public regarded these reservations on the side of the Community as unfounded and a result of misinformation or as a sign of political bad will with regard to an improvement of the relationship between Brussels and Ankara. This Turkish view does not seem to be completely unfounded. Although a critical attitude with

---

[46] For a more detailed account of the developments in the late 1970s, see Lucille W. Pevsner, *Turkey's Political Crisis*, The Washington Papers, No. 110 (New York: Praeger Publisher, 1984); Clement H. Dodd, *The Crisis of Turkish Democracy* (Huntingdon: Eothen Press, 1990, 2nd ed.); and Mehmet Ali Birand, *The Generals' Coup in Turkey: An Inside Story of 12 September 1980* (London: Brassey's, 1987).

[47] Details of this situation are discussed at some length in Eberhard Grabitz, *et. al.*, *Direktwahl und Demokratisierung. Eine Funktionenbilanz des Europäischen Parlaments nach der ersten Wahlperiode*, Europäische Studien des Instituts für Europäische Politik, Vol. 15 (Bonn: Europa Union Verlag, 1988), pp. 207-246 and Heinz Kramer, *Die Europäische Gemeinschaft*, pp. 84-111.

respect to human-rights standards in third countries has become one of the features of a "Community" political culture, the vehemence and continuity of criticism regarding Turkey stand out.

In the very recent past, West European general criticism about insufficient human rights and democratic standards in Turkey has calmed down.[48] It is widely acknowledged that during the last years Turkish governments have brought about significant improvements in this respect. Nevertheless, the situation is widely regarded as being not fully satisfactory.[49] There is some concern about how effectively and rapidly further progress can be made given a severe resistance from parts of the bureaucracy and the "law-and-order" apparatus of the state. Their position is strengthened by the fact that they also find considerable support in all groups of parliament, even in parts of the Social Democratic Populist Party. The fate of the so-called Judicial Reform Bill which initially foundered at the cliff of the National Security Council's disapproval, is another recent striking example of the still existing limits in Turkey to initiate truly liberal reforms in a West European sense. The finally approved version of the bill gives rise to concern that violations of human rights, especially systematic torture in police custody, will not

---

[48] It should be noted, however, that such criticism was never a one-sided West European affair. Up until the present, there has always been a strong domestic criticism of the democratic and human rights standards in Turkey, which was not only the expression of "separatists" or "radicals" but could be found in circles of the Turkish "moderate left" as well. Hence, West European complaints about the situation in Turkey also were, to a certain extent, a reflection of the domestic Turkish political debate insofar as this was not suppressed by the state authorities. In this sense, the sometimes harsh rejection of West European criticism by Turkish officials always also was directed at certain domestic groups.

[49] A short account of the reconsolidation of Turkish democracy is given by Metin Heper, "Consolidating Turkish Democracy", *Journal of Democracy*, Vol. 3, No. 2, April 1992, pp. 105-117; see also Turkish Democracy Foundation, *Development and Consolidation of Democracy in Turkey* (Ankara: Sevinç Matbaasi, 1989). For a differing viewpoint, see Mehmet S. Gemalmaz, *The Institutionalization Process of the "Turkish Type of Democracy". A Politico-Juridicial Analysis of Human Rights* (Istanbul: Amaç Yayincilik, 1989).

effectively be stopped.[50] However, optimism prevails in the Community as can be seen, for example, in the latest "Turkey report" of the European Parliament, submitted by Belgian MEP Raymonde Dury.[51]

Kurdish Separatism and the "Minority" Issue

Strongly related to the issue of "democratisation" is the problem of the Kurdish minority in Turkey and its treatment by the Turkish authorities. This issue, over the last years, almost outranked the "democratisation" issue in the hierarchy of West European public concerns regarding EC-Turkish relations. An obvious reason for this is, of course, to be seen in the repercussions of the second Gulf war on the Kurdish question in general. As long as the "traditional" Turkish treatment of the Kurdish minority[52] persists along with the efforts of other countries in the region

---

[50] In early 1992, there have been open signs of dissatisfaction with the "democratic" approach of the new coalition-based government on the side of the police and representatives of other security organisations; see *das tageszeitung (taz)*, 21 February 1992, p. 9; see also *Briefing* (Ankara), Nos. 903 (31 August 1992) through 911 (26 October 1992) for continuous reporting about the "end of the democratisation hopes". The continuation of torture has been confirmed by a recently published report of the Anti-Torture Committee of the Council of Europe; see *Süddeutsche Zeitung*, 22 December 1992, p. 6.

[51] See European Parliament, Doc. A3-0193/92 (with Annexes), 21 May 1992, in which it is stated in the explanatory part that relations between the EC and Turkey, which "in future will play an ever more important, even a decisive, political role in an especially endangered region, should be strengthened and revitalised." (p. 29) The Belgian MEP saw the necessity of fully supporting the Turkish government in order to enable it to realise its promises made in the election programme. Due to controversies between the groups in the EP over how to react to the latest anti-Kurdish moves of the Turkish government, the report had been removed from the EP's agenda twice since its presentation in committee. It was finally approved at the November 1992 session of the EP after a fairly controversial debate.

[52] For a short and comprehensive overview of the history of the Kurdish issue in Turkey, see Michael M. Gunter, *The Kurds in Turkey. A Political Dilemma* (Boulder, CO: Westview Press, 1990).

to misuse the Kurdish problem and the Kurds in pursuit of their own political goals, there is always the possibility that the issue could become a serious burden on the political climate between Turkey and the Community.

A satisfactory reconciliation of West European and Turkish views of this problem seems to be very difficult. Although there certainly are some misunderstandings or misjudgments on the side of the West Europeans, as Turkish official and public opinion suggest, the main underlying factor seems to be conceptual differences with respect to the substantial content of the notions of "minority" and "nation state" and the inherent relationship between them.[53]

In Turkey there is a widespread conviction that there are no minorities in the country except those explicitly stated in the Treaty of Lausanne of 1923. This is a very narrow legal approach to the phenomenon of minorities which is mainly based on the national state doctrine of the indivisibility of the Turkish nation and Turkish state. It should be noted, however, that this approach does not deny the existence of Kurds in Turkey; it only denies their legal status as a minority. This is a distinct difference to the usage of the term in Western European political discourse. Here, it is applied to a much broader and multifarious pattern of social and political reality.

In the prevailing and overwhelmingly accepted Turkish doctrine, the nation and the nation state form an inseparable whole which, if coupled with the principles of political democracy and rule of law, render

---

[53] In taking this position, the author denies Turkish claims that West European opinion leaders are victims of misinformation campaigns organised by Kurdish separatist groups and their fellow travellers in Western Europe. A careful reading over time of, for instance, the leading West European dailies such *Le Monde*, *The Financial Times*, *The Independent*, *The Times*, *Neue Zürcher Zeitung*, or *Frankfurter Allgemeine Zeitung*, gives no justification to the claim of one-sided reporting about the Kurdish issue in Turkey. It may be diplomatically wise to cover differences of opinion with the notion of "misunderstandings", but this view does not find any justification in the factual situation with regard to the availability of widespread and balanced information about the Kurdish issue in leading West European media.

meaningless any differentiation between citizens based on ethnic criteria. This Turkish (majority) position with regard to the links between "minority", "nation", and "nation state" is but one possible view of the substantial meaning of these concepts and its linkage. It mainly holds true for nation states that are organised after the principles of a "unitary state" whereas nation states that are organised after the principles of a "federal state" display a different understanding of the terms and their linkage.[54]

This more abstract discussion of some basic concepts which are connected with the actual Kurdish issue in Turkey leads to the conclusion that, in order to become a member of the Community, Turkey does not necessarily have to grant a special minority status to its Kurdish citizens or even change its state organisation into a "federal state". There are unitary states within the EC which are also very reluctant to grant special status to their minorities or to officially accept the existence of different peoples within their borders. Hence, Turkey would not be an exception in this respect.

This leaves as a final point of contention between Turkey and parts of the Western European public and governments the issue of how to cope with the separatist terrorism of the Kurdish Workers Party (PKK).[55] West European positions vary markedly. One reason for this seems to be the existence or non-existence of separatist political movements or inclinations in Community member states. Hence, France, Spain and the United Kingdom display a more moderate attitude than, for instance, Germany or Denmark.

Another important factor seems to be the existence of considerable large

---

[54] For the various forms of "nation state", see the article "Political Systems", *The New Encyclopaedia Britannica*, Vol. 25, 1987 (15th edition), pp. 987-988 with references to further literature on the issue. See also the relevant contributions in *Journal of International Affairs*, Vol. 45, No. 2, Winter 1992.

[55] For the most comprehensive documentation and analysis of this issue to date, see Ismet G. Imset, *The PKK. A Report on Separatist Violence in Turkey (1973-1992)* (Ankara: Turkish Daily News, 1992).

groups of Kurds within some of the EC member states. This is especially the case in Germany where about 300,000 of its 1.75 million Turkish inhabitants are claimed to be of Kurdish origin. They have established a variety of political organizations some of which are "civilian" offsprings of the PKK. Some of these organizations have established links to various German political and social organizations, thus introducing the Kurdish issue much more intensively into the general political and social discourse of Germany than is the case in most of the other EC member states.[56]

The majority of the political parties and the German government, however, like officials of the Community and its member states in general, never have shown any sympathy for PKK and its activities. Official criticism which has been directed at anti-terrorist activities of Turkish authorities, has consistently warned against overstepping the limits set by the rule of law and about infringements of human rights with respect to the civilian population in southeast Anatolia. It did, however, not deny Turkey the legitimate right of defending its political and territorial integrity against separatist terrorism.[57]

Turkish officials, however, prefer to uphold their opinion that, first, West European governments and Community institutions tend to unduly confuse PKK terrorism with the Kurdish issue proper and, secondly, do not undertake thorough enough measures to prevent PKK and its sympathisers from acting on their territory. Hence, part of the Turkish

---

[56] A comprehensive overview of Kurdish organisations in Germany and other West European countries is provided by Berliner Institut für Vergleichende Sozialforschung, et al. (eds.), *Kurden im Exil. Ein Handbuch kurdischer Kultur, Politik und Wissenschaft*, Vol. 1 (Berlin: Edition Parabolis, 1991).

[57] For the official German position, inter alia, see the respective declarations of Minister of Interior, Mr. Rudolf Seiters, and of the governmental spokesman, Mr. Dieter Vogel, of 25, 26 and 30 March 1992, as documented in Presse- und Informationsamt der Bundesregierung (ed.), *Bulletin*, No. 33, 1 April 1992, p. 323. The almost identical official French position was expressed by President Mitterrand at his press conference during his visit to Turkey in April 1992; see Ambassade de France (à Bonn), *Bulletin d'information*, No. 76, 21 April 1992, p. xi.

public earnestly believes that some Western European states, at least implicitly, support Kurdish separatist terrorism against Turkey.

However, as long as the Turkish government continues with its present approach to curbing separatist terrorism of PKK mainly by means of large-scale military operations which also tend to severely affect large portions of the civilian population in the region, West European criticism, especially in Germany and the European Parliament, will not stop. This will continue to negatively affect EC-Turkish relations.

3. The "Cultural" Issue

public discussion in the EC and in Turkey as well as between representatives of both sides about the human rights and democracy issue in the context of EC-Turkish relations sometimes tends to be affected by arguments about the "cultural" or "religious" factor.[58] The Turkish opinion seems to imply that the EC's attitude in its conduct of relations with Turkey is often influenced by a continuation of the defence of the Christian occident against the Muslim threat or, even worse, by a sort of crusader's mentality.

Of course, this feature plays an unspoken role in forming the attitude of certain parts of public opinion and of some politicians as well in EC member states. This is an indication of the fact that the answer to the questions of what constitutes European or "Community identity" and if and how far Turkey fits into this concept, is by no means clear. This is no contradiction to the fact that the question of Turkey being a "European" country in a political sense has been positively answered, at least since 1963. It points, however, to the difference between the

---

[58] For an attempt at a more "objective" discussion of this issue, see Metin Heper, *et al.* (eds.), *Turkey and the West. Changing Political and Cultural Identities* (London/New York: I.B. Tauris & Co, forthcoming 1993); see also Nüshet S. Özertan, *Türkei: Mittel oder Mittler? Zu den politisch-kulturellen Grundlagen eines EG-Beitritts*, Studien zur Politikwissenschaft, Vol. 55 (Münster/Hamburg: Lit Verlag, 1990).

political level and the attitudinal or "ideological" basis of EC-Turkish relations.

A closer look at the underlying motivations that determine the culturally-based anti-Turkish argumentation in some circles of the EC reveals that, in general, it is not "Turkish culture" as such, and often even not "Islam" that is feared. What drives the attitudes of these groups and/or persons is the fear of an "invasion" of and eventual "occupation" by elements of an alien way of living that are regarded as a threat to one's own identity or way of living. This phenomenon, however, is not particular to the EC member states or to problems of EC-Turkish relations. One can, for instance, find it, in a certain way, also in Turkey where "Kemalist" parts of society feel threatened by Islamic "fundamentalist" forces or phenomena.[59] In Western Europe, on the other hand, xenophobic resentments are not exclusively directed against Turks but include a wide range of "alien" people like Sinti, Roma, Maghrebines, Africans, or Pakistani. Hence, the more general issues of xenophobic traits in West European societies more incidentally gain a foreign-policy implication with regard to EC-Turkish relations.

This state of affairs does not mean that one should content oneself with the situation as it is. Quite to the contrary, those political groups which are interested in a positive outlook for the future conduct of these relations are confronted with the task of correcting the balance in the West European public with regard to cultural and religious prejudices against Turkey and its eventual accession to the Community.

On a more "technical" level, one has to stress that the EC does not have many competencies in the fields of culture and education. The Community in its present form is officially based on the rule of law and on economic interdependence but not on cultural or religious homogeneity. An evaluation of the eventual membership of any

---

[59] The most prominent example for this is the so-called "turban issue", i.e. the debate about wearing "religious" dress, like head scarves, in public institutions, especially university classes. The growing number of student boarding houses that are run by religious foundations is another issue at hand.

applicant country, thus, has to ask, first, if the country is ready and able to comply with the legal acquis communautaire as established in the treaties and secondary European Community law. Secondly, it has to ask if the applicant country is ready and able to shoulder the economic consequences of membership.

With regard to this, one must state that Turkey's legal system is in full concordance with the European system of law and that, in Turkey, the application of laws does not fundamentally deviate from the practice as established in EC member states.[60] Hence, there would be no difficulties in Turkey for the implementation of EC law after entry into the Community. Furthermore, if law can be regarded as an important part of a society's culture, one would, consequently, have to conclude that in this important respect Turkish culture is part of European culture.

With regard to the more "non-technical" or "psychological" aspects of the issue at hand, the West European public should become more aware of the fact that realities of Turkey's "civilisation" do, to a large extent, coincide with the range of realities of daily European life as is expressed by the factual situation in the area from Copenhagen to Crete and from Lisbon to Görlitz. There are more common features in the culture and civilisation of a Muslim central Anatolian village and of a Catholic rural Spanish village than between the "culture" of these villages and, say, that of Ankara or Barcelona respectively. Taken objectively, the issue of cultural differences comes down to an issue of difference of *Lebenswelt*, which often is more of an intra-societal problem than an inter-societal or inter-ethnic one.[61]

In this context, it seems appropriate to point to another facet of the issue. As experience of about forty years of EC integration shows, this process generally does not tend toward significantly abolishing the spatial

---

[60] See Franz Mayer, "Die Türkei, ein Glied der europäischen Staaten- und Rechtsgemeinschaft", in Klaus-Detlev Grothusen (ed.), *Die Türkei in Europa* (Göttingen etc.: Vandenhoeck & Ruprecht, 1979), pp. 247-259.

[61] For this argument, see also Zentrum für Türkeistudien (ed.), *op. cit.*, pp. 103-113.

separation of the people of the member states. Ethnic amalgamation, to the present, has not been a result of EC "community building". There is no obvious indication that this would be different in the case of closer relations with Turkey. It can even be doubted that the probability of mass labour migration in case of Turkish membership would be as high as is generally assumed.[62]

In addition to this, "multiculturalism" or cultural heterogeneity is stressed to be a "trademark" of EC integration as can be seen by the most recent intra-EC debate about certain aspects of the Maastricht Treaty. Up to now, no convincing argument has been put forward in public discussion that European Muslim societies have to be excluded from this.[63] Hence, closer relations with or an eventual accession of Turkey to the EC cannot be excluded only because EC member states have not been able so far to realise the much cherished principle of cultural heterogeneity in daily Community life to such an extent that it no longer poses domestic problems in various member states.

4. The "Greek Factor"

The paramount political problem posed for a revitalisation of EC-Turkish relations and for an eventual Turkish membership in the EC is, however, the conflict with Greece. This conflict has its origins far back in history and both sides face each other in this conflict with a reciprocal and

---

[62] For this argument, see Volker Nienhaus, "Ökonomische und politische Vorteile einer EG-Vollmitgliedschaft der Türkei für die Europäischen Gemeinschaften", *Zeitschrift für Türkeistudien*, Vol. 5, No. 1, 1992, pp. 59-74.

[63] Without going into details here, it should, however, be stressed that Turkey cannot be regarded as a Muslim society in the popular understanding of the term. One may argue about the scope of secularisation that has taken place in Turkey since the foundation of the Republic by Mustafa Kemal, but there can be no doubt that the Muslim society of Turkey significantly differs from its Arab neighbours, not to speak of Iran. For substantiation of this argument, see Metin Heper, "Islam, Polity and Society in Turkey: A Middle Eastern Perspective", *The Middle East Journal*, Vol. 35, No. 3, Summer 1981, pp. 345-363.

unfathomable mistrust. These predispositions born respectively from the mutual threats to national identity make it extremely difficult to work out effective compromises and solutions for the disputed issues. There are at present hardly any recognisable traces on either side of a fundamental preparedness to solve the conflict by way of a comprehensive compromise with mutual concessions.

With regard to the influence on EC-Turkish relations, the majority of the Turkish political public is convinced that Greece abuses its membership in the Community for spoiling EC-Turkish relations. It is equally convinced that the EC institutions as well as Greece's partners do not show enough resistance against this.[64]

In general terms, this Turkish view is not completely unfounded given Greece's continuous attempts at blocking any new movement in EC-Turkish relations by pointing to the unsolved Cyprus problem and to the, in Greek eyes, still unsatisfactory human-rights situation in Turkey. What is, however, either a fundamental Turkish misconception or an exaggeration of facts is the description and evaluation of the reaction of Greece's partners to Athens' behaviour. It is totally misleading to interpret this reaction as an active support of Greek ambitions. More often than not, the eleven have tried hard to change the Greek attitude, but they are bound by the Community's decision-making rules. Most of the decisions for the implementation of Community activities within the framework of EC-Turkish association need unanimity in the EC Council, i.e. Greek consent. There is also no chance of changing the rules

---

[64] For a more recent overview of Greece's "Turkey policy" in the context of European politics, see Heinz-Jürgen Axt, *Griechenlands Außenpolitik und Europa: Verpaßte Chancen und neue Herausforderungen*, Aktuelle Materialien zur Internationalen Politik, Vol. 26 (Baden-Baden: Nomos Verlagsgesellschaft, 1992), especially pp. 61-83; see also Heinz-Jürgen Axt and Heinz Kramer, *Entspannung im Ägäiskonflikt? Griechisch-türkische Beziehungen nach Davos*, Aktuelle Materialien zur Internationalen Politik, Vol. 22 (Baden-Baden: Nomos Verlagsgesellschaft, 1990). Views from Greek, Turkish and third-country scholars are included in Semih Vaner (ed.), *Le différend Gréco-Turc* (Paris: Editons L'Harmattan, 1988) and in Dimitri Constas (ed.), *The Greek Turkish Conflict in the 1990s. Domestic and External Influences* (London: Macmillan, 1991).

because this, too, requires an unanimous decision of the Council. This situation, certainly, is deplorable from the Turkish point of view but it seems unfair to blame Greece's partners.[65]

Greece's attitude is strongly linked to the Cyprus issue. Since its entry into the Community, Greece sought to rally her EC partners behind its national position in the struggle with Turkey. This effort was not really successful until the late 1980s. It was only in preparing for the meeting of the Association Council of 25 April 1988, that the Greek government succeeded in having a formula included in the EC's opening statement to the effect that "the Cyprus problem affects EC-Turkey relations". This formula was reason enough for the Turkish side to blow up the meeting because Ankara was and remains convinced that the Cyprus problem has nothing to do with EC-Turkey association.

Since then, the issue of the "Cyprus formula" in the EC opening statement remained a point of disagreement. The Community, nevertheless, hardened its position by including this formula in the Presidency Conclusions of the Dublin meeting of the European Council of 25-26 June 1990. Since then it can be seen as part of a Community acquis in EC-Turkish relations. The Turkish government immediately denounced the EC's position by repeating its opinion that the Cyprus question is not connected to EC-Turkish relations and by declaring that the Community has given up its constructive approach with regard to the Cyprus issue and sided with Greece, thus losing any political credibility concerning the international political process for a solution of the Cyprus problem.[66] During the next meeting of the Association Council on ministerial level on 30 September 1991, however, the Turkish side restricted its reaction to a verbal rejection of the Community's position but did not abort the meeting.

---

[65] For a similar view from a Turkish scholar, see Haluk Günugur, "Certains problèmes juridiques qu'entrainera l'adhésion de la Turquie à la CEE", *Turkish Yearbook of Human Rights,* Vol. 7/8 (1985/1986), Ankara, 1987, pp. 119-136, especially p. 122.

[66] See the statement of the Undersecretary of State of the Turkish Foreign Ministry, Turgay Özceri, *Newspot*, No. 28, 12 July 1990, pp. 3 and 6.

A new facet has been added to the Cyprus issue in the context of Turkish-EC relations with the application for accession of Cyprus to the Community by the (Greek-)Cypriot government, dated 3 July 1990. The Turkish-Cypriot government supported by Ankara argued that the application was illegal both from the point of view of Cypriot constitutional law and from the point of view of international law.[67] As the Council ignored the Turkish concerns and passed the Cypriot application to the Commission for the preparation of an "opinion", the Community added another element of complication to the already very complex situation regarding its political position in the Eastern Mediterranean area. However, the behaviour of the Council can be interpreted as a logical result of the EC's position with respect to Cyprus and as an indication of the other members' unwillingness to create an internal crisis in the Community, which would have been inevitable in case of rejection given the strong Greek support to the Cypriot move.

It is, however, highly improbable that the Commission will advocate an opening of membership negotiations with Cyprus unless the conflict between the two communities on the island is completely solved. At present, the Community upholds association relations with Cyprus under the assumption that the whole island is included, although deliberations and activities between the Community and the association partner only involve representatives of the Greek-Cypriot community. This may be possible in the framework of an association relationship but it seems completely unimaginable to do the same in the case of membership. A situation which would pretend that Cyprus, i.e. the whole island, is an EC member with only the Greek-Cypriot side actively taking part in this is too fictitious to ever become reality. Hence, the only logical result of the Commission's effort in formulating an opinion on the Cypriot application

---

[67] See the text of the Turkish-Cypriot memorandum of 12 July 1990, and the text of a complementary note of 3 September 1990 in Necati Münir Ertekün (ed.), *Le Statut de deux peuples à Chypre* (Lefkosa: L'office d'information publique de la République Turque de Chypre-Nord, 1990), pp. 31-45. This position, of course, has been fully supported by the Turkish government in a letter from the Foreign Minister, Mr. Ali Bozer, to his Italian counterpart who was then the acting president of the EC's Council of Ministers; see *Newspot*, No. 30, 26 July 1990, p. 2.

could be a decision to postpone the opening of entry negotiations until a solution has been found for the Cyprus question proper. An outright rejection of the application seems to be unlikely because this would create intra-EC strains in relations with Athens. A positive response, however, could irrevocably damage relations with Ankara.

From all this, it is evident, that Turkish accession to the EC is unthinkable unless the Cyprus problem has been solved to the satisfaction of all sides involved. There seem to be no possible other developments which could induce Athens to lift its veto against Turkey's membership. Hence, any argument about furthering a solution to the Cyprus question and other Greek-Turkish disputes within the framework of the EC institutions after Turkish accession, as is sometimes heard in Turkish and some European circles,[68] simply ignores political reality. This situation may, for Turkish spectators, create the impression of a partisan Community position with regard to Greek-Turkish relations and of a certain application of a double-standard by the EC with regard to Turkey and Greece respectively. This impression, to a certain degree, is objectively justified but the underlying situation cannot be changed since Greece is a member of the Community and Turkey is not.

IV. A Look into the Future: Ambiguous Perspectives

The four main recurring issues debated in EC-Turkish relations will continue to make an impact on Turkey's links with the Community, but within a radically changed international context. The end of the cold war is about to create a completely new environment for the conduct of EC-Turkish relations. The leitmotif will remain the same: Is Turkey a part of Europe, and if so, how far and in what way? The melody, however, will be different.

---

[68] For an example of the latter, see Volker Nienhaus, *op. cit.*, p. 64.

1. An Uncertain Future for the Community

Uncertainty is not only the motto for the future of the "new world order" but also has become an issue in intra-EC debate about the Community's future. Two developments have led to this situation. On the hand, the attempt at transforming the single market into an economic and monetary union as another step toward the completion of European Union somewhat unexpectedly reopened a political debate about the final goals of Western Europe's integration process. Secondly, the opening of the border toward the former "East" and the breakdown of the system with its concomitant "reawakening" of old European nation states and the creation of some "new" ones added quite a new dimension to the discussion about the future of the EC. Both issues have become interlinked in the revival of another recurrent intra-EC discourse: the one about "deepening" and/or "widening".

The debate about "Maastricht" has shown that the publics of some important member states are not ready to follow their governments whole-heartedly into what is regarded as a European "superstate". As a consequence, it has become highly doubtful if over the coming years an economic and monetary union plus the first stage of a common foreign and security policy will emerge between the EC member states.

The possibility and the probability of the Community's transformation into a multi-tier system have grown. With the very likely accession of three to five EFTA member states within about three years, this development could gain further momentum. All of these candidates wish to join the EC for basically economic reasons and all of them would add problems to the creation of a political union in one way or the other, although most of them would have no problems with the creation of EMU. Hence, in an EC of 17 members, by 1996, tendencies toward "multi-tierism" may become more pronounced. The possibility of a fundamental transformation of the present EC into a system of overlapping but not completely identical "market", "monetary", and "political" Communities over the coming decade cannot be completely ruled out.

Such a development, however, would not give an answer to the problems of the "new East". Here, the outstanding political challenge is the creation of a new "European order" which is capable of eliminating or, at least, containing the risks of violent clashes in and between most of the "new democracies" in Central, Eastern, and Southeastern Europe. The best way to achieve this generally is seen to be massive Western assistance for the rapid establishment of functioning democracies and market economies in these countries. The record of Western efforts, to date, however, is not very promising. What seems to be in the making is not a fairly homogenous "new order" but rather a process of political and economic differentiation and segmentation into more or less stable, more or less prosperous, and more or less "Western" states.

Debate within the Community and between the EC and its eastern neighbours about if and when to include some of the former socialist countries into the EC system will continue. This debate will inevitably also have to address more thoroughly than done at present the question of the eventual eastern borders of the Community. If the process of an "eastern enlargement" is launched, it is difficult to see how and where to draw the line unless some of the "new" states obviously disqualify themselves for potential membership. In any case, a far-reaching "eastern enlargement", even only at the beginning of the next century, will cause another change in the political quality of the integration process. What would be created then may present more of a "European" character in geographical terms but less of a "Community" in political terms than the present EC system. Hence, in a long-term view, the *finalité politique* of the European integration process becomes less and less clear.

2. New Horizons and New Problems for Turkey's Foreign Policy

It is, however, not only European integration that is being tested by the end of the cold war. Turkey, too, is confronted with a totally altered foreign- and security-policy environment which is likely to influence the future of its relationship with the EC.[69]

The country today finds itself encircled by highly unstable and tension-ridden regions in which small-scale violence is spreading and large-scale violence can erupt at any time: the "traditional" crisis region of the Near and Middle East, the newly emerging states of Central Asia and Transcaucasia, the reestablished Russia with its unsolved internal and external problems, and the Balkans which are on the way to once again becoming the European "powder keg". With regard to any of these new "hot points", Turkey runs the risk of becoming involved in an emerging crisis with the potential of spill-over into military activities. The conflict between Armenia and Azerbaijan over Nagorno-Karabagh is only the most evident case to come to mind but in no ways is the only one.

In this situation it is only small consolation that the former great threat from the north, for the time being, has disappeared. What seems of greater importance in this respect, although hardly in a positive way, is the equally diminished role of NATO, which has evolved as a consequence of the end of the antagonistic systemic conflict. By implication, this also means a weakening of the security-policy bonds between Turkey and Western Europe which in the past have constituted the strongest element of the EC member states' consistent interest in close relations with Turkey. In the future, there is a growing probability of diverging risk and threat perceptions on the part of Turkey and West Europe, thereby further diminishing the feeling of security-policy solidarity, especially on the EC's side. It doubtful that an eventual Turkish military involvement in any violent conflict in its immediate vicinity will be regarded by its alliance partners as a "NATO case". The growing divergence between Turkey and the EC members of their respective understanding of their strategically relevant regional environment poses the danger of spilling-over into a more general

---

[69] This new situation is analysed in more detail by Duygu Bazoglu Sezer, "Turkish Risk Perceptions in Turkey's Future Political-Strategic Environment", unpublished paper prepared for a SWP research project, November 1992. See also Ian O. Lesser, *Bridge or Barrier? Turkey and the West After the Cold War* (Santa Monica: RAND, 1992).

estrangement between the two sides.

This trend will be reinforced by another consequence in the wake of the breakup of the former Soviet Union: the emergence of a new "Turkish world". The newly created independent states in Central Asia and Azerbaijan in Transcaucasia pose the opportunity for Turkey to become the centre of an ethnically and linguistically homogeneous region stretching from Western Thrace in Greece to the Chinese borders with some more insular "annexes" in the Balkans. Turkey sees this development as a chance to establish itself as a major actor in the process of restructuring the Soviet heritage. It has acted accordingly by establishing close and intensive ties with all of these new states and by offering them generous possibilities for intense cooperation across a wide spectrum of issues, ranging from trade and cultural affairs to education.

This new horizon of Turkish foreign relations, however, is not without repercussions in the domestic situation. In Turkey one can find a growing awareness of the fact that Turkish identity is no longer limited to the Anatolian heartlands. More important than this reemergence of pan-Turkish traits in the consciousness of the Turkish public, however, could be the concomitant development of ethnically orientated "pressure groups" in Turkey. There is also a growing awareness of the different ethnic roots of the Turkish population living in Turkey. People rediscover, for instance, their Tatar, Kirgise, Albanian, or Bosnian ancestors and, as a consequence, develop an intensified interest in the fate of the respective contemporary people and their new states. This contributes to the development of a dimension in Turkey's national interest, i.e. extending active solidarity to these states. The actual Turkish deep concern for the fate of Bosnia-Hercegovina and Albania is but the most visible example of this development. [70]

Relations with other European countries and with Europe in general cannot remain unaffected by this. There is the, albeit rather slim, possibility, that growing pan-Turkism in a coalition with nationalist groups and Islamic "traditionalists" may lead to a stronger national

---

[70] See especially Sezer, *Turkish Risk Perceptions, op. cit.*

self-assertiveness in Turkish foreign policy. This could express itself in a stronger emphasis on a special national and regional political role of Turkey, thereby gradually diminishing the Turkish interest in closer integration with Europe. Talk of "the 21st century being the Turkish century" point in this direction.[71]

3. Turkey and Europe: Integrated or "Singularised"?

The likelihood that these tendencies will acquire a leading influence in the process of Turkish foreign-policy formulation will be greatly influenced by the Community's reaction to the new international role of Turkey. Without a doubt, the EC member states have developed a great interest in Turkey's new strategic position, not so much because of the risks it involves for Turkey but because of the opportunities it offers to exert a stabilising influence via Turkey on the highly volatile forces in Central Asia and Transcaucasia. This part of the world, in the European view, and even more so in the American one, runs the danger of becoming part of the Islamic fundamentalist threat to the West which is increasingly styled as being the new strategic challenge to Western security interests. Hence, Turkey should get all Western support it needs in order to effectively play its role as the anti-fundamentalist "model" for the development of the new states. What seems to be much less clear, however, is the transformation of this general Western interest into substantial policy.

One option could be to incorporate Turkey as firmly as possible into the emerging European security order by including it fully in all efforts to create a genuine foreign and security policy of the Community. In this view, Turkey's special status of association with the WEU would be regarded as a transitory state leading to eventual membership. By implication, however, this would not be possible without membership in

---

[71] According to press reports, the Turkish President Turgut Özal made such a remark at the recent first "Turkish summit" which gathered the heads of state of Turkey and all new Turkish republics in Central Asia (with the exception of Tajikistan) in Ankara on 31 October 1992; see *Frankfurter Allgemeine Zeitung*, 2 November 1992.

the European Union as envisaged by the Maastricht treaty, and Turkey, for many years to come, will not be in a position to enter the EMU, for the reasons outlined earlier. This scheme, therefore, would run into problems. Conceivably, these problems could be avoided if a stronger differentiation of Western European integration would come about allowing for an EU membership "à la carte". If and how much Greek resistance would to have be overcome, in any case, is another question which cannot be answered today but which can never be completely neglected in all plans to bring about a closer link with Turkey.

Alternatively one could think of creating a "special strategic status" for Turkey on the periphery of the EC by making full use of the possibilities offered by Turkey's membership in all other European organisations except the Community. Added to this would have to be the establishment of strong special bilateral relations between Turkey and some key EC member countries including France, Italy, and the United Kingdom. These relations should mainly be aimed at improving Turkey's economic capabilities in assisting the Central Asian states. However, the sensitive question of how to strengthen the links in the field of security relations, too, cannot be left aside. What Turkey needs here, is a reliable assertion by its partners that the country can count on their active solidarity in cases where it would be involved in one of the military eventualities implied in its new foreign-policy horizon. As already mentioned, however, it is highly doubtful that such an assertion will be politically feasible for most of the important EC countries, especially Germany.

All of this, in conjunction with the other elements discussed in this paper, leads to a gloomy forecast of the future relations between Turkey and the EC. What seems to be the most probable mid-term scenario for these relations on the official level is the continuation of the state of "half-way integration" of Turkey into the Community accompanied by strong but empty rhetoric on both sides pointing to the necessity for considerable improvement. At the same time, however, the problematic factors mentioned in this paper will continue to exert their influence on the relationship, and most likely not in a positive manner. Against the background of the fundamentally changed international constellation in which the relations will be conducted in future, this enhances the danger of a growing estrangement between the EC and Turkey.

A more positive future can only be envisaged if either the Community is ready and able to fundamentally change its policy towards Turkey or if the future development of the EC goes in the direction of "multi-tierism" and/or a drastic enlargement of the Community's geographical scope by the inclusion of some former socialist countries in the near future. In such an enlarged EC, Turkey would easily find a place. The question would remain, however, of just how attractive such a perspective would then be to Ankara.

4. Possible "Intermediate Paths" for Intensifying the Relationship

As most of the determining factors of future EC-Turkish relations are themselves still in a state of flux, one could think of "intermediate paths" for intensifying the relationship -- leaving open (and aside) the final answer to the issue of Turkish membership of the Community. The following considerations should be regarded in this perspective as an endeavour in "intellectual speculation" with the aim of broadening what has been a fairly narrow scope of discussion on the issue.

The first, and most "natural" path would be a serious attempt to finalise the association as agreed upon in the Ankara Agreement and the Additional Protocol. At a minimum, this would imply, in addition to the establishment of the customs union for industrial products, the following:
- solution to the problem of financial cooperation;
- solution to the problem of free movement of labour;
- adaptation of Turkey's agricultural policy to the Common Agricultural Policy to enable the full inclusion of agricultural produce in the customs union as stipulated in article 33 of the Additional Protocol;
- accelerating the process of legal harmonisation as stipulated, inter alia, in article 48 of the Additional Protocol;
- starting the process of free trade in the service sector (including public procurement) as stipulated in article 41, para 2 of the

245

Additional Protocol;
- starting the process of freedom of settlement for professionals as stipulated in the same provision; and
- extending the EC's transport regulations to Turkey as stipulated in article 42 of the Additional Protocol.

The fulfilment of this programme would more or less automatically enable the inclusion of Turkey into the single market. Moreover, it would bring the country in its relation with the EC to a position which is far more advanced than that of any other European country whose eventual membership is currently under discussion.

A less ambitious programme of intermediate measures has been established by the Association Council meeting of 9 November 1992, mainly along the lines of earlier suggestions of the Commission. The basic intention could be termed "improvement of association relations à la carte". Efforts would concentrate on those issues which are non-controversial and where some progress seems likely. The focus of attention will be the finalisation of the customs union as envisaged in the Ankara Agreement until the end of 1995. Issues like financial cooperation and the free movement of workers will rank less prominently in order to avoid unnecessary quarrels. Instead, additional efforts will be concentrated on alternative ways and means for overcoming the "built-in" obstacles of association relations, for which intensified political dialogue seems to be regarded as an appropriate political approach.

Full implementation of this programme will bring Turkey considerably closer to the EC by the mid-1990s but would not enable it to fully participate in the single market. For this to happen, additional measures in the fields of legal harmonisation and tax policy would be necessary. The establishment of a customs union, however, would be an important benchmark concerning a reevaluation of Turkey's request for membership. A country which has achieved a partial degree of integration into the EC could hardly be denied the opportunity to open negotiations on membership so long as a single market based on the customs union lies at the core of EC integration.

Such a development could be further underpinned by upgrading and strengthening Turkey's relations with European Political Cooperation (EPC) or the Community's Common Foreign and Security Policy (CFSP) as it is termed in the Maastricht Treaty. This could happen by creating an "association status" for CFSP parallel to that already created in the framework of WEU. There is no logical reason for allowing Turkey a nearly full-scale participation in security-policy cooperation but assigning foreign-policy cooperation the minor status of political dialogue. This situation, moreover, could run into larger problems once security-policy cooperation develops further and the WEU becomes a closer part of the EC system. Turkey, then, would participate in this process of integration as an associate partner without being able to play the same role in the more general foreign-policy deliberations which form the broader basis for security policy. This imbalance does not seem to be sustainable over a long period of time. Hence, it would only be logical and meaningful to include Turkey in foreign-policy cooperation to same degree as it is included in security-policy cooperation. In practical terms, this would mean allowing Turkish participation in "normal" EPC meetings with a qualified participation in decision-making.

Aside from the possibility of upgrading EC-Turkish relations in the field of foreign-policy cooperation, the Community should in any case, establish and develop institutionalised relations with the Black Sea Economic Cooperation Zone which was founded in 1992 under Turkish initiative by 11 countries bordering the Black Sea. The EC should organise its relations with this new institution on the European periphery based on the model of its relations with ASEAN or the group of Latin American states, i.e. development cooperation and political dialogue should form the basis of the relationship. Such a move would favourably complement EC-Turkish relations and, at the same time, assist Turkey in diversifying its political and economic linkages. Furthermore, such a policy could also function as a welcome complement to the Community's policy toward some of the CIS republics.

The "intermediate paths" proposed so far would more or less lead to a point where the issue of Turkey's membership in the EC would have to be decided within the next five to ten years. Furthermore, they would create a situation in which a negative decision would hardly be possible. If for any reason, the EC and its member states would like to avoid taking this decision that soon,[72] they will have to look for alternative "intermediate paths" for structuring their future relations with Turkey.

One such alternative could be the European Economic Area (EEA) which had been designed for bringing EFTA states closer to the Community after the establishment of the EC's single market. In light of the likely accession of three to four EFTA members to the EC within the next three years[73] and Switzerland's recent rejection of participation in the EEA, this scheme will lose very much of importance unless its geographical scope can be extended to other European states. Here, one can think of Turkey and some of the more advanced "transformation states" of Central Europe such as Hungary, the Czech Republic, and Poland. Such a move would, however, require some modifications to the original EEA scheme such as, for example, dropping the obligation of EEA members to contribute to the EC's structural funds. It would, nevertheless, be very much in line with the policy content of the Association Agreement and could bring Turkey one step closer to eventual membership. Furthermore, it would incorporate the country into the group of states that are regarded as members of the next generation of EC enlargement after the EFTA members.

An alternative formula for designing an "intermediate path" of EC-Turkish relations could be the negotiation of a new agreement along the lines of the so-called "Europe Agreements" concluded by the

---

[72] Some reasons for such an attitude are brought forward by Michael Cendrowicz, "The European Community and Turkey. Looking Backwards, Looking Forwards", in Clement H. Dodd (ed.), *Turkish Foreign Policy* (Huntingdon: Eothen Press, 1992), pp. 9-26. He mainly argues that the prevailing uncertainty about the future of all of Europe should caution the EC against developing too ambitious a scheme for "widening" in the near future.

[73] In February 1993, the Community began entry negotiations with Sweden, Finland, and Austria and, most likely, will do the same with Norway later in the same year.

Community with former socialist countries.[74] This new type of association agreement would replace the Ankara Agreement, hence somewhat downgrading the present status of EC-Turkish relations. It would, however, bring them more into accordance with political reality and feasibility. The economic obligations of Turkey would not be as far-reaching as the stipulations of the present agreement; the possibility of eventual membership, however, would be kept on a more loosely defined basis; and the issue of democratic standards and human rights would be expressively addressed under a formula of "political conditionality". And again, Turkey would be aligned with other European countries that are regarded as being in a special situation of close relationship with the EC. "Singularisation" of the country vis-à-vis the Community would be effectively avoided.

This very sketchy outline of some "intermediate paths" for EC-Turkish relations shows that there is ample room for upgrading the present situation beyond its fairly unsatisfactory state of affairs without concentrating too much on the issue of Turkey's eventual membership. Given the openness of the present all-European political situation, some of these "intermediate paths" for forging EC-Turkish relations over the coming years may be more in accordance with the general political developments of the EC, of Turkey and of the wider Europe than a strict adherence to the paths set out in a quite different past.

---

[74] For a preliminary analysis of this type of association agreement, see Heinz Kramer, "The European Community's Response to the 'New Eastern Europe'", *Journal of Common Market Studies*, Vol. 31, No. 2, 1993, and Rolf J. Langhammer, *Die Assoziierungsabkommen mit der CSFR, Polen und Ungarn: wegweisend oder abweisend?*, Kieler Diskussionsbeiträge 182, (Kiel: IWW, 1992).

8 Turkey and the European Community: A Change in the Offing?

Seyfi Tashan

As an observer of both European Community affairs and Turkish foreign policy since the mid-1970s, I would remark that the paradoxes in these relations have never been so evident as they are today. This observation applies to both European and Turkish interests and is equally valid from either perspective.

The European Community entered into an Association Agreement with Turkey in 1964, in the belief that the latter, an economically marginal but strategically important ally, could thereby be anchored in Western Europe and eventually become a full member in the distant future. From the Turkish viewpoint, the Association Agreement was both an instrument to reaffirm Turkey's Ataturkist tradition and a source of economic and financial assistance to develop its economy, aside from its contribution as a prop to Turkey's military alliance with Western Europe. The first ten years of the association passed so smoothly that the preparatory period was swiftly completed, and the association entered into its second phase, namely, the transition.

Several developments then occurred in the world that adversely affected Turkish-EC relations, the first being the introduction of détente in East-West relations. Beginning with President Nixon's historic trip to Moscow and culminating in the signing of the Helsinki Declaration of 1975, this process reduced the value that politicians attached to Turkey as a strategic ally even though the military strategists continued to value the relationship. The second development was the oil crisis of 1973, which brought the growth-type economies of Western Europe to a halt, and hence reduced their need for foreign workers. Since 1961, Turkey had been an important supplier of foreign workers to Western Europe, particularly to Germany, but these workers now became undesirable guests in the face of increasing unemployment. Thus, politicians sought

250

means to restrict the entry of Turks to Western Europe and became extremely worried about the implications of the provision in the Association Agreement to permit the free circulation of labour by 1985.

A third source of tension in EC-Turkish relations was the extended Turkish-Greek dispute over Cyprus. A bloody coup by the Greek Cypriots in 1964 designed to remove Turkish nationals from the island's administration, was followed in 1974 with another attempt by the Greek Cypriots to annex the island to Greece. The ensuing Turkish military intervention increased the rift between Turkey and the Western powers who considered the Greek Cypriot government as the legitimate government of the island. Turkey considered this attitude to be unjust and indefensible. Last, but not least was the impact of the Islamic revolution in Iran which brought a militant fundamentalist government to power in 1979. Events in Iran had the effect of resurrecting the centuries-old Western European image of the Turks as the enemy of Christian Europe. After 1980, Western Europe also began to worry about human rights in Turkey -- an issue largely instigated by extreme leftist opposition in Turkey.

Throughout this period, Turkey itself was experiencing internal political problems which revealed a certain ambiguity in its attitude towards Europe. In the 1970s, the series of coalition governments between the left and extreme right, the right and extreme right, and finally a minority of the left turned Turkey's European policies into a shambles, so much so that the Turkish Prime Minister asked for a freeze in the relations in 1978. Turkish attempts to revive the relationship in 1980 were short-lived and were abruptly interrupted by the military intervention in September of that year.

What was the impact of these developments on Turkey's relations with Western Europe and the European Community? In the first place, the provisions of the Association Agreement and its protocols became an *à la carte* menu from which individual items could be selectively chosen. For example, the Community granted third countries certain privileges that equalled and even surpassed those given to Turkey, without taking the latter's interests into account as had been provided for in the

Association Agreement. Secondly, Greece was admitted after the Cyprus crisis to full EC membership, despite Turkey's objections. And as soon as it became a member, Greece began to use its veto rights to block the Community's financial assistance to Turkey. Thirdly, the Community simply ignored its obligations to permit the free circulation of Turkish workers in its member countries and imposed quota restrictions on Turkey's chief export item (textiles) and non-tariff barriers to many of Turkey's agricultural exports. For its part, Turkey delayed reducing customs duties in favour of Community products; failed to establish its Economic and Social Council; and lagged behind schedule in harmonising its legislation.

The military intervention of 1980 brought a new dimension to its relations with Europe, that of concern for Turkey's respect for human rights. The public image of Turkey was badly tarnished by the Western media, which portrayed the country as a cross between a military dictatorship (Latin American-junta style) and a fundamentalist Islamic state, such as had arisen in Iran. Of course, Turkey resembled neither. To prove the point and challenge the European Community to improve the relationship, Turkey applied for full membership in 1987.

More than five years have elapsed since its application, and it was only in 1992 that Turkey received a clear response from the European Community. The Commission's much delayed report unequivocally stated that "Turkey was eligible for membership", which had the effect of striking at least from the official agenda the often repeated arguments about Turkey's European character, but raised other reservations regarding Turkey's suitability for Community membership, based on questionable criteria. The Commission's analysis of the Turkish economy, for example, was based on a static review of the conditions, and objections to Turkish treatment of human rights were based on hearsay or politically tendentious arguments.

Cyprus, which had never been previously mentioned as a handicap in Turkish-EC relations, gradually became another factor that had a bearing on Turkey's application for membership. It is hard to say whether this factor has become a scapegoat or represents an attempt to appease the

Greeks or to pressure Turkey to relinquish Cyprus as a price for improved relations with the Community. Nevertheless, most Turks have come to bitterly resent the introduction of this extraneous item into its discussions with the Community as blackmail, especially in light of the solemn promise Turkey received at the time that Greek membership would not harm its relations with the Community.

Polemics aside, Turkey may at last look forward, although cautiously, to what appears to be a promising future in its relations with the European Community. Since the middle of 1980s, Turkey's fortunes have changed dramatically, both at home and abroad. At home the economy has improved, and Turkey has evolved from being a recipient of foreign assistance to now being also an aid donor. Its standard of living has also improved significantly. The GNP per capita, for example, in terms of purchasing power parity, today exceeds $7,000, and its exports, imports and invisible earnings have all increased substantially. Today Turkey is the tenth largest exporting country in the European Community, and ranks twenty-first as a supplier of Community imports.

Even more important changes have been taking place in Turkey's strategic role in world events. At a time when many Western politicians had begun to regard the country as irrelevant to Western defense in light of the Conference on Security and Cooperation in Europe (CSCE) and the decline of Soviet power, the Gulf crisis brought home once again that Turkey was the only stable, strong and reliable Western ally capable of defending their common interests. The Western European security marriage had the promise of being a long and lasting one. Turkey would no longer be a spectator to the happenings in the Middle East where most of its interests coincided with that of the West, but would become a player on behalf of its own interests and could become a partner of the West.

The breakup of the Soviet Union into its component republics opened the doors of its Turkish-speaking states. Turkey was the first country to recognise their statehood along with other republics of the Commonwealth of Independent States (CIS). Turkey has helped these countries to the best of its ability, with official development assistance to date having reached a figure of around $2 billion. Most of these countries have expressed a desire to emulate the Turkish example in the transformation of their economies into a free-market system and of their state structures into secular democracies. More than 10,000 students from the Turkish-speaking republics are studying at Turkish universities or are receiving training at Turkish institutions.

Relations with other republics of the former Soviet Union and the Balkan countries are also being rapidly established. In order to create a framework in which regional bilateral and multilateral relations could be developed in an orderly and satisfactory way, Turkey has initiated the Black Sea Economic Cooperation Zone, which brings together the Balkan and Caucasus countries in the west and east and Russia in the north and Turkey in the south. Considering the unrest in the Balkans and Caucasia, at least for the moment, Black Sea Cooperation presents the most significant multinational framework in which conflicting states can find a forum where they can discuss their differences and seek common economic security.

In the context of Turkish-European relations, I should like now to give brief attention to the situation in the Balkans and the former Soviet Union and to consider the feasibility of enlarging the concept of "European space" in order to gain or regain these countries in the European system. Common problems face all of these countries: economic transformation and development; reconstruction of their political and bureaucratic systems along democratic lines respecting common norms of human rights; and establishing national and ethnic harmony without the dictatorial imposition of a central authority.

Let us first turn to the Balkans. Turkey's interest in this region results from several strategic, ethnic and political factors. In the first place, the Balkans constitute the main communications link between Central and Western Europe and Turkey. The free flow of goods and persons through the Balkans is of the utmost importance not only to Turkey but to many European and Middle Eastern countries which rely on this route. Secondly, as a residual part of the former Turkish empire in the Balkans, significant Turkish and Ottoman Muslim communities remain there whose security and human rights are of serious concern to Turkey. And thirdly, Turkey's security and well-being cannot be isolated from that of the Balkans.

Considering the magnitude of their problems, the challenge before Turkey to effectively assist the Balkan countries is immense. The ethnic Turks and Muslims live in scattered areas in various areas of former Yugoslavia, Bulgaria and Greece. The only country where they are now truly integrated into the political system is Bulgaria -- a fact which has greatly contributed to the development of Turkish-Bulgarian relations. A similar situation exists also in Macedonia, but there are problems in Kosovo and Western Thrace of varying degrees. The most tragic situation, however, is the one in Bosnia, where attempts by the Serbs to present the fighting there as a Muslim-Christian conflict is simply disgraceful. The callousness with which the Western world looks on the bloody "ethnic cleansing" is deplored by the Turkish public. It would be a tragedy if this mentality contributed to the growth of xenophobic movements in Europe.

Turkey's policy aims in the Balkans should in no way be misunderstood. They are not aggressive or expansionist in nature but, rather, cooperative in spirit with the aim of assisting the economic transformation and development of democratic institutions and protecting the rights of Turks and Muslims. It might be appropriate here to ask what should be the role of European Community in this area. Naturally, before these countries successfully make the transition into democracies and free economies, their application for EC membership would be extremely difficult. However, the European Community might help Turkey and other countries in the region to develop further regional cooperation arrangements, such as the Black Sea Economic Cooperation Zone, or a possible Balkans Cooperation Area, as a step to encourage the people of the Balkans to rise above their national, ethnic and religious parochialism.

The Caucasus area faces a similar situation of ethnic, religious and national conflicts. Like the Balkans, the Caucasus region presents a gateway to other areas where Turkey has powerful interests: Russia and

Central Asia. A stable Caucasia is very much in Turkey's interest, and they are doing their best to bring about a multilateral dimension to their relations in order both facilitate their integration in the international system and to provide a dialogue forum for their disputes. It was with this intention in mind that Turkey promoted the participation of all former Soviet republics in the Conference on Security and Cooperation in Europe (CSCE) and the NATO Advisory Council. During the Turkish term as Presidency of the Council of Europe, which ended in November 1992, the Foreign Minister took initiatives to increase contacts between the Council of Europe and the former Soviet republics.

All of these measures may be considered a modest contribution by Turkey to the restructuring of Europe along the lines adopted by all Community countries and Turkey. It would have been most desirable to have conducted these activities in cooperation with the European Community. Up to now, however, the political consultation mechanism (the famous "Troika Formula") has not been adequate or conducive to effective political cooperation in this area.

In 1991, Turkey signed an agreement with the EFTA countries, thereby bringing Turkey's economic relations with these countries at a par with that of the European Community. Similar arrangements are being worked out with the Visegrad countries (Hungary, Poland, the Czech Republic, and Slovakia). Thus, Turkey is preparing a place for itself within the European Economic Space. An economic agreement with Israel is also pending.

After a long standstill, we may at last expect a change in the relationship between Turkey and the European Community. The first signal came from the European Commission. In its report to the Lisbon Council on the subject of the enlargement of the Community, the Commission made the following comment about Turkey:

> . . . this country would experience serious difficulties in taking on the obligations resulting from the Community's economic and social policies. In order to speed up its rate of development in the coming years, the Association Agreement

should be more actively and effectively applied. The Commission recalls that already in 1990 it suggested to the (European) Council measures to complete the customs union, to undertake wide-ranging sectoral cooperation, to resume financial cooperation, and to raise the level of political dialogue. Events have highlighted Turkey's geopolitical importance and the role which it can play as an ally and as a pole of stability in its region; the Community should take all appropriate steps to anchor it firmly within the future architecture of Europe.

Having studied the Commission's report on enlargement at its Lisbon meeting, the European Council issued the following statement:

With regard to Turkey, the European Council underlines that the Turkish role in the present European situation is of greatest importance and that there is every reason to intensify cooperation and develop relations with Turkey in line with the prospect laid down in the Association Agreement of 1964 including a political dialogue at the highest level. The European Council asks the Commission and the Council to work on this basis in the coming months.

It might be worthwhile considering what these two statements signify and what they don't. In the first place, the Commission and the Council accept Turkey's increasing geopolitical role in its region and in Europe. Both express the importance of intensifying cooperation with Turkey; the Council especially in calling for a high-level political dialogue.

In their statements, both the Commission and the Council refrain from making direct reference to Turkey's membership application. The Commission talks about anchoring Turkey firmly within the future architecture of Europe, but this does not necessarily imply membership in light of the persistence of the idea for integration at different velocities or for the creation of satellite European regions. The European Council, although also reticent to make reference to full membership, goes somewhat further and says that the intensification of cooperation and development of relations (should be) in line with the prospect laid down in the Association Agreement. Since it is absolutely clear that the prospect envisaged in the Association Agreement of 1964 is customs union and membership, there may be objective reasons for the Community not to make a direct reference to Turkey's prospective membership. This is noteworthy particularly because such a statement was not eschewed in the cases of Malta and Cyprus.

It seems evident that at least for the time being the European Community is not willing to commit itself to Turkey's membership, nor to deny it. Instead, it seems that Turkey must follow the same path that the EFTA countries have travelled: to first establish the customs union and then be granted membership at a later time when it will not create a political, economic and social burdens for the Community.

The present government in Ankara as well as almost all major political parties are anxious to take part in the construction of Europe and do not wish to choose alternative political objectives. Therefore, the present challenge is how to intensify work in the direction laid out by the Council.

Turkey has announced that it is ready to fulfil one important obligation of the Association Agreement, namely the creation of a customs union with the EC by 1995, and has begun to take measures in this direction. The establishment of the customs union will impose substantial burdens on Turkish industry and agriculture because of the stiff European competition and will exacerbate Turkey's trade balance. If the European Community continues its protective policies in areas where Turkish industry is competitive, the current trade deficit of $2.2 billion per year will increase to immense proportions. In addition, it is estimated that the reduction in Turkish customs will cause a cumulative revenue loss on the order of $50 billion by the year 2000. Nevertheless, Turkey still hopes to establish the customs union in 1995 as foreseen in the Additional Protocol, but the Communal Housing Fund, used for industrial development, will be reduced gradually and ended probably in 1998.

If there is to be progress made towards intensifying EC-Turkish cooperation in line with the Association Agreement and as called for by the Commission and the Council, certain measures need to be taken by the Community. These were included in the famous Matutes Plan which awaits the approval of the Council.

The Association Council meeting in November 1992, has probably been the only serious one to have met in the past 12 years, where both parties expressed a desire to work together. If the Council, the Commission bureaucracy and the Turkish government work together efficiently, it is feasible to create a customs union in 1995. Significant Community economic assistance as provided for in the earlier agreements is unlikely, because of the near-certainty of a Greek veto. Nevertheless, if the Community is serious in wishing to develop its relations with Turkey at least at the point of achieving a customs union, it ought to take the steps that fall within its obligations, such as removing the quotas and non-tariff barriers that prevent Turkey from materially reducing its trade deficit.

Aside from trade matters, there are several other issues that require attention, such as the circulation of persons and services; harmonisation of economic and commercial policies; protection of intellectual property; and a host of other issues that have been neglected for nearly two decades. It may now be hoped that we are on a path leading to integration. According to a decision of the Association Council in November 1992, there will be a political dialogue at the highest level as suggested earlier by the European Council.

In the field of political cooperation and security, the fact that Turkey and members of the WEU (Western European Union) have signed an Association Agreement may prove helpful for several reasons, even though such an arrangement falls short of Turkey's expectations. As long as the WEU did not encompass all of the European members of NATO, there was a danger of creating a division in European defence and thereby causing varying threat and risk perceptions. This danger has now been averted to a significant degree. Secondly, the establishment of high-level dialogue, even though far short of the political cooperation foreseen in Maastricht, may be helpful in creating mutual understanding and possibly some form of cooperation.

In attempting to define the present stage in Turkish-EC relations, one might call it the beginning of a "restoration period". How far can the relationship go? As far as the majority of Turkish public opinion is concerned, there has been little deviation from the original ambition to achieve full integration. The Turkish hope is that the European partners share that ambition, even if they may view it as a longer-term prospect than do the Turks. It is conceivable that the processes of harmonisation, cooperation and integration may occur simultaneously.

There are certain pitfalls, however, which should be avoided, and while not directly related to the actual processes, they may seriously affect them. One such pitfall is the potentially negative influence that the mass media may exert on questions that are particularly sensitive to public opinion. One can observe, for example, a link between the unfavourable attention Turkey has received in the Western media over the past few years with the lack of progress in talks with the European Community. Recently there seems to have been a decided improvement in the public image of Turkey. Undoubtedly, fuller knowledge of the actual changes taking place in Turkey will continue to enhance its image and hopefully its prospects for closer relations with the EC.

The second pitfall may be the bureaucracies in both Brussels and Ankara. Traditionally, bureaucrats are overly cautious in taking radical decisions and sometimes prefer litigation to cooperation in instances where they do not have a clear political mandate. Furthermore, they will face strong protectionist pressures from national industries which may suffer, if only in the short term, from the elimination of customs. This pressure will be greater in Turkey, because the country does not expect financial support from the Community at least in the foreseeable future, in terms of either EIB credits or assistance from other Community funds. Furthermore, most of Turkey's industry has a weak structural base and lacks competitive experience.

A final pitfall may be a desire on the part of the Community to substitute Turkey's associated status for full membership on a permanent basis. The same may be said for Turkey's associate or non-voting membership within the WEU. Turkey intends to establish the customs union fully by

1998, which will create a rather unique situation in which a non-member country enjoys the customs union but does not participate in the decision-making mechanisms of the single market on matters concerning the economy, commerce and other major policies. Such an arrangement, however, is clearly untenable on a permanent basis. The Turkish population expects that any arrangements made for implementing the customs union will adequately protect Turkey's interests and will be transformed into full adhesion as soon as it is possible and feasible for both sides.

Glossary of Abbreviations

ACP	African, Caribbean and Pacific (countries)
AMU	Arab Maghreb Union
CAP	Common Agricultural Policy
CIS	Commonwealth of Independent States (formerly USSR)
CSCE	Conference on Security and Cooperation in Europe
CSCM	Conference on Security and Cooperation in the Mediterranean and the Middle East
CFSP	Common Foreign and Security Policy
EBRD	European Bank for Reconstruction and Development
EEA	European Economic Area
EFTA	European Free Trade Association
EIB	European Investment Bank
EMU	Economic and Monetary Union
EPC	European Political Cooperation
EUA	European Units of Account
FIS	Front Islamique du Salut (Algeria)
FAO	Food and Agricultural Organisation (UN)
GCC	Gulf Cooperation Council
GMP	Global Mediterranean Policy
HDI	Human Development Index
MFA	Multi-Fibre Arrangement
MFN	Most-Favoured Nation
MNMC	Mediterranean Non-Member Country
MOF	Multinational Observation Force (in Sinai)
MTCR	Missile Technology Control Regime
NAFTA	North American Free Trade Agreement
NATO	North Atlantic Treaty Organisation
NGO	Non-Governmental Organisation
NPT	Nuclear Non-Proliferation Treaty
NTB	Non-Tariff Barriers
0DA	Official Development Assistance
PKK	Kurdish Workers Party (Turkey)
PNC	Palestinian National Council
PNF	Palestine National Front
RMP	Renewed Mediterranean Policy
UNDP	United Nations Development Programme
WEU	Western European Union